'Some Big Bourgeois Brothel'

Contexts for France's culture wars with Hollywood

'Some Big Bourgeois Brothel'

Contexts for France's culture wars with Hollywood

Bill Grantham

UNIVERSITY
OF LUTON

press

British Library Cataloguing in Publication Data

A catalogue record for this book is available from the British Library

ISBN: 1 86020 535 6

In memory of my mother

Mary Margaret McCormack Grantham
1935-1995

Published by
University of Luton Press
University of Luton
75 Castle Street
Luton
Bedfordshire LU1 3AJ
United Kingdom

Tel: +44 (0)1582 743297; Fax: +44 (0)1582 743298
e-mail: ulp@luton.ac.uk
website: www.ulp.org.uk

Cover Design Gary Gravatt
Front Cover: Jack Lemmon in *Irma la Douce* (Billy Wilder) courtesy of BFI Stills
Typeset in Van Dijck MT
Printed in United Kingdom by Whitstable Litho, Whitstable, Kent

Contents

Acknowledgements

I hope it is not too obvious from reading it that this book did not start out as a book at all. I originally planned a 30 or 40 page affair for a seminar on administrative policy at the Boalt Hall School of Law of the University of California, Berkeley. The paper got out of hand, and, by the time I finished, I had a book-length manuscript. My thanks go first, then, to Professor Edward L. Rubin at Boalt Hall, who indulged the "paper's" length, subject matter and approach, and then contributed characteristically shrewd and helpful comments to make it better.

I also benefited from the advice, good sense and superior knowledge of those friends and colleagues who read all or part of the original manuscript, notably Bruce Alderman, Lenny Borger, Pascal Bourdon, Ian Christie, John Dick, Alice Kaplan, James Saynor and Neil Watson. Dudley Andrew, Thomas Guback, Peter Monteith and Kristin Thompson kindly helped with various questions. Camille Treacey of LEXIS arranged for online database access when I needed to update my research. I was lucky to be able to use excellent libraries and enlist the help of excellent librarians at Boalt Hall, the Main Library at Berkeley (in particular the newspaper and government documents collections), the Academy of Motion Picture Arts and Sciences, Los Angeles, the law library at the Université de Paris II and the Institut Henri-Desbois, Paris. Professor Manuel Alvarado of the University of Luton was an unfailingly encouraging editor. Martha Rose Shulman, was, as ever, bemused at, but tolerant of, my enthusiasms.

Finally, I should acknowledge the work of others on whose efforts, as the endnotes make clear, I have much relied. The research of Kristin Thompson and Ian Jarvie on the relations of the early American film industry and Europe have been essential resources for this book, as has the important study by Charles W. Brooks of French attitudes to America. Two invaluable books appeared after this one was written: Richard Abel's *The Red Rooster Scare* and Geoffrey Nowell-Smith & Steven Ricci's (eds.) *Hollywood & Europe*. Finally, a deft translation of Georges Duhamel by Donald Ray Allen provided this book's title.

Introduction

At the end of 50 years journeying the American Motion Picture Industry stood on a mountaintop from which the beacon of its silver screen was sending rays of light and color and joy into every corner of the earth.

Will H. Hays, president of the Motion Picture Producers and Distributors of America.[1]

In England one is always running into people who are anti-American although they've never set foot in this country. And I always tell them, 'There are no Americans. America is full of foreigners.'

Alfred Hitchcock[2]

This is a book in two parts, each sufficiently distinct that either part could be read alone without reference to the other. Nonetheless, the two parts are best read together, because the first, which describes a cultural pathology, informs the second, which depicts a political process. The first part takes the form of separate but connected vignettes, each illustrating aspects of the cultural relations between France and the United States since their respective republics came into being in the late eighteenth century. The second part describes as apparently undramatic a subject as the mesh of international trade politics and the regulation of television program imports. The essential thesis of the book is that what the first part describes is what makes the events of the second part both interesting and singular.

The subject of this book is a strange policy, which strangeness makes for an odd analysis. The policy is strange because, despite having little rational basis and even smaller impact, it nearly caused the derailment of another policy, a rational one with global effect. The analysis is odd because, deprived of the comforting instrumentalism of typical considerations of policy (reason, analysis of interests, and so on), the book is obliged to consider more occult bases: confusion, error, ignorance, prejudice, atavism, history and culture. Odder still, these steamy imperatives surface in the driest of stories, a tale of committee rooms and paper-pushing, of treaties and multilateral negotiations.

In late 1993, world trade talks involving more than 100 nations, and aimed at concluding the so-called Uruguay Round of the General Agreement on Tariffs and Trade (GATT), came close to foundering. At issue was the implementation by the then 12 nations of the European Union, under a policy unblushingly called "Television Without Frontiers", of quotas on US -made programs and films shown on European television screens.[3] The Europeans, led by France, claimed a "cultural exception" to the GATT. The huge social and cultural influence on the fabric of European life of massive numbers of American programs should not, it was argued, be subject to a treaty aimed merely at reducing barriers to trade. The US, for its part, claimed that Europe was wrapping itself in the flag of culture to justify old fashioned commercial protectionism. The mutual accusations and recriminations as the GATT talks teetered on the verge of breakdown were unusually bitter and undiplomatic. And then, at the last minute, the two sides agreed to disagree. No "cultural exception" was incorporated into the GATT, but the quotas stayed in place. The issue, it was decided, could wait another day.

That day has yet to come. When (and if) it does come, two baffling facts will probably once more go unacknowledged as the US and Europe next square off. These facts are:

- The quotas cause virtually no economic damage to United States commercial interests.

- European audiences, unhelped by governments, overwhelmingly prefer domestic programs to foreign ones, including those from the US As a reflection of this, most European television networks voluntarily show fewer American programs than the quotas allow.

Despite this, American fury at these nugatory, innocuous quotas remains undimmed. And the European – or rather, the French – conviction that its culture must hold the line against an invasion of corrosive, alien pap remains as steadfast as ever.

This book is about how policy may be formed by largely irrational, atavistic forces. It examines both the commercial and cultural arguments concerning the quotas in both historical and current perspectives. It shows how the impasse between the two parties owes much more to mutual suspicion than to any genuine, verifiable commercial or cultural threat the one poses the other.

The book is organized as a series of contextual discussions of cultural, historical, political and industrial factors. The book first shows how the present quota dispute is the latest incarnation of a 90-year-old transatlantic face-off with its roots in the film business. It looks at the deep roots of Franco-American distrust, and how they came into being. It traces the history of French fear of contamination by American culture, in particularly by Hollywood feature films. It then shows how this fear was exacerbated by highly divergent views of the function of cinema itself and, in particular, the nature of cinema authorship, both in creative and legal terms.

In its second part, following an explanation of the industrial and economic organization of the international television industry, the book examines the events of the dispute, from the perspective of the GATT, the European Union and the United States. Because these events are sometimes inexplicable otherwise, they are often viewed from the perspective of the players: strong, smart, exasperating personalities who occasionally substituted the strength of their wills for the substance of their arguments.

The focus of this book is on how these issues played out between France and the United States, although at times, examples from other European countries are used to support some arguments. In particular, two sections draw heavily on discussions of other countries: the introduction of motion picture quotas in Germany and Britain in the 1920s, which predated the first French quotas; and the discussion of television quotas in Europe between the 1950s and 1980s, which focuses on Britain rather than France because of the ready availability of detailed information on the policy discussions that brought about the quotas.

The choice of France as the principal exemplar of these arguments is for three reasons. First, France was the leading voice on the European side throughout the GATT dispute. Secondly, France has historically been the most prominent European critic of American culture. Third, the concept of French national culture, while not unbothered by definitional and subjective questions, is less troubling than the idea of some kind of homogeneous transfrontier European culture, no matter how ancient that latter idea might be. It has become a truism that the nation-state is an "imagined political community," wherein a contest for control of the nation's identity may lead to attempts to "seize the popular spirit and fill it with ideas of loyalty." [4] Nevertheless, "France" is something one understands the moment once crosses the French border. "Europe," and the idea of a European culture, may have emerged in the sixteenth century as a humanist successor to the idea of Christendom,[5] but there is not yet, despite the efforts of the past half century, a "European" identity as strong as that of any of the continent's many nation-states.

The book concludes with a discussion of the ramifications for policy making of making analysis in a state of what, for want of a better term, might be called "false consciousness." It also suggests how policy outcomes might be affected if the various parties could see their positions more clearly.

---

1   "What's Right With America", speech to the Poor Richard Club, Philadelphia (Jan. 18, 1938), in Post-Presidential Papers, File Hays, Will H. (National Archives, Herbert Hoover Presidential Library), cited in Ian Jarvie, "Dollars and Ideology: Will H. Hays' Economic Foreign Policy 1922-1945" *Film History* 2 (1988), 216. New York, London. Taylor & Francis.

2   François Truffaut, *Hitchcock* (rev. ed. 1986), 97. London, Paladin.

3   *Council Directive of 3 October 1989 on the coordination of certain provisions laid down by law, regulation of administrative action in Member States concerning the pursuit of television activities.* 89/552/EEC, 1989 O.J. (L 298) 23-30. This is often known as the "Television Without Frontiers" directive, from the title of the consultative document that led to the promulgation of the directive. *Television Without Frontiers: Green Paper on the Establishment of the Common Market for Broadcasting, Especially by Satellite and Cable, Communication from the Commission to the Council*, COM(84) 300 final, 14 June 1984.

4   Benedict Anderson, *Imagined Communities* (rev. ed. 1991), 6. London. Verso. See also, Monroe E. Price,
"The Market for Loyalties: Electronic Media and the Global Competition for Allegiances" , *Yale Law Journal* 104 (1994), 681, which applies this idea to the mass media.

5   For example, John Hale, *The Civilization of Europe in the Renaissance* (1994), 3-50. London, HarperCollins.

Part 1

Culture

1

American culture and France

[Q] - How, in your opinion, are the influences of the United States manifesting themselves upon Europe and in Europe?

[A] - Through the most emphatic garbage, the ignoble sense of money, the indigence of ideas, the savage hypocrisy in morals, and altogether through a loathsome swinishness pushed to the point of paroxysm.

Benjamin Péret, 1928.[1]

God damn the continent of Europe. It is of merely antiquarian interest. ... France makes me sick. Its silly pose as the thing the world has to save. ... Culture follows money, and all the refinements of aestheticism can't stave off its change of seat. ... We will be Romans in the next generations as the English are now.

F. Scott Fitzgerald, 1921.[2]

Any discussion of how groups as large, diverse – and to some extent supposititious – as nations come to view each other inevitably runs the risks of both speculativeness and over-generalization. Yet it is also a truism that names of nations such as "America" or "France" evoke meanings which extend far beyond the topographical, political and legal definitions which provide their formal delimits. If the act of physical travel has become atavistic, as the Swiss writer Max Frisch suggested,[3] how much more so has the imaginary travel of the mind involved in constructing the meaning of an entire country?[4] The atavism of the traveler, imaginary or otherwise, entails the engagement of his own cultural imperatives with the country in which he travels. When the country in question is the United States, with its immense size, population, resources and presence, the level of this engagement is correspondingly magnified. Conversely, American voyaging is always refracted through the American's view of him or herself.

While there are obvious pitfalls to discussing the way nations see each other on a cultural level it does not seem too extreme to state that there is something in the view France has of America – and vice versa – that goes beyond the empirically verifiable and that resides in the worlds of attitude, ignorance, fear, prejudice, projection and incomprehension. To an extent this is one way traffic: for reasons that will become clearer, France is more preoccupied with America than the other way round. But as F. Scott Fitzgerald's outburst shows, there is something in France's insistence on the importance of its own culture that sends others reaching for their revolvers. The roots go deep.

Early attitudes

Africa, Asia and America have successfully felt [Europe's] domination. The superiority, she has long maintained, has tempted her to plume herself as the Mistress of the World and to consider the rest of mankind as created for her benefit.[5]

Alexander Hamilton

AMERICANIZE [amerikanize] tr[ansitive] v[erb]. To give an American character. – (1866) Pronom[ial].

To Americanize (Often pej[orative]). Europe is becoming Americanized.[6]

With the fall of the Soviet Union, France and the United States are probably now the two countries whose modern political discourse most constantly evokes the principles – real or imagined – of their establishing revolutions, of "Republican values" on the one hand and those of the "Founding Fathers" on the other. Yet these the systems that were the product of these two revolutions – arguably the main political events that shaped the contemporary western world – were, despite superficial similarities and affinities, at odds with each other within a very short time following their creation.

Geopolitics had a big part to play in this rupture, as these two proud, powerful nations vied for influence in the north Atlantic, and elsewhere. France may have assisted America in its war of independence, and the subsequent French revolution owed inspiration to the American example; however, relations between the new United States and France were already frosty by the end of the eighteenth century. There was widespread revulsion in America towards the French experiment in regicide and the massacres of aristocrats and political enemies of the revolution. In addition, the constant flux of post-revolutionary France – fourteen changes of government in 26 years – made for an uncertain and unpredictable foreign policy. This manifested itself in a series of diplomatic outrages. In April 1793, when the American republic was barely 10 years old, the French minister to the United States, Edmond Charles Edouard Genêt, landed in the new nation and attempted to enlist men and fit out ships for France's wars. Rebuked by Washington, Genêt tried appealing over his head to the American people and was quickly recalled to France at the request of the government. Five years later, the so-called "XYZ affair" was exposed to Congress by John Adams: three American peace envoys to France were asked for bribes and a $12 million loan before negotiations could begin. And, in the closing years of the eighteenth century, France and the United States fought a "limited and undeclared" naval war which further poisoned relations.[7]

However, an even more profound division between the two countries centered on how each saw itself, and others. It is a commonplace that in the conscious effort to develop its own culture, the new American Republic was anxious to emphasize what it was not. Notoriously, thanks to its constitutional arrangements, it was not black, or Indian. But there is also an important sense in which the white men of European stock who created the United States were determined not to be European. "Why," George Washington said in his farewell address, "by interweaving our destiny with that of any part of Europe, entangle our peace and prosperity to the toils of European Ambition, Rivalship, Interest, Humour or Caprice?"[8] Washington, a politician and soldier, presumably had politics and war on his mind. His contemporary Alexander Hamilton, quoted at the beginning of this section, went further and perceived in Europe a set of attitudes that went beyond mere power.

It is perhaps not surprising that Washington and Hamilton declined the gift of French citizenship from the National Assembly in Paris, although James Madison accepted.[9] (Even Madison, however, with Hamilton, "warned against the creation [in America] of large European-style cities with their physical congestion, frustrated mobs, and social dislocations" and "deplored the factionalizing effects of European politics".)[10]

One pioneer historian of American cultural attitudes, Howard Mumford Jones, concluded that early Americans, to the extent that such can be generalized, embraced a range of attitudes to France, all of which denoted a particular strength of feeling towards that country. Thus, some were held by Jones to feel "a sense of religious difference," which "carries with it a suspicion of French morality, of French infidelity, and of French Catholicism."[11] However, Jones argued that among those who possessed "the cosmopolitan spirit" the religious sense was weaker, yielding to the "important element which has developed in our history ... that things French came to *possess social prestige* for the Americans."[12] Between these two "contradictory attitudes":

> ... the Americans, and the middle-class Americans in particular, have developed a third belief concerning the French which has been powerful in the relations between the two people ... the idea that the French are predominantly a *fickle and unreliable people*. The very fact that the most unchanging factor in the cultural relation has been social prestige given French manners and French arts has likewise helped to build up this notion. To the average American in our period the most obvious facts about the French were, first, that they were politically unstable, and second, that their principal production were articles of luxury, fashions, millinery, the dancing master, an exaggerated sense of punctilio, and various other things or qualities which seemed to him unworthy of serious consideration by a truly great and important people.[13]

Nevertheless, and probably because of the books we read, it is perhaps more natural to see the American view of France and Europe refracted through the eyes of such nineteenth and early twentieth figures as Henry James, Edith Wharton, F. Scott Fitzgerald, Ernest Hemingway and Mark Twain – all possessors of Howard Mumford Jones' "cosmopolitan spirit" – than of the great middle class, still more than ever the talismanic exemplars of the American soul who, despite their mistrust, are still bound to Europe and its culture. One American critic, Leslie Fiedler, has equated this bond, the embrace of European culture among nineteenth-century American travelers, as a kind of apostasy, "which is to say the surrender of essential 'Americanism,' as defined in the WASP tradition."[14] Yet this apostasy still beckoned the nineteenth century middle classes:

> ... in whose name Mark Twain [in *The Innocents Abroad*] pretended to speak; for Twain represents merely the other side of the old WASP ambivalence, its secular Puritanism, that rear of High Art and High Church worship which the followers of Henry Adams had rejected in favor of the religion of Art. Twain may refuse the virgin and choose the dynamo, but he remains immeasurably closer to the first American travelers in Europe than any latter-day American Catholic or Negro or Jew. Whatever sense of alienation he may feel from Dante, Shakespeare, and Michelangelo, to Shakespeare at least he is bound by a kinship of blood and tradition he can never quite disavow.[15]

Europe had become a kind of forbidden fruit, fascinating but threatening. And France was not only totemically European: it had taken on the cultural value of being inversely American. The idea of the two cultures residing at opposite poles was something with which the French, too, would grow comfortable.

Although the term "Americanize" was apparently first used in Britain in the 1830s, it spread quickly to France.[16] The earliest recorded use of the verb "to Americanize" in French is contained, predictably, in a bitter tirade against America. The poet Charles Baudelaire expressed his pity for the "poor man" who is:

> ... so Americanized by his zoocratic and industrial philosophers that he has lost the idea of the differences which characterize the phenomena of the physical world and of the moral world, of the natural and of the supernatural.[17]

For Baudelaire, Americanization was not only an idea, but a process wherein the surrender to brutish desires inevitably entailed a loss of moral sense. The concept of Americanization as a force – a malign force – would never be lost from the French language. The philosopher Elme-Marie Caro, who was wrongly credited with introducing the term "Americanize" . . .

> ... employed the verb *s'américaniser* to describe, not the real America, but the disappearance of a society of cultivated people which had reached its apogee in eighteenth century France, and its replacement by one dominated by the vulgar and crassly commercial concerns of the contemporary world. *S'américaniser* did not really refer to America at all.[18]

This idea of America as a projection of France's darkest fears had its apogee in another work of Baudelaire's, his hugely influential essay of 1852, *Edgar Poe, Sa Vie et Ses Oeuvres*, which situated Edgar Allan Poe as a European mind imprisoned in the physical surroundings of the United States:

> The various documents that I have just read have created in me this conviction that the United States were for Poe a vast cage, a great accounting establishment, and that all his life he made feeble efforts to escape the influence of this antipathetic atmosphere. In one of the biographies it is said that, if M. Poe have wanted to wanted to straighten out his genius and apply his creative faculties in a more appropriate fashion on American soil, he could have been "un auteur à argent," a *money-making author* ...[19]

[Poe, of course, has been widely expropriated for different reasons. As Leslie Fiedler has pointed out, if for Baudelaire, Poe was the "*poète maudit*, ... the *Edgairpo* of the Europeans, which to this day baffles visitors from our side of the Atlantic," in his home country he "became for the American imagination the eternal prototype of the American Writer," particularly in the self-destructive form of a F. Scott Fitzgerald or a Hart Crane.[20] The American "Poe" may have taken longer to grip the national imagination: arguing about American literature in 1947 with the editors of *Partisan Review*, Simone de Beauvoir noted dryly – and shrewdly – that Poe appeared to be "a French author."[21]]

The idea that the choice between art and money was imposed by American society was thus an early and potent one for the French imagination. It was not a choice simply created by specific American conditions: it was intrinsic to the idea of America, the invasive value of a new, unexpected and alarming force in the world. For Europeans in general, and not merely the French, the newness of America signified a lack of traditions and roots, a source of horror to many. Although, for others, precisely this characteristic contained America's mythic appeal. Goethe, for instance, hoped that God would preserve America in future "from Europe's mournful legacy, from romantic ruins, from tales of bandits, knights and ghosts".[22]

In fact, French attitudes to the United States always contained a more enthusiastic current, which, like Alexis de Tocqueville, looked to America favorably – if questioningly – for a social model that would overtake the old European ways.[23] In other words, the enthusiasts located in the United States precisely what appalled America's antagonists: an unstoppable force for unfettered change. This opposition mirrored the crucial faultline in French society, that created by the 1789 revolution[24] and which would never cease to underlie the constant upheavals of political and private life. In 1815, 1830, 1848, 1871 and 1940, the pendulum of power would swing decisively between Republican forces – heirs of the Revolution – and monarchist or dictatorial forces, counter-revolutionaries never fully converted to democracy.[25] Even the modern French Republic, the Fifth, was created in 1958 out of a barely-thwarted military *coup d'état*.[26]

Poe may have been a European *manqué* in some French eyes, but Europeans knew there was a distinctive American culture – a very different one. Literature provided the romance of the American west, from the respectable works of James Fenimore Cooper to the "hugely popular" and "widely imitated" dime novel.[27] In the wake of the western novel came the western show, a new and heroic form that barnstormed across nineteenth century Europe, often appearing at the world trade fairs that celebrated Victorian invention and entrepreneurism, where the cowboys seemed to present an alternative version of the possible world:

> At the world fairs, civilization was often symbolized in the form of a woman in classical garb. Buffalo Bill offered a strikingly different image: a virile, violent male, independent of domestic life and of the growing realm of consumer society represented by the department store or the World's Fair itself.[28]

Whatever his symbolic weight, however, Buffalo Bill was himself a product of consumer society, a spectacle marketed and sold by impresarios and showmen. P.T. Barnum may have been the first – in print, at least – to speak the language that would later be commonplace in the world of Hollywood.

> The show business has all phases and grades of dignity, from the exhibition of a monkey to the exposition of that highest art in music or the drama, which entrances empires and secures for the gifted artist a world-wide fame which princes might well envy. Such art is merchantable, and so with the whole range of amusements, from the highest to the lower. The old word "trade" as it applies to buying cheap and selling at a profit, is as manifest here as it is in the dealings at a street-corner stand or in Stewart's store covering a whole square. This is a trading world, and men, women and children, who cannot live on gravity alone, need something to satisfy their gayer, lighter moods and hours, and he who ministers to this want is in a business established by the Author of our nature. If he worthily fulfills his mission, and amuses without corrupting, he need never feel that he has lived in vain.[29]

Long before the arrival of the cinema, America appeared synonymous with mass entertainment and the cheerful business of making money thereby. As far as Europe – and particularly France – was concerned, "Hollywood" had been invented before the film makers had even found it.

Twentieth century attitudes

In the 1960s the Black Panther Party leader Eldridge Cleaver, meditating on America's worldwide influence, wondered what it must be like for non-Americans to watch the US and its Cold War-era dominance. They had to feel:

> ... like passengers in a supersonic jet liner who are forced to watch helplessly while a passel of drunks, hypes, freaks, and madmen fight for the controls and the pilot's seat.[30]

Cleaver, an American, captures the mixed feelings of fear, bafflement, bemusement and amazement found in European accounts of the United States, its power and its culture. (Being a somewhat alienated American, he does not acknowledge a final feeling – admiration.)

It is also telling that Cleaver uses the image of non-Americans trapped inside a high-tech American-run machine. For it is the America of the machine age, at once awesome and loathsome, that magnifies and intensifies European, particularly French, attitudes to the US and its culture. As the great inventions and discoveries of the later 19th and early 20th centuries – the typewriter, the telephone, electric light, the internal combustion engine, powered flight – were harnessed, when they were not actually American inventions, by American entrepreneurism, the image of the inexorability of American growth became fixed. A Thomas Edison was not simply a pure scientist or disinterested savant in the classic mold: he was also entrepreneur, businessman, monopolist and robber-baron, a man with genius but without culture. In one formulation, "American had machines and no culture; France had culture and few machines."[31] This technological hegemony was not the only troubling factor that differentiated America from France; American democracy also seemed threatening, a social unleashing that did not also appear to threaten disintegration and revolution; indeed, it appeared to be ideologically engaged in the same mission as the entrepreneur-technologists. As one French observer, Paul Bourget, noted:

> Equal social possibility – such is the democratic formula in America. Equal social reality – such is the formula in Europe, and primarily in France, since the Revolution of 1789. I know nothing so contradictory. ... It is a conservative democracy – that is to say, exactly the opposite of ours.[32]

The rise of Hollywood coincided with the rise of the machine, so that the American cinema came to be considered exemplar, infant and victim of its age, On the eve of the Second World War, a French cultural critic, Bernard Faÿ, would declare that the "American cinema was massacred by the engineers and the inventors."[33]

As will be seen, one feature of France's success in defeating US attempts upon its television quotas was political unity: in the key period of the quota battles, 1984-1993, there were changes in government between left and right, but little discernible shift in policies, regardless of political ideology. On the French left, anti-Americanism was largely a post-war phenomenon, fueled partly by the French Communist Party (PCF), which mounted attacks on the US during the great struggle for influence in Europe between Moscow and Washington after the 1945 victory. In addition, the non-Communist New Left that emerged after the Hungarian uprising of 1956 culpabilized the US as well as the USSR for the Cold War and found massive support in its attacks on the American war in Vietnam.

This longstanding political consensus of left and right (although not the entire right) can make us lose sight of the fact that, before 1945, the European left had a more nuanced view of American power. Partly this was because conventional Marxism-Leninism held that advanced capitalist societies were meant to be closer to their inevitable transformation into socialist economies. Karl Marx himself, in the mid-nineteenth century, had regarded the US' burgeoning and unchecked capitalism as a far better candidate for socialist revolution than, say, Russia. What is more, the New World seemed refreshingly free of the clogging sedimentation of petit-bourgeois, rentiers, bureaucrats, clergy, military castes and others whose persistence in Europe only obscured and obstructed the historic opposition between fundamental economic forces. As described by the Italian marxist Antonio Gramsci:

> This condition could be called "a rational demographic composition" and consists in the fact that there do not exist numerous classes with no essential function in the world of production, in other words classes which are purely parasitic. European "tradition", European "civilization", is, conversely, characterized precisely by the existence of such classes, created by the "richness" and "complexity" of past history.[34]

Of course, Gramsci's view simply recalibrates the classic opinion of America as a place without culture, except that this lack is to be approved of. Indeed, Gramsci believed that American culture was simply purloined from the Old Continent: "all that they do in America is to remasticate the old European culture."[35] Of greater interest was the way in which a new approach to production, sometimes called Fordism (after its putative founder, Henry Ford), appeared to be transforming the social order in the United States. In this view – although he may not have meant to say it – Gramsci linked Hollywood to the wealthy class that must be swept away by revolution. The argument ran thus: Advanced production creates greater wealth. This wealth continues to be concentrated in the upper classes. The upper classes squander their wealth in extravagance and moral degradation. Upper class women are more morally degenerate because, unlike their industrialist husbands and fathers, they have nothing to do. They thus, in Gramsci's words, become "luxury mammals." The accompanying standards of beauty and femininity "stimulate the mental attitudes of prostitution." And, to prove it, look how "30,000 Italian girls ... sent photographs of themselves in bathing costumes to Fox in 1926."[36]

It is not to be imagined that these 30,000 girls were from the upper classes. or that Gramsci really thought so. But what is striking is how production techniques so impressive that their application to the Soviet economy had been seriously considered,[37] were viewed, in the context of a capitalist system, as corrosive and immoral. Given that, for better or worse, a capitalist system was what Europe and the United States had, the Gramscian view (not of itself influential until the "rediscovery" of Gramsci in the 1960s) reflected the more widely-held attitude that American industrial dynamism produced a social and cultural impact that was transforming Europe.

Fordism gave rise to pessimism, and pessimism to dystopianism. Aldous Huxley's *Brave New World* was set in an explicitly Fordist future (the late Henry having been apotheosized as the Christ like "our Ford") where all individualism has been excised from a completely industrialized system, where no history is taught, and where the highest form of pleasure is instant self-gratification.[38] Fritz Lang's film

Metropolis,[39] the big-budget, German production that the UFA studio hoped would show it capable of matching Hollywood at its most lavish,[40] evoked the vast, dehumanizing machine age with a dehumanizing vastness of its own[41] – 36,000 performers, 500 skyscrapers, four million feet of film.[42]

The meditations of Gramsci, Ford and Lang on Fordism point to the intersection of three features of Hollywood that made it a particularly intense exemplar of the new age. Its films were themselves a product of the machine revolution that was transforming America and the world: when Europe tried, as with *Metropolis*, to match Hollywood's industrial might, it courted disaster and ruin. Through these films, Hollywood depicted the transformational values of this new epoch, where mass-production of objects produced a parallel mass-generation of imitative mores and attitudes. Finally, Hollywood's audiences, feasting on these depictions, themselves appeared to be a dopey embodiment of these enormous changes, a mass seeking entertainment, not culture, valuing novelty, not tradition.

These themes came together in a French dystopian book of 1930, George Duhamel's *Scènes de la vie future* (translated, lest the lesson be missed, as *America The Menace*). For Duhamel, the luxury movie palaces that had sprung up in the previous decade were the epitome of the ugliness of the machine age:

> And, indeed the place had the luxury of some big bourgeois brothel – an industrialized luxury made by soulless machines for a crowd whose own soul seems to be disappearing and looking for a uniform, since you find it in all establishments of the kind from one end of the Union to the other.[43]

Nor did Duhamel spare the films or the audiences in such places:

> It is a diversion for Helots,[44] a pastime for the illiterate, for miserable creatures, stupefied by their drudgery and their cares. It is skillfully poisoned, the food for a multitude that the forces of Moloch have judged, condemned and which they finish by degrading.[45]

Not all French commentators saw in America the embodiment of the forces of Moloch. As with Tocqueville in the 19th century, some were exhilarated – or at least impressed – by the vitality of American democracy, even in the machine age:

> The machine, engine of social peace, is a precious supplement to national unity. The American people do not live, as in our old countries, on accumulated wisdom, on joys and sadness suffered in common, on innumerable experiments attempted and turned into habits; it is not its past that keeps it united, but the desire and hope that it has for a magnificent future promised to its children and to itself, if it know how to work.... The machine is turned entirely towards the future.[46]

Both optimists and pessimists paradoxically saw in America the same thing: the future. While the majority may have joined with the Dadaist Tristan Tzara, in excoriating America's "glorification of work, that stupid ideology which has engendered the idea of material progress,"[47] an influential minority saw in the US the lessons that had to be drawn in order to modernize Europe – and to resist

American economic power.[48] From the dawn of Hollywood, the French in particular have used America as a blank slate upon which to write their own version of both present and future, from Blaise Cendrars, intoxicated by the new, young film industry that had sprung up from nowhere,[49] to Jean Baudrillard, perpetually bemused by the "real" America that, for him, exists as the America of the cinema.[50]

However, fascination also breeds fear, particularly where culture is concerned. Fears of American newness, of its industrial power, of its mass tastes, of its lack of traditions – and the way in which all these values meshed and appeared to depend on each other – have been seen to exist virtually since the birth of American democracy. But when the focus of European and French concerns has been purely on culture, and on the impact and influence of American culture, the debate takes on a different tone, embodying a particular kind of anti-Americanism characterized by one French writer by "a quality of obsession, and by the rejection of any attempt at rational appraisal – or even irrational, but intelligible appraisal."[51] In the years following 1945, the United States saw itself transformed by military victory and economic strength into a superpower, into what once would have been called an empire. In the eyes of America's critics, where there was an empire, there had to be imperialism. And where there was imperialism, there resided always one particularly virulent form of domination without war: cultural imperialism.

Cultural imperialism

The attack on American cinema for what it represented culturally began early in France. In 1918, Edmond Rostand, author of *Cyrano de Bergerac*, proposed setting up a French Cinema League; others, at around the same time, called for a cinema equivalent of the national theatre, the Comédie Française: all called for tax benefits and subsidies for the national cinema.[52] By 1930, American cinema in France was said to have engaged in an "invasion," and the general American economic project qualified as "imperialism."[53] As will be seen in the discussion of the first introduction of quotas in Europe, there was always concern about the influence of the *content* of American film, parallel with fears about their economic *impact*. Nonetheless, while such films were often regarded as vehicles for American propaganda, often at the expense of the truth – for instance, the 1919 victory parade at the Arc de Triomphe through which, according to MGM, only the American army marched[54] – it took time for this phenomenon to be regarded by critics as a fully-fledged and conscious project to conquer the world with American values.

The picture was complicated by the ideological polarization of the post-Second World War period, where the American and Soviet systems were vying for influence across the globe and where the opposing sides each proclaimed moral and political superiority derived from their economic and cultural systems. Before 1945, Hollywood's worries about the impact of the content of its films in foreign markets were concerned above all with offending governments and thereby losing market access:

Sinclair Lewis's book *It Can't Happen Here* was shelved [as a film project]. It might offend nations governed by dictators. Mexico raged furiously against Hollywood cowboy pictures which always made the villain a Mexican. This had to be stopped and was. Certain Balkan countries objected to their countrymen being portrayed as spies. This was immediately done away with. The Chinese Government has raised protests against the consistent showing of their nationals as back country bandits with long, drooping moustaches. Hollywood watches that carefully .... The reason that Hollywood is so careful to avoid offending foreign nations and foreign audiences in its films is the fact that receipts on pictures from outside this country have been growing more and more each year.[55]

After 1945, American industrial, political and cultural interests increasingly were identified, particularly on the left, as products of the same ambition: in order to conquer markets, the US needed to conquer the minds of consumers. This congruity of interests was important, because it distinguished what came to be called cultural imperialism from the more explicitly ideological efforts of the sinking empires of Europe, notably Britain and France, to stamp their cultures directly upon their colonies around the world.

European resistance to American culture was also conditioned by imperial decline, in marked contrast to the soaring arc of American influence. In both Britain and France, post-1945 attitudes were also conditioned by differing forms of disdain for the war's clear victor, the United States. Britain, although on the winning side, had a shattered economy and a clearly reduced role in the postwar world: there was also the popular view that the Second World War was "its" war, and that American intervention, while welcome, merely provided a backup.[56] In France, first defeated by Germany, then liberated largely by the US, a "deep collective sentiment of inferiority" was forged into a "nationalism of humiliation," characterized by anti-Americanism and an equally uncritical pro-Soviet sentiment.[57] American goods and services were not merely products – they were vehicles for American culture, conveyors of taste that turned foreign consumers from a preference for native products towards favoring the alien alternatives. This "unambiguous domination of one dependent culture by a clearly demarcated other"[58] was pejoratively labeled cultural imperialism.

This essentially Marxist-Leninist view of the imperialist motives of American capitalism was developed in critiques of the American television industry by scholars based in the US Indeed, it was this apparent American capacity for self-criticism that gave fuel to the cultural imperialism thesis in Europe and elsewhere, and respectability to the anti-Americanism on which it attended.[59]

One influential exponent of the cultural imperialism thesis, Herbert Schiller, saw the expansion of American-style commercial television worldwide as an essential ingredient to create advertising vehicles that would promote global American products:

Nothing less than the viability of the American industrial economy itself is involved in the movement toward international commercialization of broadcasting.[60]

Another American-based researcher, Alan Wells, documented the symbiotic connections between the spread of American-style advertising, consumerism and television in the economies of Latin America, concluding that these phenomena blocked the development of those countries.[61]

This cultural imperialism model was widely criticized, partly on methodological grounds, including the lack of adequate empirical data, "subjectivism" and insufficient analysis of audience reactions to television programs.[62] The cultural imperialism thesis, as limited to the US, was also attacked for failing to "confront the presence of strong regional exploiters in various parts of the world," such as Mexico, Argentina, Egypt, India, Britain, France, Germany, Italy, Spain, Japan, Sweden and the USSR.[63] Further, the vulnerability of "traditional culture" to American influence was itself a problematic concept. Cultures had their own internal faultlines that might lead to disruption without outside influence, as in the case of civil wars. They depended on ideas that might in any case be in decline, such as religious beliefs. Further, such traditional cultures could have within them "unpopular characteristics" – attitudes towards women, the young, the poor – by contrast with which imported culture might seem more attractive.[64] In other words, cultural imperialism's use of the term "culture" was insufficiently nuanced, while its use of the term "imperialism" crudely stacked the deck:

> A ... fundamental problem is [cultural imperialism's] implicit assumption of 'culture' as an organic, self-contained entity with fixed boundaries, whose traditional wholesomeness is presumed to be crushed by the superimposition of another, equally self-contained, 'dominant culture'. As a result, talk about cultural imperialism often tends to collude with a defense of conservative positions of cultural puritanism and protectionism, To put it differently, this perspective too easily locates the 'global' as the site of cultural erosion and destruction, and the 'local' as the site of pristine cultural 'authenticity'.[65]

However, regardless of the academic critique now so widespread as to represent a consensus, the cultural imperialism model lost little of its *popular* force. Cultural imperialism had a comforting Manichean simplicity, dividing the world into good guys and bad guys (or rather, one bad guy). It was fed by an important half-truth. American culture was everywhere. In France, after the war, this was not limited to films. American comic strips flooded the country, menacing the local comic book trade which, like the cinema, had flourished under the insulation of the occupation.[66] Jazz music, pulp fiction, the radio – all provided other venues where the values of the New and Old Worlds seemed to battle.[67] The post 1956 New Left in France and elsewhere abandoned Soviet Communism, but not the anti-Americanism it had taught them: instead, they were able to apply the rhetoric of cultural imperialism to the new dynamic of struggle and liberation they now espoused. American popular culture was simultaneously embraced, for its own liberating impulses, and reviled for its corporate and institutional roots. The most superficially innocent of American cultural products, the Disney cartoon, was revealed by this approach to be dragged along in the undertow of imperialist ideology.[68]

It is tempting to psychoanalyze the cultural imperialism thesis, to see in it, as in its fellow-traveler anti-Americanism, a form of scapegoating by both Left and Right, a common desire to expunge humiliation and failure through finding a blameworthy target. Indeed, Jean-François Revel did just this, in accusing the Right of employing anti-Americanism to express rage at France's postwar decline, and the Left of doing the same to mask the global failure of the socialist experiment.[69] But for our purposes here, the main importance of cultural imperialism is phenomenological: it is the ever-present motif, cross-political and unifying, that stands as a permanent critique of American cultural power. It can be evoked without even mentioning it. When Jack Lang, France's culture minister, made a notorious attack on the United States during a speech in Mexico in 1982, he never used the term "cultural imperialism." Everyone knew what he meant however: under Lang, French cultural policy was lastingly transformed into an instrument for fighting this insinuating enemy.

1   From Benjamin Péret's contribution to Eugène Jolas, "Inquiry Among European Writers Into The Spirit Of America," *transition* no. 13 (Summer 1928), 248, 250. Paris: Eugene Jolas.

2   Letter from F. Scott Fitzgerald to Edmund Wilson (May, 1921), in *The Letters of F. Scott Fitzgerald*, (Andrew Turnbull ed., 1963), 326. New York: Scribner. Some Europeans, however reluctantly, came to see things Fitzgerald's way, as notably exemplified by future British prime minister Harold Macmillan's famous wartime letter to a future cabinet minister, Richard Crossman:

> We ... are Greeks in this American Empire. You will find the Americans much as the Greeks found the Romans – great, big, vulgar, bustling people, more vigorous than we are and also more idle, with more unspoilt virtues but also more corrupt. We must run the [allied forces headquarters at which Macmillan was stationed] as the Greek slaves ran the operations of the Emperor Claudius.

Quoted in Joseph Frankel, *British Foreign Policy* 1945-1973 (1975), 163. London. New York: Published for the Royal Institute of International Affairs by Oxford University Press.

3   C.W.E. Bigsby, "Europe, America and the Cultural Debate," in *Super Culture: American Popular Culture and Europe* (C.W.E. Bigsby, ed., 1975), 2. Bowling Green Ohio: Bowling Green University Press and London, Elek.

4   For another account of the nation as imagined community, see Eric Hobsbawm, "The Nation as Invented Tradition," in *Nationalism* (John Hutchinson & Anthony D. Smith eds., 1994), 76. Oxford: Oxford University Press.

5   Howard Mumford Jones, *O Strange New World: American Culture: The Formative Years* (1964), 325-26. New York: Viking Press.

6   Josette Rey-Debove & Gilberte Gagnon, *Dictionnaire Des Anglicismes* (1988), 17-18 . Unless otherwise noted, all translations from French are mine. Paris: Le Robert.

7   *O Strange New World*, 322; Howard Mumford Jones, *America and French Culture 1750-1848*

(1927; reissued ed. 1973), 546; Westpont Conn.: Greenwood Press, Maldwyn A. Jones, *The Limits Of Liberty* (1983), 86. Oxford: Oxford University Press.

8   *O Strange New World*, 327.

9   Paul Merrill Spurlin, *The Enlightenment In America* (1984), 23-24. Athens, Ga: University of Georia.

10   Richard Pells, *Not Like Us: How Europeans Have Loved, Hated and Transformed American Culture Since World War II* (1997), 4. New York: Basic Books.

11   *America and French Culture*, 569.

12   *America and French Culture*, 570 (emphasis in original).

13   *America and French Culture*, 569-71 (emphasis in original).

14   Leslie A. Fiedler, "Afterword," to Mark Twain, *The Innocents Abroad* (1869; reissued, 1980),495. New York: Signet New American Library; London: Signet, New English Library.

15   Ibid, 495-96.

16   *Not Like Us*, 7.

17   Charles W. Brooks, *America in France's hopes and fears, 1890-1920* (1987), 1:60. New York, London: Garland. Baudelaire defined "zoocractic" thus: "... from the impious love of liberty is born a new tyranny, the tyranny of beasts, or zoocracy, which by its savage insensibility bears a resemblance to the idol of Juggernaut." Brooks, 1:61-2.

18   Ibid, 1:58.

19   Charles Baudelaire, *Oeuvres Complètes* (Claude Pichois, ed., 1975), 2:249-50 (emphasis in original). Paris: Gallimard.

20   Leslie A. Fiedler, *Love and Death in the American Novel* (rev. ed. 1966; reissued, 1984), 424-25, 428. Harmondsworth: Penguin.

21   Simone de Beauvoir, *L'Amérique au jour le jour* (1948), 58. Paris Éditions Paul Morihien

22   Quoted in Peter Duignan and L.H. Gann, *An Ambivalent Heritage: Euro-American Relations* (1984), 5. Stanford: Hoover Institution on War, Revolution and Peace, Stanford University Press.

23   See generally, *Democracy in America* (1835). London: Saunders and Otley.

24   See. eg. François Furet, *Interpreting the French Revolution* (1981). Cambridge: Cambridge University Press.

25   For material on French history, I have mostly relied on the various volumes of the Cambridge History of Modern France: André Jardin, *Restoration and reaction*, 1815-1848 (1983); Maurice Agulhon, *The Republican experiment*, 1848-1852 (1983); Alain Plessis, *The rise and fall of the Second Empire, 1852-1871* (1985); Jean-Marie Mayeur and Madeleine Reberioux, *The Third Republic from its origins to the Great War, 1871-1914* (1984); Philippe Bernard and Henri Dubief, *The decline of the Third Republic, 1914-1938* (1985); Jean-Pierre Azema, *From Munich to the Liberation, 1938-1944* (1984); Jean-Pierre Rioux, *The Fourth Republic, 1944-1958* (1987); Serge Berstein, *The Republic of De Gaulle, 1958-1969* (1993). Cambridge: Cambridge University Press.

26   The tension between Republican and reactionary or counter-revolutionary values cannot, of course, account alone for French attitudes towards America. Jean-Philippe Mathy, for instance, has described six "interpretive clusters" to classify the various views in the twentieth century while warning that the coherence of even this larger group of categories should not be overemphasized. Jean-Philippe Mathy, *Extrême-Occident: French intellectuals and America* (1993), 9. Chicago, London: University of Chicago Press.

27   John F. Sears, "Bierstadt, Buffalo Bill, and the Wild West in Europe," in *Cultural Transmissions and Receptions: American Mass Culture in Europe* (R. Kroes et. al., eds., 1993), 5. Amsterdam: VU University Press.

28   Ibid 12.

29   P.T. Barnum, *Struggles and Triumphs* (1869; Carl Bode ed., 1981), 79-80. Harmondsworth: Penguin.

30   Eldridge Cleaver, *Soul on Ice* (1968), 114. New York: McGraw Hill.

31   *America in France's Hopes and Fears*, 1: 40.

32   Paul Bourget, *Outre Mer: Impressions of America* (1896), 417. Mark Twain found Bourget rather cold-blooded: "One learns people through the heart, not the eyes or the intellect." *America in France's Hopes and Fears*, 56. London, T. Fisher Unwin.

33   Bernard Faÿ, *La Civilization Américaine* (1939), 239.

34   Antonio Gramsci, "Americanism and Fordism," in *Selections from the Prison Notebooks* (Quentin Hoare & Geoffrey Nowell-Smith eds. & trans., 1971), 281. London: Lawrence & Wishart.

35   Ibid 317.

36   Ibid 305-306.

37   Quentin Hoare & Geoffrey Nowell-Smith, Introduction to "Americanism and Fordism," 277.

38   Aldous Huxley, *Brave New World* (1932). London: Chatto & Windus.

39   UFA, 1926.

40   Klaus Kreimeier, *Histoire du Cinéma Allemand: la UFA* (Olivier Mannoni trans., 1994) 234-241. Paris, Flammarion.

41   *Histoire du Cinéma Allemand*, 236. *Metropolis* was seen by many as more of a comment on German industrialization and perfectionism than on America and Fordism. But, visually, Metropolis was a city of the future in the American fashion.

42   One foot of 35 millimeter film is 16 frames, and will last two-thirds of one second when projected at the industry standard 24 frames per second. Ephraim Katz, *The Macmillan International Film Encyclopedia*. London: Macmillan (3rd ed. rev. Fred Klein & Ronald Dean Nolen, 1998), 472. Lang's four million feet therefore equaled more than 740 hours of uncut film.

43   Georges Duhamel. *Scènes de la vie future* (1930), 24-25. Paris: Mercure de France. The translation of this paragraph is taken from Donald Roy Allen, *French Views of America in the 1930s* (1979), 224. New York: Garland.

44   "Subservient person, reduced to the last degree of misery, of ignorance." Paul Robert, *Le Petit Robert* (A. Rey & J. Rey-Debove, eds. 1985) 1: 960. Paris: Le Robert.

45   *Scènes de la vie future*, 58.

46   Faÿ, *La Civilization Américaine*, 88.

47   *transition* 13:273.

48   See, eg, Jean-Jacques Servan-Schreiber, *Le défi américain* (1967). Paris: Denöel.

49   Blaise Cendrars, *Hollywood, La Mecque du cinéma* (1936; reissued 1987). Editions Bernard Grasset.

50   Jean Baudrillard, *Amérique* (1986; paperback edition 1992). Paris, Editions Bernard Grasset.

51   Jean-François Revel, *Without Marx or Jesus* (J.F. Bernard trans., 1971), 125. London: MacGibbon and Kee.

52   Victoria de Grazia, "Mass Culture and Sovereignty: The American Challenge to European Cinemas, 1920-1960," *Journal of Modern History* 61 (1989), 53.

53   René Jeanne, "L'Invasion cinématographique américaine," *Revue des deux mondes* (15 February 1930), 857.

54   "L'Invasion cinématographique américaine," 879.

55   Samuel Goldwyn, "What's the Matter with the Movies," New York Times Magazine, Nov. 29, 1936, quoted in John Eugene Harley, *World-Wide Influences of the Cinema* (1940), 23. Los Angeles: the University of Southern California Press.

56   See, eg, John Keegan, *Six Armies in Normandy* (1983), 1-19. Harmondsworth: Penguin.

57   Tony Judt, *Past Imperfect: French Intellectuals 1944-1956* (1992), 256-257. Berkeley, London: University of California Press.

58   Ien Ang, "Cultural studies, media reception and the transnational media system," in *Living Room Wars: Rethinking Media Audience for a Postmodern World* (1996), 145. London: Routledge.

59   Peter Duignan & L.H. Gawn, *An Ambivalent Heritage: Euro-American Relations* (1994), 34-35.

60   Herbert I. Schiller, *Mass Communications and American Empire* (2d. ed., 1992), 139 (emphasis in original). Boulder, Oxford: Westview Press, and New York: Augustus M. Kelley.

61   Alan Wells, *Picture-Tube Imperialism?* (1972), 137. Maryknoll N.Y: Orbis.

62   See, eg, Geoffrey Lealand, *American Television Programmes on British Screens* (1984), 4-7; London: British Film Institute, Broadcasting Research Unit. Jeremy Tunstall, "Media Imperialism?" in *American Media and Mass Culture* (Donald Lazare ed., 1987), 540. Berkeley, London: University of California Press.

63   "Media Imperialism?" 550.

64   "Media Imperialism?" 550

65   Ien Ang, "Global media/local meaning, in *Living Room Wars*, 152-153.

66   Michael Kelly, et al., "Modernization and Avant-gardes" in *French Cultural Studies: An Introduction* (Jill Forbes & Michael Kelly eds., 1995), 142. Oxford: Clarendon Press.

67   Kelly, *et al.*, "Modernization and Avant-gardes," 142-145.

68   See, eg, Ariel Dorfman & Armand Mattelart, *Para leer el Pato Donald* (1971). Chile: Ediciones Universitarias de Valparaiso, translated as *How to read Donald Duck: Imperialist ideology in the Disney comic* (David Kunzle trans., 1975). New York: International General.

69   *Without Marx or Jesus*, 144.

2

The culture of cinema

In a debate seemingly fated to be sempiternal, the gulf between France and Hollywood over the cinema can be expressed very simply: We French regard cinema as an art, you Americans view it primarily as a business. (This opposition appears to be nearly as conventional as the cinema itself: hence George Bernard Shaw's famous inversion of the theme in 1920, when he turned down an offer to write films for Samuel Goldwyn: "There is only one difference between Mr. Goldwyn and me. Whereas he is after art I am after money.")[70] Simple, and simplistic, this formula also represents a more thorough divergence on what the cinema was for, and who it was for. Both issues concern the industrial organization of the cinema: the first, in inquiring what the cinema is for, involves the different ways in which films are made in Hollywood and France. The second issue, asking who the cinema is for, investigates the beneficiaries of the production process, and the competing interests of producers and authors. The answers to these questions explain the fundamental culture issues that separate the Hollywood from the French view of the cinema – another line of discord in the troubled relations between to the two.

The commodification of cinema

Cinema was originally organized industrially, because few conceived of it as art. An entire film might consist of workers leaving a factory at the end of their shift,[2] a train arriving at a station,[3] of views across a city during a snowstorm,[4] or of a bull during a bullfight.[5] The marvel was that such things could be recorded at all. The original film magnates were themselves industrialists, manufacturers of cameras, projectors and film. They owed their position to ownership of industrial property, for instance patents on the sprocket system that looped film through projectors. Just as in the 1920s, wireless set manufacturers would start radio stations to boost sales of their equipment, the film equipment entrepreneurs went into production in order to sell more cameras and projectors.

And yet, in the earliest days of cinema, some filmmakers wanted to use the medium to tell stories – in particular, stories loved by the public. One of the earliest American films simply enacted the removal of a foreign flag and its replacement with the Stars and Stripes.[6] According to its director, J. Stuart Blackton, "the people went wild."[7] In France, George Meliès graduated from shooting street scenes to stage illusions,[8] what would now be called drama-documentary,[9] as well as fairy and fantasy tales.[10]

The development of narrative cinema gave greater value to the narrators, notably directors and writers, who conceived films as structured dramas, first lasting only a few minutes, but ultimately stretching to the length of the modern feature film. Nevertheless, in the early years of the cinema, the worldwide structure of the film business was primarily industrial. On interesting feature of the outcome of the First World War was that Hollywood had come to resemble a Fordist assembly line (not for nothing was it called the "dream factory"[11]), while the European industry was weakened by the fragility of the local economy and by poor management. France, in addition, had been resistant to some of the narrative techniques involving camera movement and editing that had been pioneered and adopted by Hollywood.[12] Pioneer American directors such as Edwin S. Porter and D. W. Griffith were from the early days of film history credited with either the development or the perfection of such continuity-based technical cinema enhancements as editing, direct story construction, the moving camera, the cut, the spot-iris, the mask and the fade.[13] The significance of the narrative continuity editing methods of these film-makers that they were strongly rooted in storytelling, and consequently highly adapted to cinema as a popular medium. Indeed, the critique of this style by such admirers of Griffith as Sergei M. Eisenstein, Vsevolod I. Pudovkin and Lev Kuleshov was that this form of editing was rooted in the literary technique of the nineteenth-century novel and was not well-adapted to the form of intellectual and symbolic commentary these Soviet masters believed the cinema was capable of. Although the years of the First World War produced a small number of important French film directors, notably Abel Gance, Marcel L'Herbier and Louis Delluc, "their lack of interest in narrative meant that these film makers were to be marginalized in terms of world cinema..."[14] In other words, by the dawn of the 1920s, the French film sector could be sharply differentiated by Hollywood both in terms of industrial organization and style of filmmaking.

There was also the question of what people thought of as the essential element of cinema. Hollywood was founded largely by showmen, wealthy business entrepreneurs who owned theatres and other attractions and who diversified into making films. They were in the tradition of P.T. Barnum and the mass popular entertainment already established in the US In France, cinema too was popular entertainment – indeed, a pioneer such as Meliès would turn his hand to almost everything from conjuring tricks to "adult" entertainment.[15] But as evidenced by the efforts of the likes of Rostand and the French Cinema League, the analogy was also drawn between cinema and more "highbrow" entertainment, such as drama. Further, although film was regarded virtually everywhere, including the US, as having an important educational and training role, it is noteworthy that in France, political control of the cinema was confided in part in the ministry of education, which adopted a cultural posture when dealing with Hollywood's success in dominating the French market.

Finally, the rallying of the French cinema in the later 1920s was mainly due to the efforts of creative individuals, who experimented with narrative continuity while maintaining an experimental approach to storytelling, and who operated in a less structured industrial system:

> The most successful films of the decade were superproductions with an exotic, historical or literary flavor and in the absence of a strong production system of the kind that had emerged in Hollywood, the director was the undisputed master of film making who, although often pushed into making commercial concessions, was never constrained by a tight studio system.[16]

These individuals – a Dane, Carl Theodor Dreyer, a White Russian, Ivan Mosjoukine, a Belgian, Jacques Feyder, three Frenchmen, Abel Gance, René Clair and Jean Renoir – were among those who rejuvenated the film in France with strongly personalized films, even if their content ranged widely from tragedy through historical drama to broad comedy. Although Hollywood, too, built its success on the creative efforts of talented individuals, the means of selecting, developing and executing film projects was substantially industrial. This became even more clearly so in the economic crisis of the 1930s. Hollywood studios teetered on the verge of bankruptcy, but survived. French studios, by contrast, went under. In the Depression, Hollywood studio values plummeted as cinema audiences dwindled. At one point, RKO stock fell from 50 to 1⅞; Fox Films saw its stock plunge in less than three years from $100 per share to 25 cents. Paramount went into receivership.[17] In 1933, Louis B. Meyer, "red-eyed and unshaven" successfully begged his staff to take a 50 percent cut in pay for his MGM studio to survive.[18] Warner Brothers' went from profits of more than $14 million in 1929 to a loss of similar size in 1932; profits climbed back to nearly $5.9m in 1936, only to fall again, building once more to just $5.4 million in 1941.[19] However, one way or another, they all pulled through. In France, plagued by bad management and actual fraud, Gaumont crashed in 1934, and Pathé in 1936 As a result of the eclipse of these two pioneer-giants, French film production "became an intensely speculative activity indulged in by a myriad of tiny, undercapitalized companies."[20] Gaumont was ultimately rescued by the intervention of a state-owned bank.[21]

All these distinctions are capable of exaggeration. The industrialization of Hollywood was real – but it also fed the general image of America's machine age that, as had been seen, so sharply shaped French attitudes towards Hollywood and the US. The impoverishment of the French cinema was also real – but it is striking that the country's leading cinema industry names of the 1990s still include, in restructured forms, Gaumont and Pathé, which continue to be active distributors, theater-owners and producers.

Nevertheless, by the 1920s, from a mixture of rational and irrational factors, the relationship in cinema between France and America was regarded in France as that between David and Goliath, or as the creative individual versus the impersonal machine. This struggle on the macro level, between two nations, two cultures, two systems, was also apparent on the more intimate creative level, through a fundamental cultural difference over what constituted authorship of a cinematic work.

The ascendancy of the author

Andrew Sarris, the most influential proponent of the *auteur* theory[22] of cinema in the United States,[23] listed 14 "pantheon" directors – who had "transcended with a personal vision of the world" – in his landmark work, *The American Cinema*, in 1968.[24] Eight of the key "American" directors, according to Sarris, were European.[25] The men who employed these pantheon-dwellers, the founders of most of the leading Hollywood studios, were also largely Europeans.[26] These moguls engaged a lot of other Europeans, too: in all, some 73 of the 185 directors listed in Sarris' book came from Europe. In fact Sarris is responsible for the English term "*auteur* theory," this being his rendering of the French expression "*politique des auteurs*," first developed by François Truffaut in the French film journal *Cahiers du Cinéma* (although the actual phrase, coined by Truffaut, first appeared elsewhere). The original term literally means "author policy," and refers to the editorial approach of the journal in how the work of major directors was discussed, rather than a complete theory of how films are made.[27]

Yet these *auteurs* produced work that appeared at the time – and that still seems – quintessentially American. A Sicilian, Frank Capra, Preston Sturges – American-born, but educated erratically across Europe before and after the First World War[28] – the Viennese, Billy Wilder: these were the European talents responsible for such definitive Hollywood output as *It Happened One Night* (Capra),[29] *Sullivan's Travels* (Sturges)[30] and *Sunset Boulevard* (Wilder).[31] Other Europeans over the years discovered a kind of stylistic polyvalency, alternating work at home and in Hollywood, but adapting to the creative demands of each place – directors ranging from René Clair[32] to Costa-Gavras,[33] Louis Malle[34] and Stephen Frears.[35] Of course, the traffic has not all been one-way. Many American directors have produced their best and most important work in Europe: for example, Joseph Losey,[36] Richard Lester,[37] Stanley Kubrick[38] and Jules Dassin.[39]

Yet despite this constant cross-fertilization, "Europe" and "Hollywood" have never ceased to be separate in the minds of both. The industrial organization of Hollywood put power into the hands of producers, essentially product managers who supervised the conception, development, manufacture and market launch of new films. As the studio system reached its height in the 1930s, a studio production chief such as Hal B. Wallis at Warner Brothers would be absolutely in charge of supervising the script, dealing with pre- and post-production censorship concerns, hiring the director and overseeing casting. Above all, Wallis would have the final word on the musical score, editing, and the preparation of the finished film for its ultimate promotional campaign and theatrical release.[40] Indeed, it was claimed that 80 per cent of Hollywood directors shot scenes "exactly as they are told to shoot them without any change whatsoever, and that 90 per cent of them have no voice in the story or the editing."[41] Only a small handful of leading Hollywood directors – Preston Sturges, John Huston, Charles Chaplin, John Ford, Howard Hawks, William Wyler – had greater control over their films, either through being writer-directors, or through assuming the producer's role. Even then, they were often ultimately answerable to a studio production executive.[42]

Strangely, postwar French criticism purported to see through this system and to anoint the director with an influence that broke free of the studio straitjacket. André Bazin, the spiritual father of the *auteur* theory and later founder of *Cahiers du Cinéma*, said as much in reflecting on Hollywood films in 1946, the first year since 1940 that American cinema had been widely seen in France:

> We've come to the end of the myth of a standardized Hollywood in which anonymous technical crews pre-masticate the director's work so that he is unable to express himself in his own style. The formidable Hollywood machinery seems to have finally achieved that degree of perfection which frees the artist from technical concerns. A director now thinks in cinema with a variety and precision of syntax and vocabulary that are equal to that of writing. As a result we see a multiplication of the names of directors whose presence in the credits signifies something.[43]

On one level, Bazin simply spoke an obvious truth: no matter how homogeneous the studio system became, there was clearly a wide stylistic gulf between, say, Howard Hawks and John Ford. But Bazin's view is also an echo of Baudelaire's image of the *poète maudit*, the genius who emerges despite the constraints of a mechanistic and oppressive industrial system. The great Hollywood directors turn the table on the studio world that is so highly evolved and programmed that it leaves the director with nothing to do, no role to play, save that of the *auteur*. Indeed, Bazin, like his successors, had very little time for the industrial aspects of Hollywood, among which he counted screenplays, which he found to be banal and crippled by an "automatic ... sociological censorship aimed at seeing to it that the public is never really upset."[44] In taking this approach, Bazin consequently elevated the remaining "creative" element in a film – that of the director – even higher. One reason for this may have been severe limitations in Bazin's command of English.[45] While theatrical releases were available in subtitled forms, these could not communicate many of the audiences of the original writing. Further, many of the American films in the archives of the Cinémathèque Française, the cradle both of postwar French film criticism and the New Wave of directors, were unsubtitled original versions, tending to focus the attention of all but the most fluent English speakers on the visual and technical elements of the film – those that were mainly in the director's domain. Even in those American films appreciated in France where the director's role was not particularly prominent, the non-script elements tended to be highlighted: the hugely-popular Marx Brothers, for instance, whose films are still a permanent feature in Left Bank theaters, are regarded more for the clown-like elements of their performances than for the writing contributions of S.J. Perelman or Arthur Sheekman, authors of many of the "Grouchoisms" so widely quoted in English-speaking countries.

In France, as has been seen, the underdeveloped industrial structure of the cinema had already made the director into the predominant figure in defining and shaping the style and content of feature films. The *Cahiers du Cinéma* critics and the New Wave directors (often the same people) further cemented the primacy of the director – as opposed to the producer – in the French sense of cinematic propriety. There was, however, another factor separating French and American concepts of the cinema: a legal framework that, in the different countries, regarded the ownership and authorship of films in quite different ways.

---

1   A. Scott Berg, *Goldwyn* (1989), 97. London: Hamish Hamilton.

2   *La Sortie des usines Lumière* (Lumière 1895).

3   *Arrivé d'un train à La Ciotat* (Lumière 1895). On Lumière, see Roy Armes, *French Cinema* (1985), 8-10. London: Secker & Warburg.

4   *New York in a Blizzard* (Edison 1901).

5   *The Great Bull Fight* (Edison 1901).

6   *Tearing Down the Spanish Flag* (Vitagraph 1898).

7   Lewis Jacobs, *The Rise of the American Film* (1939), 11. New York: Harcourt Brace & Co.

8   *Escamotage d'une dame chez Robert Houdin* (Meliès 1896).

9   *L'Affaire Dreyfus* (Meliès 1899).

10   Eg, *Cendrillon* (Meliès 1899); *Voyage à la lune* (Meliès 1902) On Melies, see *French Cinema*, 10-13.

11   By an anthropologist, Hortense Powdermaker, in *Hollywood: The Dream Factory* (1950). Boston: Little Brown and Co.

12   See, eg, the discussion of the development of narrative continuity in the early cinema in Karel Reisz & Gavin Millar, *The Technique of Film Editing* (2d. ed. 1968), 16-40. London & New York: Focal Press.

13   *The Rise of the American Film*, 35-36, 98-99.

14   *French Cinema*, 50.

15   *French Cinema*, 11.

16   *French Cinema*, 62-63.

17   *Goldwyn*, 208.

18   Ian Hamilton, *Writers in Hollywood* (1991), 90. London: Minerva.

19   Nick Roddick, *A New Deal In Entertainment: Warner Brothers in the 1930s* (1983), 20. London: British Film Institute.

20   *French Cinema*, 68.

21   Georges Sadoul, *Le Cinéma français* (1962), 67. Paris: Flammarion.

22   "The theory that the director is the 'author' of a film. The reasoning that leads to this conclusion is that a film is a work of art, and since a work of art is stamped with the

personality of its creator, it is the director, more than anyone else, who gives the film its distinctive quality." *The Macmillan International Film Encyclopedia*, 64.

23   Among many other positions in both film academia and criticism, Sarris was, from 1965-1967, Editor-in-Chief of the English-language edition of the vanguard publication of auteurism, *Cahiers du Cinéma*. Andrew Sarris, *The American Cinema* (1968), 2. New York: Dutton. The bitter critical row over the auteur theory in America was principally engaged in by Sarris and Pauline Kael in a series of exchanges which in some ways embody the Euro-American divide: Andrew Sarris, "Notes on the Auteur Theory in 1962," *Film Culture*, Winter 1962-63; Pauline Kael, "Circles and Squares," *Film Quarterly* 12 (Spring, 1963); Sarris, "The Auteur Theory And The Perils Of Pauline," *Film Quarterly* 26 (Summer, 1963).

24   *The American Cinema*, 5, 39.

25   Charles Chaplin (born London, England), Alfred Hitchcock (born London, England), Fritz Lang (born Vienna, Austria), Ernst Lubitsch (born Berlin, Germany), F.W. Murnau (born Bielefeld, Germany), Max Ophuls (born Säarburcken, Germany), Jean Renoir (born Paris, France) and Josef von Sternberg (born Vienna, Austria). *The American Cinema*, 5. Of the remaining six directors, two – Robert Flaherty and John Ford – were of Irish origin, though American born. Both made "Irish" films and Ford, certainly, remained sentimentally Irish. A third pantheon director, Orson Welles, began his professional stage career at the age of 16 in Ireland, created a memorable Irish fall guy in *The Lady From Shanghai* (Columbia Pictures, 1948), and even appeared in one of the rare pre-1980s Irish movies, *Return to Glennascaul* (Dublin Gate, 1951) – although his "Irish" scenes were actually shot in Italy. For directors' birthplaces, see generally *The Macmillan International Film Encyclopedia*. On Orson Welles' early career, see generally Christopher Fitz-Simon, *The Boys* (1994); London: Nick Hern Books; on his Irish films, see Kevin Rockett, *The Irish Filmography* (1996), 18, 400. Dublin: Red Mountain Media.

26   Carl Laemmle (Universal Pictures) was German; Adolph Zukor (Paramount Pictures), Hungarian; William Fox (Fox Film Corporation, ultimately 20th Century-Fox), Hungarian; Louis B. Mayer (Metro-Goldwyn-Mayer), Russian. The four Warner Brothers were sons of an itinerant Polish peddler: one was born in Europe, the others in the US. In addition, Harry Cohn (Columbia Pictures) was born to a German and a Russian. See generally, Neal Gabler, *An Empire Of Their Own: How The Jews Invented Hollywood* (1988). London: W.H. Allen. The four founders of United Artists (now part of Metro-Goldwyn-Mayer) included Charles Chaplin. Steven Bach, *Final Cut* (1985), 28-29. The legendary Samuel Goldwyn was born in Warsaw, Poland. *Goldwyn*, 5. The one Hollywood "major" unconnected with these studios and not founded by Europeans is the Walt Disney Company, whose eponymous creator, against the Hollywood grain, was an American from Kansas City, Missouri. John Taylor, *Storming The Magic Kingdom: Wall Street, The Raiders And The Battle For Disney* (1987), 7. London: Viking. For a definition of "major studio," see John W. Cones, *Film Finance & Distribution: A Dictionary Of Terms* (1992), 292. Los Angeles: Silman-James Press.

27   The definitive reconstruction of the evolution of the *politique des auteurs* has been conducted in Antoine de Baecque & Serge Toubiana, *François Truffaut* (1996), 144-51. Paris, Gallimard. Although the term became indelibly associated with *Cahiers du Cinéma*, Truffaut in fact first used it in print in 1954 in the magazine *Arts*.

28   See Preston Sturges, *Preston Sturges on Preston Sturges* (Sandy Sturges, ed.) (1990). New York: Simon and Schuster.

29   Columbia Pictures 1942.

30   Paramount Pictures 1941.

31   Paramount Pictures 1950.

32   Eg, *Sous les toits de Paris* (Tobis 1930) (France) and *I Married a Witch* (United Artists/Cinema Guild 1942) (US).

33 Eg, *Z* (Reggane/ONCIC 1968) (France/Algeria) and *Missing* (Universal/Polygram 1982) (US).

34 Eg, *Zazie dans le Métro* (Nouvelles Editions 1960) (France) and *Pretty Baby* (Paramount 1978) (US).

35 Eg, *My Beautiful Laundrette* (Working Title/SAF/Channel 4 1985) (GB) and *Dangerous Liaisons* (Warner/Lorimar/NFH 1988) (US).

36 *The Servant* (Springbok 1963) (GB); *King and Country* (BHE 1964) (GB); *The Go-Between* (World Film Services 1970) (GB); *Monsieur Klein* [Mr. Klein] (Lira/Adel/Nova/Mondial Te-Fi 1976) (France/Italy).

37 *A Hard Day's Night* (Proscenium 1964) (GB); *The Knack* (Woodfall 1965) (GB).

38 *2001: A Space Odyssey* (Stanley Kubrick 1968) (GB); *A Clockwork Orange* (Polaris 1971) (GB); Barry Lyndon (Hawk/Peregrine 1975) (GB).

39 *Night and the City* (TCF 1950) (GB); *Du Rififi chez des hommes* [Rififi] (Indus/Pathé/Prima 1955) (France); *Pote tin Kyriaki* [*Never on Sunday*] (Lopert/Melinafilm 1959) (Greece). Dassin and Losey were among several Hollywood figures who departed for Europe after difficulties with the House Committee on Un-American Activities: others included Lester Cole, Edward Dmytryk, Adrian Scott, Howard Koch, Donald Ogden Stewart, Carl Foreman and Abraham Polonsky. David Caute, *The Great Fear: The Anti-Communist Purge Under Truman and Eisenhower* (1978), 516-18. London, Secker & Warburg. Having been judged "Un-American," it was perhaps natural these artists should "become" European.

40 *A New Deal In Entertainment*, 29-63.

41 Letter from Frank Capra to the New York Times, Apr. 2, 1939, quoted in *The Technique of Film Editing*, 57.

42 Capra, letter to the New York Times; *A New Deal in Entertainment* 24.

43 André Bazin, "The Cannes Festival of 1946", in *French Cinema of the Occupation and Resistance* (François Truffaut ed., Stanley Hochman trans., 1981), 135, 139. New York: F. Ungar Publishing Company.

44 "The Cannes Festival of 1946," 139.

45 I am grateful to Bazin's biographer, Dudley Andrew, for confirming that Bazin spoke very little English.

3

The legal culture
of authorship

The idea of the separation of incorporeal and physical rights in an object such as a written or painted work goes back at least to Roman law.[1] However, to discuss the difference between French and American concepts of authorship is to enter immediately into parallel, barely intersecting worlds – even the terminology is untranslatable. French lawyers speak of *le copyright* to distinguish the Anglo-American system of protection from their own; Americans will refer to *droit d'auteur* to signal discussion of an essentially different body of law. To simplify – inasmuch as any simplification is possible – this book uses the term "literary and artistic property" (taken from French usage) to identify the different bundles of rights comprehended by copyright and *droit d'auteur*, and to distinguish these rights from "industrial property," which covers protections for trademarks, patents, model drawings, plant varieties and the like.

Facially, copyright – the exclusive right to publish and sell a work – and *droit d'auteur* – the author's rights in a work – address different issues. But the first English copyright statute, the Statute of Anne,[2] was titled "An Act for the Encouragement of Learning, by Vesting the Copies of Printed Books *in the Authors* or Purchasers of such Copies ..." (emphasis added). Further, the House of Lords in 1774 rejected the longstanding claim that stationers (ie, printers and publishers) – as opposed to authors – held common law copyright.[3] Instead, under the Statute of Anne regime, the author had the sole right, subject to certain formalities, to print a book for a period of fourteen years, renewable for a further fourteen if the author was still alive.

The essentials of the English scheme passed into American law. The United States Constitution empowered Congress to grant authors exclusive right to their writings for limited times.[4] The federal Copyright Act of 1790[5] imitated the Statute of Anne in granting authors a 14-year copyright term, subject to registration formalities, with renewal for a further 14 years if the author survived the first term. As in England, the courts rejected the existence of common-law copyright in published works, either at federal or state law.[6]

In France, the rights of authors over their works had been claimed at least as early as 1586, when a lawyer, Simon Marion, pleaded that every man is "lord of what he makes, invents or composes," and that just as God owned the heaven and earth, the author of a book was:

> ... the complete master of it, and as such may freely dispose of it, even keep it always under his private hand, like a slave, or emancipate it, by conceding it common liberty and granting it, either purely and simply without keeping back any of it, or instead subject to reservation through a kind of right of patronage that no other than him may print it, except after a certain time.[7]

Marion appears to have won his case, although possibly not on these grounds.[8] However, decisions of French courts progressively allowed the benefit of the privilege to publish, granted by the Crown, to shift from booksellers and printers to authors.[9] Indeed, throughout Europe in the eighteenth century, there was general pressure from authors for their rights of control over their work to be recognized, resulting in statutes first in England in 1710, then in Denmark and Norway in 1741 and Spain in 1762.[10] Laws passed by in France by Louis XVI in 1777 and 1778 defined the privilege to publish as a temporary monopoly, granted by the Crown to authors and subsidiarily to publishers, in order that each be recompensed for his work.[11]

The French Revolution abolished all royal privileges in 1789, causing a vacuum in artistic and literary property rights that did not begin to be addressed until 1791, when playwrights received protection, and 1793, when authors of written works, composers, painters and illustrators were granted the "exclusive right to sell, provide for the sale and distribute their work in the territory of the Republic."[12] These laws remained in force, with only slight modification and numerous additions, until 1957.[13]

So far, both the Anglo-American and French artistic and literary property schemes are quite similar. Indeed, commentators have frequently remarked on the similarities between the origins of French and Anglo-American copyright law and the closeness of the concept of the author in both systems at their inception.[14] Even this view may have been overstated. In France, the revolutionary regime's version of the author has been argued to be one "intended to dethrone the absolute author, a creature of privilege, and recast him, not as a *private* individual (the absolute bourgeois), but rather as a *public* servant, as the model citizen."[15] In modern American discussions of the purpose of copyright laws as created under the eighteenth-century constitution, copyright protection is usually seen in terms of social welfare and the welfare of the author. But authorship itself – other than as a necessary means of generating shared knowledge – is not generally regarded as a separate social value.[16] France's contrasting veneration of the intrinsic value of authorship helps to account both for the emergence of the moral right and for its persistence in viewing apparent threats to authors as a public policy issue. This argument, wherein the concept of authorship is determined by ideology, follows Foucault, among others: "[T]he ... 'author-function' is not formed spontaneously through the simple attribution of a discourse to an individual. It results from a complex operation whose function is to construct the rational entity we call an author."[17] Moreover, even if the claims of conceptual closeness of the French and American copyright systems do hold for the eighteenth century, it would be wrong to take this closeness as an index of harmony between the contemporary schemes of literary and artistic property protection in the US and France. The crucial divergence between the two systems occurs not in their way of resolving the question of pecuniary or patrimonial rights, but in the presence in the French conception of a highly elaborated network of non-pecuniary or moral rights, which have been defined as a "legally protected link, uniting the creator with his work and conferring on him sovereign prerogatives with regard to users, the work having entered into economic circulation."[18]

The moral right, or *droit moral*, is of both surprisingly obscure origin and recent vintage. The doctrine of moral rights has been said to have emerged in Germany and France in the 1880s as a response to the supposed insufficiency of then-current notions of property rights to cover the emerging principles of intellectual property protection.[19] (Some have seen in the moral right the influence of Kant on some nineteenth-century French jurists, but this has been the subject of some hot dispute: the first theoretical articulations in France of moral rights emerge in the 1860s and 1870s.)[20] Even before the emergence of the fully-fledged moral rights doctrine, courts forged rights that ultimately were assimilated into the *droit moral*. Thus, the rights to be acknowledged as author of a work by its publisher, and for its integrity to be respected, was recognized in 1814. Elements of the rights to control the divulgation of a work were acknowledged in cases in 1828 and 1845.[21] It has been suggested that the right to withdraw a work was not recognized until much later in 1902, and then only in the context of a marital dispute. The term "moral right" was not used by a court until 1946.[22] The law of moral rights was not actually codified in France until 1957.[23]

The current form of the moral right in France is contained in the 1992 intellectual property code.[24] Moral rights have equal standing with patrimonial rights under the *droit d'auteur* regime.[25] The author is granted the right of respect of his "name, its quality and of his work," such right being personal, perpetual, inalienable, indefeasible, and transmittable by rights of succession to heirs.[26] The author has the sole right to divulge – that is, to display, perform or publish – his work.[27] He also may, notwithstanding any prior contract assigning rights, withdraw the work from exploitation, either permanently or for modification before returning it.[28]

In addition to the moral right, there is one other important distinction between the French literary and artistic property regime and the American system: in France, the *droit d'auteur* is vested in the creator of a work by the fact of its creation,[29] and is unaffected by any work-for-hire or service contract between the author and another party.[30] One result of this is that French *droit d'auteur* can generally only be held by a physical person, not a corporate entity.[31] This is in contrast to the "works made for hire" concept in the US copyright regime, which allows an employer, including a corporate entity, to own all the rights comprised in the copyright.[32]

There is some argument over whether equivalent rights to those found in the French system exist in the US The United States explicitly recognized moral rights when it acceded to the Berne Convention in 1988. (Moral rights are covered by article 6*bis* of the Convention, which bestows on an author the right to claim authorship and to object to any prejudicial distortion, mutilation or other modification of the work, even after it has been transferred. However, Berne, unlike the French code, does not bar waiver of this right.) The legislation ratifying the American accession to Berne explicitly declined to expand or reduce existing federal or state law concerning claims of authorship to a work or objection to prejudicial distortion, mutilation or modification.[33] Instead, it was asserted that existing law provided reasonable alternatives to moral rights.[34] Visual artists were given separate moral right protection by legislative enactment;[35] however, motion pictures and other audiovisual works were expressly excluded from the law's definition of visual art.[36]

However the state of current American law may be viewed, there is still an essential difference between it and the French regime. French literary and artistic property law goes much further than the requirements of the Berne Convention, and, through its refusal of the work made for hire principle concentrates rights in the hands of creators, not their employers, such as film companies. Indeed, the creators are thereby protected against the excesses of their employers. This is a cultural as well as legal value, and was recognized by the French courts well before the enactment of the 1957 law: in 1949, for instance, it was held that Marcel Carné and Jacques Prévert were entitled to damages for cuts made to a film by producers, despite their prior cession of pecuniary rights in the film.[37] In 1990, a filmmaker was entitled to damages from a television network that broadcast a film with a break for advertising and failed to obtain prior authorization.[38]

However, in the case of films and television, much of the protection of moral right in France is somewhat illusory. The law names as authors of an audiovisual work the writers of the scenario, adaptation and dialogue, the writers of music and lyrics specially created for the work, and the director.[39] (This part of the law provides that only "physical persons" [ie, not companies] may be regarded as authors of audiovisual works. Further, it has been suggested that the list of people potentially considered as authors of an audiovisual work may not be limited by the language of this provision and could conceivably extend to performers, editors, camera and sound operators, the person responsible for dubbing, and even the author of a pre-existing work who took no part in the adaptation of the work for the film.[40]) The producer, as a non-author, thus has no moral rights. However, the law provides that in the case of audiovisual works, moral rights can only be exercised where the work has actually been completed.[41] (This provision is a significant derogation from the overall moral right scheme: in other media, artists have succeeded in actions to force patrons to allow work to be completed.)[42] Further, the determination that the work has been completed is arrived at jointly by the producer and the authors.[43] Moreover, an author refusing to complete a contribution to a film, or failing to because of *force majeure*, may not invoke moral rights to oppose the use of any contribution already completed.[44] These provisions give film producers significantly greater power over the works they produce than, say, the publisher of a book. It means that the coveted "final cut" is something a director has to negotiate carefully with the producer: if not, there will be no consent to the work being deemed finished and consequently subject to the exercise of moral rights.

In addition, there are practical limits on moral rights. If an author exercises the right to withdraw a work being supplied under contract, the author must indemnify the concession-holder – publisher or producer – for the costs of the withdrawal. Further, if the author then later decides to publish the work after, all, it must be offered to the original concession-holder under the original terms.[45] The effect of this provision is to make it practically impossible for the author of an audiovisual work to withdraw it: few directors could afford the cost of an entire feature film as indemnification for exercising the moral right. In other words, in the audiovisual sector at least, the moral right often has great symbolic importance than practical significance for authors.

Nevertheless, it is precisely the symbolic importance of things that carries greater weight in the determination of outcomes. One of the most significant moral rights cases in recent years fell directly on the faultline between France and Hollywood, between culture and barbarism, and between the profit motive and the respect for the integrity of a work. It concerned plans by a French television network to broadcast a Hollywood film, *The Asphalt Jungle*,[46] in a colorized version. The film was directed by John Huston and written by Ben Maddow. It was the production studio, however, that obtained a copyright registration certificate in respect of the film, not the "authors," whose work was made for hire under American law.[47] Under the law of the contract between the original parties, Huston and Maddow had no moral right in their work. Under classic conflict of law principles (used to decide which law should apply to analysis of legal disputes), the law of the contract should have been applied to establish who was the author in an alleged infringement case.[48] Article 5 of the Berne Convention, to which both France and the US have acceded, provides that foreign authors should receive equal treatment to nationals under domestic copyright laws. This principle is recognized by article L. 111-4 of the French intellectual property code, which creates a framework of reciprocity "subject to the provisions of international agreements to which France is party." However, the issue in *Huston* was, first, whether the plaintiff authors (or their families) had any standing to sue – that is, whether their legal status allowed them to be parties to a copyright infringement action. If they were not the holders of copyright in the film, they would not have standing and accordingly could not bring an action. US federal copyright law, applied to the contract drawn up under California law, made MGM the copyright holder. Thus, French law – including the moral right – could only be applied if there was a means of ousting American laws and thereby giving the plaintiffs the standing to sue in pursuit of a right which was inalienable according to national principles.

The Court of Appeal took the classic conflicts of law position that American law applied and rejected the moral rights claim by the Huston and Maddow families against the showing of the colorized film. On further appeal, France's highest court reversed the decision, declared that France's moral right law was of "imperative applicability" in the case, and declined even to consider the conflict of laws question.[49] Having decided that French law applied, and that Huston and Maddow, who did not count as authors of the work in the US, were to be so considered in France, the actual implementation of the law in this instance was straightforward: the Huston and Maddow families could intervene to ensure respect of the work.

The decision was a strong demonstration of France's attachment to the moral right, which operates in constant tension with other patrimonial laws, such as those of contract and succession. For the Cour de Cassation in the *Huston* case, the inviolability of the moral right was a question of *ordre public*, of public policy. Although the legal reasoning of the decision has been strongly questioned,[50] the *Huston* decision is important because of its strong emotional pull in favor of the protection of an artist's work by the purely commercial forces of Hollywood. The court's position is symptomatic not merely of the differences in the two legal systems, but of the underlying belief, that France and America's approach to literary and artistic property rights embody fundamentally divergent cultural philosophies. Even if this view, as has been seen, is only partly true, it is more important, for our purposes, that it is widely held, by, for instance, the screenwriter Jean-Claude Carrière:

> This fundamental contradiction between two traditions explains why American film, never considered an art, has for so long been the work of producers. In Europe, on the other hand (and particularly in France), the idea that film is a form of artistic expression (and even an art in its own right) has taken root and matured.[51]

For Carrière, as for so many in France, the obliteration of the author, the director, by the cultural, industrial and legal nexus that is Hollywood, is the key to the gulf diving France and the United States. To make his point, he tells this anecdote about the television series *Dallas*, which for a short while in the 1980s was so extraordinarily popular in Europe that it became the emblem of Hollywood's apparent cultural dominance:

> [I]n the ... case [of television] the director is scarcely more than a faceless technician. During the 1986 Venice Festival, the German director Peter Fleischmann asked an audience of two or three hundred film people:
>
> "Who is the director of *Dallas*?"
>
> No one could tell him.[52]

Not many people in Hollywood, it can be imagined, would have known the answer to the question either. But a very great many would have known the name of Aaron Spelling, the producer of *Dallas* and to most minds the "creative" inspiration behind the series. The inability of either side to conceive of alternative forms of authorship to meet their individual cultural approaches to audiovisual production was just one symptom of the permanent state of incomprehension between America and Europe.

1   See, eg, Justinian, *Institutes*, 2.33-34.

2   8 Anne ch. 19 (1710) (England).

3   *Donaldson v. Becket*, 98 English Reports 257 (House of Lords, England, 1774).

4   United States Constitution. article I, section 8, clause 8.

5   1 Stat. 124 (US).

6   *Wheaton v. Peters*, 33 US (8 Pet.) 591 (1834) (US).

7   A. & H.-J. Lucas, *Traité de la propriété littéraire et artistique* (1994), 6-7. Paris: Litec. Some also see in Marion's pleading the seed of the moral right of divulgation. See, eg, Claude Colombet, *Propriéte littéraire et artistique et droits voisins* (7th ed., 1994), 3. Paris: Dalloz

8   *Traité de la propriété littéraire et artistique*, 7.

9   *Traité de la propriété littéraire et artistique*, 7.

10   Claude Colombet, *Grands principes du droit d'auteur et des droits voisins dans le monde* (2d. ed., 1992), 3. Paris: Litec.

11   Pierre-Yves Gautier, *Propriété littéraire et artistique* (1991), 17. Paris: PUF.

12   *Traité de la propriété littéraire et artistique*, 11 and n.

13   Colombet, *Propriété littéraire et artistique*, 5.

14   See, eg, Jane C. Ginsburg, "A Tale of Two Copyrights: Literary Property in revolutionary France and America," *Tulane Law Review* 64 (1990), 991; Paul Goldstein, *Copyright's Highway: From Gutenberg to the Celestial Jukebox* (1994), 170-172. New York: Hill and Wang.

15   Carla Hesse, "Enlightenment Epistemology and the Laws of Authorship in Revolutionary France, 1777-1793," in *Law and the Order of Culture* (Robert Post, ed., 1991), 130 (emphasis in original). Berkeley, Oxford: University of California Press.

16   See, eg, the United States Supreme Court's discussion of this question in *Sony Corp. of America v. Universal City Studios*, 464 US 417, 429 (1984) (copyright a limited grant intended to motivate creative activity of authors and to allow public access to the products of their genius after limited period of exclusive control has expired).

17   Michel Foucault, "What Is an Author?" in *Language, Counter-Memory, Practice* (Donald H. Bouchard, ed. & trans., Sherry Simon, trans., 1977), 127. Oxford: Blackwell.

18   Gautier, *Propriété littéraire et artistique*, 147.

19   Pierre Recht, *Le Droit d'Auteur, une nouvelle forme de propriété* (1969), 273. Paris: Librairie Générale de Droit et de Jurisprudence. Gemblonx: Editions J. Duculot.

20   *Traité de la propriété littéraire et artistique*, 16

21   *Traité de la propriété littéraire et artistique*, 15.

22   Recht, *Le Droit d'Auteur*, 306-307.

23   *Loi no. 57-298 du 11 mars, 1957, sur la propriété littéraire et artistique.* It is sometimes assumed in common law countries such as the United States and Britain that "judge-made" law does not exist in civil law jurisdictions such as France. Indeed, the post-Revolutionary order stripped the courts of their former power to issue binding precedents. Christian Dadomo & Susan Farran, *The French Legal System* (1993), 39-40. London: Sweet & Maxwell. This principle is still enshrined in the Civil Code, which forbids judges from making general and regulatory dispositions of cases. Code civil [C. civ.] art. 5 (France). At the same time, judges are forbidden to refuse to decide a case owing to the silence, obscurity or insufficiency of the law. C. civ. art. 4. Where the law is silent, as in the cases in which the moral right was developed, judges look to existing law for general principles, or *règles de droit. The French Legal System*, 13-15. While such principles, as applied to the particular case, do not constitute binding precedent, the fact of their being consistently followed in related circumstances by other courts, may lead to a *jurisprudence constante*, something akin to "settled law," but owing its force not to precedent but to its elevation to the level of customary law. *The French Legal System*, 40.

24   Code de la propriété intellectuelle [C.P.I.], loi no. 92-597 du 1er juillet 1992 (France).

25   C.P.I. art. L. 111-1.

26   C.P.I. art. L. 121-1.

27   C.P.I. art. L. 121-2.

28   C.P.I. art. L. 121-4.

29   C.P.I. art. L. 111-2.

30   C.P.I. art. L. 111.1.

31   France has created a limited work made for hire doctrine, allowing *droit d'auteur* to be held by a company, in the case of computer software and accompanying documentation prepared by employees of the software company. C.P.I. art. L. 113-9.

32   17 U.S.C. § 201(b). (US)

33   Berne Convention Implementation Act of 1988, Pub L. No. 100-568, 102 Stat. 285 (codified as amended in scattered sections of Title 17 of the United States Code), § 3(b).

34   See, eg, "Final Report of the Ad Hoc Working Group on US Adherence to the Berne Convention," *Columbia-VLA Journal of Law & the Arts* 10 (1986), 547-557, which insists rather too forcefully on the availability of alternatives to moral rights, mainly through Lanham Act provisions.

35   Visual Artists Rights Act of 1990, Pub. L. 101-650, Title VI, 104 Stat. 5128 (codified as amended in scattered sections of Title 17 of the United States Code).

36   17 U.S.C. § 101 (US).

37   Trib. civ. Seine, 1ère ch., 6-7 April 1949, *Prévert et Carné v. Sté Pathé*, Gazette du Palais 1949, 249 (France).

38   Paris, 1ère ch., 26 November 1990, *Carle v. TF1*, Images juridiques, Jan. 15 1991, 2 (France).

39   C.P.I. art. L. 113-7.

40   André Françon, *Cours de propriété littéraire, artistique et industrielle* (1994), 194-195. Paris: Les Cours de Droit.

41   C.P.I. art. L. 121-5.

42   See, eg, Cass. civ. 1ère, 8 January 1980, *Dubuffet v. Régie Nationale de Usines Renault*, Revue Internationale des droits d'auteur (April 1984),154 (France).

43   C.P.I. art. L. 121-5. In one case, France's highest court held that an author who had completed his contribution to a film could exercise his moral right even though the entire film had not been completed. This decision, apparently in direct contradiction of the text of the statute, has been widely criticized and seemingly not followed. Cass. civ., 1ère, 7 February 1973, *Sté Les Productions Fox Europa v. Luntz, Dalloz* (1973), J. 363 (France).

44   C.P.I. art. L. 121-6.

45   C.P.I. art. L. 121-4.

46   MGM, 1950.

47   The facts are drawn from the Court of Appeal decision, Paris, 4ème ch. B., 6 July 1989, *Soc. Turner Entertainment Co. v. Consorts Huston et autres*, Dalloz (1990), J. 152 (France).

48   Jane Ginsburg & Pierre Sirinelli, *Auteur, création et adaptation en droit international privé et en droit interne français. Réflexions à partir de l'affaire Huston*, Revue internationale du droit d'auteur (Oct. 1991), 5.

49   Cass. civ. 1ère, 28 mai 1991, Consorts *Huston v. Sté Turner Entertainment*, Revue internationale du droit d'auteur (July 1991), 197 (France). The normal conflicts of law approach was not explicitly applied, as Ginsburg & Sirinelli point out. *Auteur, création et adaptation*, 5. What the Cour de Cassation should have done was, first, apply French conflicts of rules to determine the applicable law; secondly, state that the application of this law (if it was American law) would be contrary to the ordre public (a term approximating to "public policy"); and thirdly, that this demanded the substitution of the law of the forum state for that of the foreign law. Pierre Mayer, *Droit international privé* (5th ed. 1994), 140. Paris: Montchrestien. A court might exclude the foreign law because it is contrary to a "universal principle of justice"; more often, the issue arises because of a perceived affront to French law, either the "political and social foundations of French civilization" or because of the necessity to ensure a "safeguard of certain legislative policies." *Droit international privé*, 140. In addition, foreign law should not be ousted unless its application would have to have an impact within the forum state. *Droit international privé*, 144-145. In the Huston case, there was no question of the impact of the affair within France, where a television network proposed broadcasting the colorized version of the film. Among questions that the Cour de Cassation might have considered – although it is not clear from the published decision that it did – were the fact that the application of French law would not inhibit the owners of the film from exploiting it elsewhere, and that there was no evidence that the purpose of the plaintiffs in bringing the suit was to renege on commitments the consequences of which they were fully aware which they entered into the contracts. Bernard Audit, Note, 1990 Dalloz Sirey (1990), J. 158.

50   Eg, by Ginsburg and Sirinelli, *Auteur, création et adaptation*.

51   Jean-Claude Carrière, *The Secret Language of Film* (1994), 194. New York: Random House.

52   *The Secret Language of Film*, 41

Part 2

Trade

1
Culture as policy: the genesis and history of quotas

The cultural gap between France and America helped produce the practical consequences that are the subject of this book: quotas on the importation of television programs. Yet there is a further context to be considered in the industrial history of Franco-American cinema and television relations. To understand both the controversial nature as well as the rationale and scope of television program quotas, it is important to recognize that the curbs that caused so much bitterness during the GATT talks were by no means a new phenomenon. Quotas on American entertainment imports have existed in Europe since the end of the First World War. Indeed, the justifications for quotas, industrial and cultural, rational and irrational, change very little over the years. The quota wars begin with the cinema, and the rise of Hollywood, fashioned like an industrial giant, devoted to global entertainment, alternatively as irresistible to the masses – and repellent to their masters – as a machine-age Don Juan. France, whose quota regime lasted longest, was originally influenced by German and British models, whose rationale was similar to France's own. Further, the French hard line was influenced by a painful memory – the effective expulsion of the French cinema industry from the US market in the years before the First World War.

The Patent Wars

Anybody visiting France in 1995 would have been forcibly and constantly reminded of a fact that is the source of both pride and ruefulness in that country: France can reasonably claim to have invented the cinema, thanks to the Lumière brothers' public demonstrations of 1895, widely and lavishly feted in their native land a century later. Within a decade, France was the world leader of the cinema. However, by the time the fledgling sector celebrated its 20th anniversary, France was virtually eliminated as a significant player in the world film industry.

In 1908, foreign – mainly French – film releases captured up to 70 per cent of the American market.[1] Like the future Hollywood studios, the leading French company, Pathé Frères, was, as equipment manufacturer, film producer and international distributor, vertically integrated with offices around the world.[2] This international presence was vital because, as the US television business later found, export represented the difference between profit and loss.[3] Although the size and rapid expansion of the domestic market may have provided a disincentive for American film companies to seek business overseas,[4] it appears that, with the exception of the Vitagraph company, US producers and distributors made few inroads into the European market in the early years of the film business.[5]

From the earliest days of the cinema, domestic film companies sought to resist the encroachment of Europeans into the American market.[6] As early as 1896, attempts by the Lumière brothers to present their pioneering dual-purpose camera-projector in the US were thwarted by boycotts, confiscations by customs and the "inexplicable" cancellation of demonstrations. The Lumières abandoned their mission: US cinema patent holders were thought to be behind the harassment. As soon as Pathé opened its first US office, in 1904, its local competitors, notably the Edison Manufacturing Company, moved to block it, filing a lawsuit alleging infringement of its film and camera patents.[7] Despite delays caused by the suit, Pathé by 1908 was the largest single source of films in the American market. The suit itself, and another against the Meliès brother's Star Films company, never came to court. Pathé, too, was capable of using its market power in an uncompromising way. Other foreign companies blamed Pathé for their exclusion from the American market. Further, by October 1907, Pathé was using "block booking" clauses – forcing customers to take the company's entire film output – in its contracts. (Block booking by Hollywood studios in their foreign operations would later be a major European grievance.)[8] In December of that year, groups headed by Edison and its rival American Mutoscope & Biograph pooled their various camera and projector patents and formed the Motion Picture Patents Co. (MPPC), the main purpose of which, in Edison's view, was to "limit the number of foreign brands allowed to circulate" in the US[9] Edison attempted – first alone, then with its partners in the Motion Picture Patents Co. (MPPC) – to corner the market in all forms of film camera and projector. Ultimately, however, the "Latham loop" patent – "on which the MPPC depended" – was struck down.[10] Then, the federal government successfully attacked the MPPC on antitrust grounds.[11]

The new association, in limiting licenses to foreign companies, had a significant effect on their business. One French company, Star Films, appears to have been forced to close its Paris studio for nine months in 1909 as a result of delays in the issue of its MPPC license.[12] While Pathé and another European operator, George Kleine, received licenses,[13] most other European firms found themselves forced to withdraw from the US market,[14] the source, until the founding of the MPPC, of more than three-quarters of the main European producers' profits.[15] The Europeans managed to re-enter the US through partnerships with independent firms,[16] and Pathé, insulated within the MPPC, continued to be a major revenue earner.[17] One success of this partnership was the successful lobby mounted against an MPPC proposal for an increase in the import tariff applied to foreign celluloid.

Despite the fact that the existing tariff was below average, Congress actually reduced it, thanks, it was said at the time, to the "social and financial standing" of the Europeans' independent ally, vaudeville manager J. J. Murdock. This would be a rare occasion when Europe actually outlobbied the American film establishment.[18] However, the overall foreign share of the American market fell steadily, until, by the time of the outbreak of the First World War, it was negligible. On 14 November 1908, just before the formation of the MPPC, foreign films accounted for 70.5 per cent of the short films in release in the US. Two month later, on 16 January 1909, the figure was 45.7 per cent. In August 1912, when the statistical methodology was changed to show only films released in a single week, the foreign share was down to 22.3 per cent. In August 1914, at the outbreak of the First World War, that figure had dropped to 15.9 per cent. In the week of 5 October 1914, just five foreign short films, or 5.4 per cent of the total, were released in the US.[19] There were, certainly, other grounds for the decline of the Europeans. Pathé, for instance, was well placed to continue operations via its US subsidiaries, and was indeed very successful as a producer of shorts by such performers as Harold Lloyd. However, the company took a strategic decision not to enter the market for full-length films and found itself at a competitive disadvantage when the war ended. Thus, despite having had strong market presence and privileged access to the MPPC, Pathé's US decline was, at least in part, due to its own business failings. In 1921, stockholders and management took over the American subsidiary from the parent country.[20] Nevertheless, by the time the antitrust laws began to break up the MPPC, the Europeans, effectively gone from the American market, were otherwise engaged.

The first European quotas

The American motion picture industry has become infected with the new spirit of internationalism which has taken such firm root in the economic and industrial life of the country as the result of the seizure of war-time opportunities. Already the infant industry has definitely embarked upon a program of world-wide expansion and exploitation which is destined to eclipse the golden era now recognized as one of the great industrial romances of America.[21]

The early slowness of American film companies to enter the European market did not last. In the period 1909-12, US films took an estimated 60 per cent of film sales in Britain (although this figure may have dropped slightly in 1913-14).[22] The US was also the source of around 30 per cent of films released in Germany in 1912-13 (France supplied 16-18 per cent).[23] However, in countries that had strong domestic production industries, such as France and Italy, American films appear to have had a harder time.[24] These countries were also the major suppliers to the rest of southern and eastern Europe.[25] However, the US began to expand its foreign distribution operation, particularly as the war began to have an impact on production in the combatant states. The film companies concentrated first on those markets which had been largely abandoned by the Europeans due to the war.[26] Nevertheless, they were soon to focus on those European nations they could reach: by 1916, US films represented 78.8 per cent of the value of films shown in

Britain.[27] By January 1917, just over 30 per cent of the footage shown in France was from the United States, compared to 37 per cent of French origin.[28] In Spain in April/May 1918, 46.7 per cent of footage imported came from the US.[29]

Europe's distress may well have been America's opportunity. But there was something else at work in the surge of US films during the war period. Hollywood[30] was changing the cinema. Not only did it show "aspects of life, landscapes, characters, of a kind absent from pre-1914 French cinema," it had also, as discussed previously, developed a "narrative continuity" style of storytelling, attractive both to audiences and young filmmakers.[31] By the time the war ended, Hollywood did not only have a lead by default: it was producing films that were actively attractive to audiences.

Quotas between the world wars

Europe's response was to attempt to restrict growing American cinema power through trade sanctions which would shelter the re-emergence of strong domestic film sectors.

Germany

One wartime impact of Hollywood movies was the propagandist success of "impressing hatred of Germany with an unrivaled force upon enemies and neutrals alike." In response to this American triumph, the German High Command organized a merger of the main national film companies, creating the UFA studio.[32] This may be the first significant European governmental attempt to organize the market so as to meet the American cultural challenge. The problem in Germany, as elsewhere, was, that the postwar economy was still more favorable to Hollywood than anyone else. The German cinema underwent vertiginous expansion in the years 1919-23, building large numbers of theaters and rapidly increasing power. Sheltered from foreign competition by import restrictions and the declining currency, "the German cinema came of age ... Contemporaries were awed by the whirlwind tempo at which casual amusement for the working classes became serious business and part of the nation's culture."[33] However, although currency depreciation aided German production and boosted exports,[34] most leading European countries had weakened economies and higher priorities than the rebirth of their film industries.[35] By 1924, it was clear that Hollywood was in Europe to stay. Across the continent, the domestic film industries struggled. The difficulties of Pathé that had led to the sale of its American subsidiaries persisted, and the company was gradually reduced to a distribution operation.[36] Even more galling for national pride, another French giant, Gaumont, was forced to merge with the Hollywood studio Metro-Goldwyn-Mayer. (The two companies demerged in 1928.)[37] In Britain, postwar attempts to build a film business collapsed amid bankruptcy and undercapitalization.[38] However Germany, which had already placed an embargo in 1916 on "inessential imports," including films,[39] decided to extend its system of protectionism and, at the beginning of 1921, imposed Europe's first quotas on foreign feature films.[40] Many other countries would follow, as Table 1 shows.

Table 1: European cinema quotas 1921-1934[41]

Country	Date	Nature of quota
Germany	1 Jan. 1921	15 per cent of negative footage produced in 1919
	1 Jan. 1925	1:1 quota for imported features
	1 Apr. 1928	Based on "needs of market": approx. 1:2 quota
	13 Dec. 1928	210 licenses for 7/29-6/30
	1 Feb. 1929	Quotas extended to 6/31: approx. 1:2.5 quota
	July 1930	Two-thirds of quota reserved for silent films
	1 July 1931	Renewal of existing quota for one year
	1 July 1932	Dubbed imports restricted to 50 per cent; dubbing to be done in Germany
Italy	1925	Exhibition quota: one week all-Italian program in two months
	1 Oct. 1927	Exhibition quota: 10 per cent of screen time
	24 Aug. 1928	Countries importing Italian films have their films classified as "Italian"
Hungary	1925	Every distributor handling 20+ films/year must produce one Hungarian film
	1 Jan. 1928	1925 rule varied to allow substitution of heavy surcharge on imports
	1 Oct. 1930	20:1 quota dropped in favor of unlimited imports with fixed fees
Austria	3 Sept. 1926	Two-year 20:1 quota
	1 Jan. 1927	Quota varied to 12:1
	1 Oct. 1927	Quota varied to 18:1; backdated to 1/27
	1 Jan. 1928	Quota varied to 20:1
	5 Dec. 1928	Quota varied to 23:1; backdated to 1/28
	1 Jan. 1929	Quota varied to 20:1
	7 Jul. 1931	Halves no. of import certificates needed per film & fixes their prices
UK	1 Apr. 1927	Quota Act sets 7.5 per cent quota for distributors, 5 per cent for exhibitors, increasing to 20 per cent by 1935-36.
Portugal	6 May 1927	One domestic short in each program
France	12 Mar. 1928	7:1 quota: licenses granted on basis of French exports
	1 May 1929	7:1 quota: no export requirement
	1 Apr. 1929	US companies begin boycott in face of threatened 3:1 quota
	1 May 1929	4:1 quota implemented; boycott continues
	19 Sept. 1929	7:1 quota reintroduced until 5/30
	1 May 1930	7:1 quota extended to 9/30
	1 July 1931	Quota abolished, except for German films
	29 July 1932	Versions not dubbed in France banned; restrictions placed on theaters showing original-language films
	24 July 1933	Quota of 140 dubbed films in year to 6/34; dubbing must be done in France
	26 June 1934	Quota of 94 dubbed films for next six months
Czechoslovakia	23 Apr. 1932	Quota of 240 features per year, ultimately reduced to 120. American firms boycott Czech market

Germany's reasons for introducing quotas were varied but typical of the mixed motives that would continue to inform European cultural quotas in the future. Cultural values such as patriotism and the need to spread the German language played a part.[42] (This, however, did not prevent the "superpatriotic" UFA, founded specifically to counter American propaganda, from scrambling, even at great financial cost, to pick up Hollywood contracts.)[43] Some groups, smarting in particular at the postwar Versailles settlement, regarded Hollywood as "a potential threat to Germany's national well-being."[44] On the other hand, the German authorities performed an economic balancing act. They wanted to maximize the chances for the domestic film business to succeed by limiting foreign – effectively, American – access. However, they did not want to limit Germany's chance to penetrate the American market which, for a time at least in the early 1920s, seemed to be highly welcoming.[45] Another issue – more specific to its time and place – was the need for the ruined German economy to restrict outflows of foreign exchange.[46] In other words, the quotas served a mixed cultural and protectionist agenda. By the Nazi period, the agenda was more purely cultural. Nazi demonstrations had forced the German censor to suspend exhibition of *All Quiet on the Western Front* (Universal, 1930).[47] Once in power, in 1935 the Nazis expelled non-Aryan employees from American company branches in Germany and imposed a new quota, with higher fees and import duties. In 1936, American film releases were reduced to 30 per year, and remittances limited, with disadvantageous exchange rates.[48]

The 1921 law allowed for importation of film equivalent to just 15 per cent of domestic production. However, the local market does not appear to have been capable of meeting demand, and by 1924, foreign imports represented 57.7 per cent of films presented for approval by the German censor; American films were 33.2 per cent of the total.[49] From the beginning of 1925, distributors were allowed to release one foreign film for every German film handled. By 1926, however, foreign films accounted for 60.8 per cent of the market, although by 1929, this figure had declined to 54.9 per cent.[50] (In 1928, the quota law had been changed yet again to permit imports up to the level of the difference between actual German production and the theoretical capacity of the country's theaters. In addition, import permits would be granted only to distributors or exporters of German films.)[51] In this period, Hollywood's market share peaked at 44.5 percent, before declining in 1929 to 33.3 per cent.[52] It is difficult to know what the proportions would have been without the quotas. In 1925, Germany produced 212 films,[53] and the US and France 600[54] and 73[55] respectively. Some 306 foreign films were submitted for German censorship that year.[56] However, the quota, or *kontingent*, bred a phenomenon that would be seen in other quota systems, the *kontingentfilme*, or quota film, many of which were never released, but which were instead used to obtain the *kontingentschein*, or quota certificate that could be traded with those wishing to import foreign films.[57] Although American films were largely very profitable in Germany, this may have been because the quota effectively forced Hollywood to send only its best films: one estimate suggested that only 40 per cent of American films could enter Germany.[58] Further evidence of the impact of quotas comes from the statistics on short films, which were not subject to the *kontingent*. In 1923, 94 German shorts were submitted to the censor, as opposed to 149 from the US. In 1929, just five German shorts were submitted, against 316 from America.[59]

United Kingdom

The German example began to be followed elsewhere in Europe. In the United Kingdom, even more than in Germany, cultural values were invoked to bolster the industrial and economic arguments in favor of limiting Hollywood while boosting the local film industry. The sense of crisis was well-founded. As early as 1916, the British domestic film-industry was close to non-existent and American films dominant: in January of that year, 53 British-made films were released, compared with 528 foreign productions, of which the US had a large share.[60] In the full year, the US accounted for 78.8 per cent of the value of films shown in the UK; Britain itself took just 9.8 per cent.[61] By 1926, Hollywood supplied 83.6 per cent of films submitted to the British censor, and Britain just 4.9 per cent.[62]

Hollywood's success released a number of anxieties in Britain. Once more, there was a mixture of cultural and industrial concerns. The cultural anxiety can be seen in this remark made in a Cabinet Office paper of 1926:

> It is clearly undesirable that so very large a proportion of the films shown throughout the empire should present modes of life and forms of conduct which are not typically British.[63]

How would mass entertainment influence a newly enfranchised electorate?[64] What of the "high national and patriotic interests" that troubled an unusual coalition of artists, politicians and business leaders – including Thomas Hardy, Edward Elgar and proprietors of the leading British newspapers – in a letter to the *Morning Post* newspaper in 1925?[65] On the other hand, the *Morning Post* editorialized on the commercial aspects of Hollywood's penetration of the British market, decrying block booking, dumping and the alleged abuse of American diplomatic power while condemning cheap American imports as "positively harmful to the children who see them."[66] More troubling, still, Hollywood seemed to attract audiences "far more magnetically than British films."[67] British industrialists and others believed that trade would be boosted by the use of British products and the depiction of British lifestyles in exported films.[68] (Conversely, those exposed to American films adopted American styles and bought American goods.) For such people, economic arguments trumped cultural ones:

> If our people are content to witness perpetual rubbish, let it, at any rate, be English rubbish in preference to American rubbish, because in producing English rubbish the money will at least be spent in this country.[69]

The result of these fears was Britain's own quota legislation, the Cinematograph Films Act of 1927. The act outlawed both block booking (requiring exhibitors to take a company's entire output) and blind booking (the sale of film to exhibitors sight unseen). The quota required distributors to include 7.5 per cent of British films in those they supplied; exhibitors were to show 5 per cent, multiplied by the number of showings.[70] Both numbers were due to rise to 20 per cent by 1936 and in fact endured until 1938.[71]

The British quotas were successful in generating "English rubbish." As in Germany, films were produced simply to satisfy the new laws, the notorious "quota quickies."[72] Unlike Germany, the regulatory regime, based on exhibition rather than production quotas, ensured that these films were not used as a form of currency, but were instead shown in theaters. While the number of feature films released each year in Britain between 1929 and 1935 remained roughly constant, at around 670, the British share rose from a low of 96 in 1930 to a peak of 190 in 1934.[73]

France

These German and British examples inspired France, whose film sector still smarted from the loss of its pre-First World War hegemony. Structurally, the French market had suffered from the near-collapse of its erstwhile leader, Pathé, through bad management and failure to adapt to the new market conditions. Creatively, and unlike Germany, France had been slow to apply the new narrative techniques, appropriate to now-popular full-length feature films, that had helped Hollywood seal its gains in the world market. Consequently, in 1927, the year before France first introduced film quotas, Hollywood owned 63.3 per cent of all films submitted for censorship and the French 12.7 per cent.[74] However, French films may have outperformed their Hollywood competitors at the box office. In 1923-24, for instance, French production represented only 15-20 per cent of films shown in Paris, home to the main showcase theaters. But throughout the 1920s the revenue share of French producers was 35-40 per cent of the market.[75] Nevertheless, overall, the French market remained enfeebled and underdeveloped, with a poor theater structure, low admissions, meager receipts and high taxes.[76] French business represented around 3 per cent of Hollywood's foreign revenues in 1925.[77]

The principal French government department responsible for film policy was the education ministry, although other departments, including the ministry of foreign affairs, the agriculture ministry, the Army department and the office of tourism, among others, also had interests – mainly educational and instructional – that touched on the workings of the film industry.[78] In February 1928, the Education Minister, Edouard Herriot gave ten days notice of the introduction of stringent film quotas in France, a decision that took many, particularly in Hollywood, by surprise.[79] The system proposed was Byzantine in its elaborateness.:

> ... French films were organized in two classes: French films of the 1st category (French producer, French technical team, interior scenes shot in France in studios belonging to French firms, at least three-quarters of leading roles taken by French actors) and French films of the 2nd category (each item comprising at least 50 per cent French elements). A publisher [ie, a producer] could not seek a visa for more than one French film of the 2nd category for [every] one French film of the 1st category. On the other hand, the number of foreign films submitted for a visa could never exceed the number of French films of the 1st category (or half of the films of the 2nd category) sold in the country of origin."[80]

Every French film exported qualified for seven import permits, of which no more than four could be used for US films – and only in respect of French films released in the US French production would have to increase by 50-100 per cent (and every one shown in America) to permit the level of films Hollywood normally exported to France each year.[81]

The reasons for the quota were spelled out by Herriot when he issued his decree of February 18: "[T]he interests of good order, and of public morality, of internal and external state security, but also the safeguarding of the customs and national traditions . . . which would be seriously compromised if the number of foreign films shown on French screens . . . continued to grow at the expense of French films."[82] In other words, and unlike in Germany and Britain, the reasons given for the French quotas were purely cultural. The Herriot decree "served as a metonymy for any future legislation aimed at protecting France's industry against America's monopolizing tendencies," although the French were also aware of Germany's success as a film exporter.[83]

However, France was not innocent of the commercial arguments for protectionism. Like everyone else, the French were keenly attuned to America's increasing economic power. They were also all too aware of one of the sources of that power: the fact that the US had, as a question of policy, moved to seize markets formerly held by the European nations while they were preoccupied with the world war. Not only was Europe weakened by the material cost of the war: it could not rely on retrieving the markets on which it had relied on before hostilities began. In this, the film business had been but a tiny, if highly visible, part of American ambitions. In 1931, a member of the National Assembly, Charles Pomaret – who went on to be interior and then labor minister in the wartime collaborationist Vichy régime before his acquittal on collaboration charges, on the ground of his resistance activities, in 1946 – sought to spell out the consequences for Europe of America's economic and financial muscle, aggressive tariff policies, and, as shown in Table 2, huge trade imbalances:

Table 2: US Trade surplus with selected European countries
(in $ millions)[84]

	1926	1927
Germany	166	281
UK[85]	589	483
Belgium	22	44
Spain	17	39
France	112	61
Italy	55	23
Netherlands	34	61
USSR	35	52

Pomaret saw in America's film business, as in all else, a juggernaut crushing Europe beneath its wheels. The statistics poured forth from his pen: Hollywood had $2.5 billion capital in 1930 and 350,000 employees who earned $50 million a year. In 1929 it spent $100 on the publicity budget alone for the 820 films it made to fill the 18.5 million seats in 20,500 cinemas. Fox made profits of $27 million, Warner Brothers $16 million, Fox $15 million.[86] Pomaret further revealed Hollywood's tactics for dominating Europe: its raids on local talent, its attempts to buy up the main theaters to give showcases to its own films, its boycott of independent theaters, and even the deliberate "stifling" of the best European films, such as Abel Gance's six-hour masterpiece *Napoléon*[87] which, Pomaret claimed, had been bought by MGM and then shown "in minimal doses on English and American screens."[88]

Pomaret's use of *Napoléon* illustrates the difficulty of separating truth from imagining in this charged environment. First, MGM may well have balked at the great length of the film, which significantly reduced the number of possible showings per day as compared to a conventional picture. (Even Gance produced a 140-minute version, in 1934) Second, a film did not need to be French to be wrecked by Hollywood's equal-opportunity vandals: it was MGM, after all, that butchered its own silent masterpiece, Erich von Stroheim's reputedly 420-minute *Greed* (MGM/Goldwyn Company, 1921), releasing it in an almost incoherent, 110 minute, version. Finally, the studio may have lost confidence in the film. *Variety*, the show-business newspaper and a reasonable barometer of the attitudes of both the theater owners and the mass public, displayed a particularly brutal sensibility when its owner and editor, Sime Silverman, reviewed *Napoléon* in New York:

> "Napoleon" doesn't mean anything to the great horde of picture-house goers over here. Nap wasn't good looking enough and they didn't put in the right scenes for the flaps over here . . . Al [sic] Gance gets the most credit. He directed. Whoever impersonated Napoleon [Albert Dieudonne] looked more like Hearst.[89]

Nevertheless, for Pomaret, predatory financial practices and the destruction of the film industry seemed to go hand in hand:

> The English film hardly exists; one can go to the finest theaters in London without seeing a British production, and yet the Americans have by their speculation on falling prices at the London Stock Exchange, pushed down the value of the English companies which were set up to benefit from the quota established by the British government.[90]

(Pomaret may have confused two factors here: the boom-bust phenomenon – whereby the value of opportunistically created British production companies was artificially inflated before crashing – does not appear to have depended specially on American capital. Some £7.2 million ($36 million) was invested in new British film companies in August 1928 as speculative cash rushed to anticipate the introduction of quotas. Contemporary British opinion blamed unscrupulous corporate promoters, not the Americans, for the *débâcle*.[91] Separately, the Fox Film Corporation did battle for several years to take control of the Gaumont-British Picture Corporation in order to secure exhibition outlets for its films. The Fox attempt failed.[92]) Hollywood's business practices, as well as the intense American reaction to the French quotas – much more intense, in a less significant market, than its response to the actions of Germany and Britain – are dealt with in the next section. In terms of the impact of the quotas on France itself, one particularly resonant effect should be noted: the Herriot decree and its successors put the French cinema business under significant economic pressure. In 1918, there were 1,444 cinemas in France: by 1929, there were 4,200.[93] However, the Herriot decree had the effect of limiting the very films that had been filling the theaters while not stimulating enough domestic replacements. French production increased quite substantially, but not enough to fill the houses. The result: by 1937, the number of French theaters had fallen to 3,700.[94] Figures for audiences were not collected until the 1930s, so it is not possible to point with absolute certainty to audience decline as a cause of the reduction in cinemas. Sadoul notes other factors that affected both the number of cinemas, the level of audiences and box office receipts, such as the arrival of talking pictures (which required substantial rewiring of theaters for sound), the depression, currency depreciation, wage fluctuations and increased leisure time. It is clear from Sadoul's figures that the number of French theaters did not decline steadily between 1929 and 1937, but appears to have moved up and down quite sharply.[95]

Even the degree to which the rise in production was due to the quotas may be debated. The number of French films submitted for censorship actually fell in 1929, from 94 to 52: by 1932, this figure had climbed once more to an historic high of 140.[96] A new factor – the arrival of talking pictures – had given temporary strength temporarily to the European cinema,[97] and brought the industries on both sides of the Atlantic into open conflict.

The response of the US government and Hollywood to the first wave of quotas

The nations of Europe were not alone in having a policy for the cinema industry. Indeed, the policies of the US and Europe dovetailed on a single issue: the Americans wanted to boost Hollywood, while the Europeans wished to curb it.

The interest of the US government in the overseas film business began early. As early as December 1916, the State Department had sought from its overseas consulates information on the exhibition, distribution and popularity of American motion pictures.[98] Overseas missions also began collecting information on foreign censorship of American films, often viewed as a veiled restraint on international trade.[99] Although Wilson administration Commerce Secretary William C. Redfield decided not to seek congressional funding in 1919 for a program to support Hollywood's overseas activities, his successor, Herbert Hoover, was exercised by "the significance of motion picture exporting both as a straight commodity trade and as a powerful influence in behalf of American goods and habits of living."[100] Hoover's two-part analysis was to provide the spine of US feature film policy between the wars. The straight commodity trade was heady enough. Hollywood had gone from nowhere to a $1 billion business by 1921. Now, it was occupying the foreign trade vacuum created by the European war: between 1918 and 1921, film exports grew 300 per cent.[101] That would have sufficed to encourage an increasingly activist Commerce Department, keenly aware that other countries were also becoming more proactive in boosting their exports.[102] However, the second prong of Hoover's description represented something unique to the cinema: the idea that "trade follows the film."[103] This widely-quoted phrase was popularly – but wrongly[104] – believed to have been coined from the Prince of Wales (later King Edward VIII, and later still the Duke of Windsor). He used it in a speech before the British National Film League in 1923. The Prince had decided to pass what turned out to be a 25-year wait for his short-lived monarchy by acting as a global ambassador for the trade of Britain and its empire. As a kind of walking clothes horse, he was quite effective:

> The Prince for some years now has been going about all over the world promoting good will for his countrymen and subjects. Incidentally he has helped trade. Everybody remembers when he was last in new York he set a vogue for blue shirts with soft collars, for a style of hat that blossomed in the ship windows even before he departed, and for gray flannels. ... The heir apparent did something to introduce and popularize English clothes, shoes, hats, pipes and what not.[105]

The US did not have a royal family, but it did have the movies, the wider commercial ramifications of which were beginning to be noted, for instance by Douglas Miller, a commercial attaché in Berlin who wrote to Hoover:

> No one has yet been able to estimate the large amount of advertising for American goods that has come through the motion pictures and the stage. The amusement world of Germany now gets its tone from across the Atlantic. American styles as seen on the film, American tunes brought over by the traveling jazz bands – all cannot fail to have a marked influence on the German habit of mind. A stranger, taking an evening stroll down the chief promenade of Berlin's new rich, cannot fail to notice the American touch in the clothing of many persons, in the advertising in shop windows and in the type of entertainment offered to the public."[106]

Businesses reported demand for American styles – and brands – in products as diverse as shoes, clothes, cars and furniture as a result of exposure of foreign audiences to Hollywood films.[107] Hollywood was said to have been responsible for the introduction of the bungalow to Brazil, and for the Americanization – through the exposure of audiences to film title cards – of European languages.[108] While Hoover may only have trade in his mind, it is equally clear that this phenomenon he wanted to encourage created a nexus between culture and commerce. Indeed, Dr. Julius Klein, head of the Commerce Department's Bureau of Foreign and Domestic Commerce, encouraged Hoover in his belief in the "trade promoting possibilities of American films," contributing an article to the Department's Commerce Reports titled "Trade Follows the Motion Pictures".[109] Other countries changed as a result of their exposure to American cinema, something the Prince of Wales, or his speechwriter, had noticed: "The film is to America what the flag once was to Britain. By its means, Uncle Sam may hope some day, if he be not checked in time, to Americanize the world."[110] In time, both the US government and Hollywood would steadfastly and constantly deny that culture was a factor in the export of films. But the "trade follows film" movement went beyond the export of American goods: it denoted the export of America itself, its lifestyle and its values. Not only did America understand this: it understood that other countries knew it, too. Clarence J. North, first head of the Motion Picture Section of the Commerce Department, said so, explaining why quota systems were being introduced:

> The film is a silent salesman of great effectiveness, and by that method much trade is being diverted to America. Moreover, through American motion pictures, the ideals, culture, customs and tradition of the United States are gradually undermining those of other countries. The film industry of these other countries must be built up as a barrier against this subtle Americanization process.[111]

The degree to which these facts were more widely recognized, in particular by a triumphalist American press, caused some alarm at Hollywood's trade association, the MPPDA (discussed in greater detail below), which urged the Commerce Department to centralize its release of data and statistics on Hollywood exports – and to allow the MPPDA to vet material before release. The request was tactfully declined.[112] In 1925 North was placed in overall charge of motion picture work in the Bureau, and on July 1, 1926, with Hoover's personal support and following a Congressional appropriation of $15,000, a stand-alone Motion Picture Section was created.[113] North was put in charge, and his staff included a special trade commissioner, George R. Canty, stationed in Europe. By 1929, the flow of information to Washington – particularly statistical information – was so great, the Section, now called the Motion Picture Division, was able to sustain a bi-weekly publication, *Motion Pictures Abroad*.[114]

Hollywood, naturally, did not remain passive as Europe normalized its quota systems. From the imposition of the German *kontingent*, America – both private and official – began to fight back. One reaction to the *kontingent* was predictable: Hollywood attempted to use its commercial power to strike a better deal. Paramount and MGM, following consultation with Universal, which initiated the deal, provided the ailing UFA company with a substantial loan, one effect of which would be to gain access to the high-class UFA theater chain, where the effects of the quota could be offset by greater screen time and higher revenues.[115]

Hollywood also exercised its commercial power by plundering Europe for talent. (Will Hays – of whom more below – would later acknowledge that one of several strategies for supporting Hollywood was "by drawing into the American art industry the talent of other nations in order to make it more truly international.")[116] By 1930, Charles Pomaret could point to a decade of departures, including Greta Garbo, Emil Jannings and Maurice Chevalier among performers and Victor Sjöström, Mauritz Stiller, Jacques Feyder, Ernst Lubitsch. E.A. Dupont and F.W. Murnau among directors.[117] One reason Hollywood had for going after Europe's best was because it felt threatened. When, in the early 1920s Germany – thanks to people like Lubitsch and Robert Wiene[118] – began to produce successful and exportable films, some in Hollywood lobbied, unsuccessfully, for higher tariffs.[119] That initiative having come to nothing, Hollywood went after the cause of the competition. In 1921, Paramount created a German-based holding company, EFA, with state-of-the-art local studios and a pocket book to sign up the best talent UFA could not afford to keep. EFA's 30 million mark investment failed within a year.[120] However, several among EFA's talent roster, including Lubitsch and Pola Negri, accepted contracts in the US, "the first of a stream of German film people who relocated to Hollywood."[121]

The second reaction of Hollywood to quotas – and this was something new – was political. In March 1922, the leading film companies had formed a trade association, the Motion Picture Producers and Distributors of America (MPPDA), under the presidency of William Harrison Hays, Presbyterian elder, presidential campaign organizer and Postmaster General.[122] Although the prime reason for bringing in Hays was to clean up Hollywood's sordid moral image and avert state intervention – in the way Judge Keneshaw Mountain Landis had recently restored baseball's reputation after the 1919 bribery scandal[123] – the MPPDA interested itself from the outset in foreign affairs, playing "a key part in formulating and implementing the strategy of Hollywood's economic foreign policy".[124] (Despite his executive and virtually plenipotentiary powers, Hays always insisted he was not the motion picture equivalent of Landis, the baseball "czar".)[125]

It has been argued that three other issues had more to do with the creation of the MPPDA than pre-empting censorship moves: overseas restrictions on US films; foreign commercial and government efforts to promote their domestic film industries; and lack of cooperation between studios and with the federal government.[126] While these concerns were unquestionably important to Hollywood, and occupied much of the MPPDA's time, as will be seen, there seems no reason to dispute the priorities set out in Article 1, Section 3 of the organization's own by-laws:

> The object for which the Association is created is to foster the common interests of those engaged in the motion picture industry in the United States by establishing and maintaining the highest possible moral and artistic standards in motion picture production, by developing the educational as well as the entertainment value and the general usefulness of the motion picture by diffusing accurate and reliable information with reference to the industry, by reforming abuses relative to the industry, by securing freedom from unjust or unlawful exactions and by other lawful and proper means.[127]

Significantly, Hays himself did not include the difficulties of foreign trade in his list of ten problems to be addressed by the industry at the time he became head of the MPPDA.[128]

The MPPDA began to work closely with government: Hays himself later described the MPPDA's foreign responsibilities as making it "almost an adjunct of our State Department."[129] The closeness of the MPPDA and its personnel to the US government may have been advantageous in terms of contacts and understanding, but has never ceased to haunt the organization in its foreign dealings, where it has often been viewed as a catspaw for national policy. As early as 1926, rumors flew overseas that Hays owed his MPPDA job to government "connivance."[130] Later, French commentators would draw sinister inferences from connections between Secretary of State James F. Byrnes and the MPPDA's successor organization, the Motion Picture Association of America. Later still, the ease of access in Washington of MPAA president (and former Johnson administration aide) Jack Valenti would be a constant source of European comment.

But first, Hays had to build his adjunct department. He hired his brother-in-law and college friend, Major Frederick L Herron, to head the MPPDA's Foreign Department (later the International Department). Despite Herron's experience as a diplomat, it took time to build the department: his first three years at the MPPDA were largely spent getting to know the MPPDA member companies' foreign managers and representatives, making government connections at the State and Commerce departments and getting to know foreign government officials in the US and abroad.[131]

Perhaps because of this need to build an organization, the MPPDA's first foreign efforts, despite the existence of the German quotas and an apparently general mobilization abroad against the strength of Hollywood, were somewhat ginger, and even naïve. For instance, Hays protested the German 1:1 import quota of 1925 on the ground – entirely conceding the German rationale for the measure – that the US exported many films but imported only a few.[132] He also tried to push his members to import more foreign films, in an effort to stave off claims that the US closed its markets the European cinema.[133] Of course, this flew in the face of what would be the MPPDA's recurring theme – an article of faith held by Hollywood to this day – that no barrier other than audience taste stood in the way of European success on American screens.

However, Hays and Herron were making progress on what would be a key feature of the MPPDA and its successor organizations: close and sympathetic contacts in Washington. The reason the MPPDA's foreign department would come to resemble an adjunct of the State Department was simple: there would come to be near-total congruence of interest and outlook between the two.

Although many papers for the period appear to be missing, it is also clear that the MPPDA was forming a close relationship with the Commerce Department. A circular sent to overseas commercial attachés and trade commissioners in 1924 described the MPPDA as one of the Bureau of Foreign and Domestic Commerce's "most valuable contacts," and called on the US representatives to make a "special point" of keeping the Bureau up to date on "all developments affecting [the film industry] throughout the world." The circular emphasized the "utmost importance" of timeliness and urged the use of cable communications to send back information quickly.[134]

Table 3: US film exports 1929-38[135]

Year	Total feet	Total value	$/ft yield
1929	274,351,341	$8,119,000	$33.79
1934	194,386,495	$4,212,000	$46.15
1935	199,690,621	$4,597,000	$43.44
1936	213,926,165	$4,655,000	$45.96
1937	220,262,588	$4,911,000	$44.85
1938	208,025,170	$4,650,000	$44.74

It has already been noted that the American attack on the French quotas was more intense than on those imposed previously by Germany and the United Kingdom. Part of the reason for this, in the case of Germany at least, may have been the newness of the MPPDA and the inexperience of Hays and Herron in their jobs. The complexity of the issues to be mastered was also a factor.[136] Further, because of the various predatory – but competitive – activities of the studios on the ground in Germany, the Motion Picture Service believed the MPPDA lacked the kind of united front required to defeat the *kontingent*.[137]

The government side was inexperienced as well: in 1925 C.J. North thought the British threat, as expressed in the House of Lords debate, was no "more than talk."[138] (However, even when North acknowledged that the British quota was inevitable, he thought the MPPDA did not.)[139] Indeed, the American approach to the possibility of British quotas in fact weakened its later position. In 1926, Col. Edward C. Lowry, an MPPDA representative,[140] offered 40 per cent American investment in what would have been around twenty British films per year.[141] The plan would have required 600 Hollywood films to released in Britain for the British total to reach twenty. The plan was rejected after apparently serious consideration.[142] This concession to British fears for its market, combined with the relatively limited initial quota, blunted the force of American opposition to the measure. Further, it was believed that demand for films in Britain was rising: therefore, Hollywood, by exporting all it could, would simply force British up production of cheap filler productions to meet the quota.[143] To an extent, this is what happened.

In the 1930s, the relations between Hollywood and the government became more streamlined, leading to a clear policy on quotas. While some in government were sympathetic to the Europeans' culture argument, they nonetheless pursued the national interest of trying to see quotas reduced. In France, insistent lobbying against the 1928 Herriot quotas led, in 1936, to the promulgation of a new regime as part of a bilateral customs agreement. The agreement established new set of exhibition quotas, modified in each of the two succeeding years, which improved Hollywood's access to the French market.

France had already relaxed its quota system from the original Herriot regime. In July 1933, a quota of 140 dubbed films was admitted for the next 12 months. The following year, the quota was raised to 94 films for a six month period. The 1936 agreement, the so-called Marchandeau accord, maintained the foreign dubbed film quota at 188 per year – but guaranteed that 160 of those films would be American.[144] Given that, at this time, MPPDA members produced some 325 films per year on average, the new quota gave the principal Hollywood studios access for virtually all its significant output (excluding low-importance "programmers").[145]

The Blum-Byrnes accords

Throughout the 1930s, the value of American film exports dropped (see Table 3). Although quotas may have had something to do with this, most analysts cite the depression as the major cause of this decline: as has been seen, the studios suffered equally badly at home.

After June 1940, when France fell, both German-occupied and Vichy France excluded American films altogether. This policy was continued by the Free French at the Liberation. There were two main consequences of this policy. First, French filmmaking underwent something of a renaissance, even as the volume of national production dropped. At the end of the war, the film industry could look back with some pride at the best of the 220 films produced between August 1940 and May 1944, notably Marcel Carné's *Les visiteurs du soir*,[146] and *Les Enfants du Paradis*,[147] Marcel L'Herbier's *La Nuit fantastique*,[148] Jean Dellanoy's *L'Eternal retour*[149] and Robert Bresson's debut features *Les Anges du peché*[150] and *Les Dames du Bois de Boulogne*.[151] Given the circumstances of censorship, repression and dictatorship under which these films were made, this fact was also a source of some troubling French reflections.

Understandably, the occupation period has produced sharp differences among historians of the cinema, as well as extensive literature.[152] Further, just as Roy Armes sees the cinema of the Vichy period more in terms of continuity with the 1930s than as a separable period, some contemporaries traced the renaissance of the French cinema to some years before the German invasion.[153] In 1937, citing such classics-to-be as Julien Duvivier's *Un Carnet de Bal*[154] and *Pépé le Moko*,[155] and Jean Renoir's *La Grande Illusion*,[156] the *New Yorker*'s correspondent, Janet Flanner noted, "French films used to be films which the French rarely went to see, American movies being their favorites. Celluloid has been changing lately. ... Already in the past year, with this list, French films have moved to the top of the European class."[157]

A second consequence of the exclusion of American films from France was the creation of a huge backlog of several hundred unreleased Hollywood features. From 1943 or so on, when it was clear that the war would be won by the Allies, Hollywood had begun to lobby for the film industry to be taken care of in postwar negotiations with both friendly and defeated governments. The continued exclusion of Hollywood from France after the Liberation was particularly irksome to the filmmakers, particularly as it violated the 1938 Franco-American agreement. (Vichy had made an issue of alleged American "cultural penetration," and by 1944 was denouncing "Jewish" America for the pre-Liberation bombing of the country.)[158] From at least 1945 on, Jean Monnet, who ran the French economic interest section in Washington, attempted to negotiate postwar credits to rebuild the country. In 1946, the negotiations for $1 billion of credits were taken over directly by the acting prime minister, Léon Blum. The negotiations had special urgency for both sides. France needed the money; the US was greatly exercised by the possibility of a Communist victory in the 1946 assembly elections and wanted to improve Blum's position by giving him the money.[159] US ambassador Jefferson Caffrey repeatedly warned the State Department of the need to ensure that Blum's mission succeeded before the June 2 elections. In the political vacuum that followed the liberation of France, a Communist election victory – or even a *coup d'état* – was a source of constant concern to Caffrey. However, from the time Monnet first raised the issue, the State Department indicated that the film industry would have to be on the agenda of any overall deal. To that end, the Truman administration's Secretary of State James F. Byrnes wrote to Caffrey on Feb. 4, 1946, instructing him to put "Motion Pictures" on the "tentative agenda for the overall financial and economic discussions" with France.[160]

And so it turned out. The 1946 Blum-Byrnes accords, as they came to be called, included the reopening of the French market to Hollywood films, albeit under a continuing exhibition quota. The agreement provided for a screen quota requiring exhibitors to show French films four weeks per quarter for a period of two years. However, the agreement lifted all numerical quotas – within the screen time constraints, Hollywood could export as many films as it wished.[161] There was uproar among the French film community, among intellectuals and in sections of the press. American films certainly poured in to France, and the public, long starved of Hollywood entertainment, went to see them. Despite their renegotiation in 1948, the Blum-Byrnes accords entered folk memory as the moment when a newly-assertive French film sector was crushed by Hollywood, backed by US political muscle.[162] The French drew comfort for their position by the fact that, as, later, in the age of Jack Valenti, Hollywood saw fit to flaunt its proclaimed closeness to American political power. Eric Johnston, Hays' successor at the MPPDA (now called the MPAA), told a French trade newspaper in 1948: "President Harry Truman told me that he considered it essential that American films be shown everywhere in the world."[163] When the issue of television quotas became news in the 1980s, the Blum-Byrnes accords were once more dredged up as a prior example of Yankee perfidiousness.

Lately, there has been some more dispassionate research into the accords, particularly by French historians.[164] One crucial discovery has been that the replacement of the numerical quota by a screen quota was in fact a *French*, not American proposal. French officials believed that a screen quota, while providing protection for national cinema, would nevertheless be more of a market-driven solution, since foreign films would compete among themselves for access to France, and French films, which could not be absorbed in their entirety by the reserved screen time, would compete with the foreigners for access to the remaining time.[165] The American negotiators pressed for a continuation of a numerical quota, as had existed under the Marchandeau accord, apparently preferring the devil they knew.[166] The US apparently accepted that such a quota would be lower than before the war, since the Vichy government had abolished the double feature in 1940, a decision that was ratified by the provisional government and its regulatory organ following the Liberation.[167] It was only later, in 1956, that the MPAA would accept the screen quota, as opposed to the numerical quota, as "the least undesirable method of affording protecting to domestic film industries."[168] The abandonment of numerical quotas and their replacement by screen quotas was a deliberate policy decision and not, as one attempted apologist for Blum has suggested, the result of being badly informed as to the likely impact of the change on the film industry.[169]

Three other features of Blum-Byrnes have also been revisited by historians. The fact that the accords simply replaced the 1938 agreement, which had been breached by France, has been acknowledged. Secondly, some of the more conspiratorial aspects of the Hollywood-State Department relationship have been downplayed (although close harmony undoubtedly existed). Before becoming Secretary of State, Byrnes had been a powerful Roosevelt-era Senator and then Justice of the Supreme Court of the United States. Following his resignation from the State Department in January 1947 (six months after he signed the agreement with Blum) Byrnes joined the Washington DC law firm of Hogan & Harrison, representing Paramount Pictures and other studio clients. He returned shortly afterwards to politics and was elected governor of South Carolina in 1950.[170] (It is often reported wrongly in French works that Byrnes actually joined the MPAA upon his resignation from the Truman Administration.) The idea that Hollywood and Washington represented some kind of nexus in conspiracy against non-American entertainment interests did not require the ingenuity of an Oliver Stone, even if it was based on a somewhat crude analysis of how the two institutions actually worked together.

Thirdly, and most importantly, the real impact of the accords has been reassessed. The reason there was an avalanche of Hollywood films was because there were so many unreleased pictures in stock. Ranged against this backlog of high-quality unreleased Hollywood films was a fairly large number of mainly low-quality French ones. (According to one French historian, these were of such low quality that 90 per cent of French production in 1946-47 was "qualitatively disqualified.")[171] The presence of the Blum-Byrnes accords in these crucial months of postwar reconstruction "probably saved the French cinema which, without shelter, would have been swept away by that Niagara, so long-awaited, that came from the other side of the Atlantic."[172] By 1948, the backlog had largely been used up, and the number of imports fell. (In the renegotiated agreement of 1948, following the outcry and upon the expiration of the two-year term of the Blum-Byrnes accords, the two countries concluded a four-year deal to raise the screen quota to five weeks per quarter, acknowledging that such an agreement was consistent with the terms of the newly-negotiated GATT. The numerical quota was reimposed, limited US films to 121 per year (all other countries combined were limited to 65).[173] The MPAA had in any case observed a voluntary quota of 124 films per year since June 1946, in an effort to defuse the fury directed against Blum-Byrnes in France.[174]

One further complicating factor is political. Much of the opposition to the Blum-Byrnes accords was industrial, but it was also fed by political interests, notably the PCF. For the Communists, attacking the deal was also a way of attacking American influence in postwar Europe. In that sense, the quota row functioned as a kind of proxy for the Cold War itself. Sometimes Hollywood appears to have seen things that way, too. Eric Johnston of the MPAA told the House Committee on Un-American Activities in May 1945 that American films provided clear proof of the lies of totalitarian propaganda.[175]

Thus, the revisionist argument goes, the accords only had short-term importance, and their "black legend" (as one historian calls it) has been overblown. Nevertheless, folk memory and passionate belief stood here, as before and later, for much more than did fact.

Hollywood's efforts to secure re-entry to France were being mirrored all over Europe. Less than two months after the end of the war, the heads of Hollywood studios visited Europe to inspect the terrain, at the invitation of the Supreme Allied commander, General Dwight D. Eisenhower. The party included Harry Cohn (Columbia), Spyros Skouras and Darryl F. Zanuck (20th Century-Fox), Jack Warner (Warner Bros.) and Edgar J. Mannix (MGM).[176] (In 1952, Zanuck and Warner would be enthusiastic co-chairs of the Hollywood committee to elect Eisenhower President of the United States; Warner had apparently tried to persuade him to run in the 1948 election.)[177] The continent had been deprived of American entertainment for six years. The tardy arrival of such films as *Gone With The Wind*,[178] of which much had been heard despite the war, was awaited with extraordinary excitement. The reaction of the countries to which these films were to be exported was more equivocal. While there was a domestic film sector to be protected, quotas were a common recourse. But even where there was no such industry, governments sought to block the repatriation of Hollywood's funds. In the years immediately after the war, when reconstructing countries were often desperately short of funds, the temptation to do so was considerable. The 1948 Franco-American agreement, for example, resulted in some $10 million per year of Hollywood's earnings remaining in France, where it was used for co-production, distribution and story rights acquisition, and studio construction.[179]

The post-war period was thus both an opportunity and a challenge for Hollywood which sought to meet the huge demand for its films while blocking attempts to limit its market to entry and tax its earnings. To this end, the MPPDA reorganized itself in 1946, creating two bodies, the Motion Picture Association of America (MPAA) and the Motion Picture Export Association (MPEA), the latter body designed to benefit from particular legal provisions for exporters.[180] The Webb-Pomerene Act of 1918[181] had created exemptions to the federal antitrust laws for associations of exporters. Theoretically, under the law, a group of American exporters might form a cartel, fix prices, engage in boycotts and other activities that would otherwise constitute antitrust activity. In so doing, they would be immune to prosecution under United States law. As a practical matter, the Webb-Pomerene Act was generally ineffective. Such an association was not entitled to protection under foreign antitrust laws[182] – indeed, a company's membership of one might draw the attention of foreign authorities to the possibility that the company might be engaging in anticompetitive practices. Generally, Webb-Pomerene is regarded as a failed and now anachronistic provision.[183] With one notable exception: Hollywood, which at least one commentator believes has been "tremendously successful in controlling the sale, distribution and licensing of US motion pictures in export markets"[184] through its Webb-Pomerene association, the MPEA.

One tool the MPEA used under its Webb-Pomerene powers was the boycott. Will Hays had apparently been authorized by the US government to threaten such action during the first wave of quota battles, at the end of the 1920s.[185] In the immediate aftermath of the war, the boycott tool had already been used in the Netherlands, Norway, Poland and Czechoslovakia where the conditions of market re-entry were unsatisfactory to Hollywood.[186] The threat of a boycott was a serious one. Not only was there substantial public interest in the return of American films; there was also no film industry in Europe capable of filling theaters without a steady supply from Hollywood. Many local businesses – theatrical exhibitors, print laboratories, subbing facilities, advertising agencies, newspapers and magazines – were to a greater of lesser extent dependent financially on the presence in the national market of American films. In the fragile reconstruction economies of Western Europe, these benefits were not lightly ignored. However, the essential feature of a group boycott, of course, was unanimity. When MPEA members failed to work together in a common action, as later occurred with boycotts in Denmark and Spain, the association's efforts were thereby compromised.[187] (As discussed later, MPEA members also failed to agree to a group boycott of a French-based television trade fair at the height of the EC quota row.) Yet despite the reality of the boycott threat in many cases, some countries that were extremely short of money to pay for essentials, such as food, were prepared to take that risk. The United Kingdom, which had seen $60 million depart for Hollywood in 1947, placed a 75 per cent customs tariff on foreign films.[188] One politician told the House of Commons:

> I have a great admiration for the acting of Mr Humphrey Bogart.... Nevertheless, as I am compelled to choose between Bogart and bacon, I am bound to choose bacon at the present time.[189]

Three days after the British imposed their tariff, the MPEA announced a boycott of the UK market.[190] Eric Johnston of the MPAA, three times chairman of the United States Chamber of Commerce and with ambitions for the presidential nomination of the Republican Party, unquestionably disapproved of the newly-emerging socialist and social-democratic governments of Western Europe with their statist, interventionist policies.[191] Nevertheless, the MPEA members were more likely to be sympathetic to Johnston's business rationale for the boycott: the British, he said, "should not expect to get a dollar's worth of film for 25 cents."[192]

As would happen 46 years later in the Uruguay Round, the US administration realized that bigger issues were at stake than the economic needs of Hollywood – even though the likely costs of the British tariff were, in real money, far higher than any Hollywood has suffered as a result of the EU television quotas. As with the Uruguay Round, the MPAA attempted to tie its sectional interests to a wider economic issue – in this case, US aid to Britain. President Harry S Truman, who received Eric Johnston personally, told him that if this were to happen, the US and the UK "might as well throw their whole Havana Charter into the waste paper basket."[193] The Havana Charter, of course, was the measure establishing the International Trade Organization which, upon its ratification being thwarted, was transformed into the GATT. Not for the last time, Hollywood was told to take a back seat to the interests of the world trading order. (As a more minor illustration of the same phenomenon, Hollywood also fell out badly with the military over the reintroduction of American films to Germany. A joint solution was blocked because of "the inability of the American motion picture industry to co-operate along policy lines laid down by the United States Government for the occupation of Germany.")[194]

Even without government backing, the MPEA had some negotiating aces – notably the overall economic impact of withdrawal from the British market. The agreement reached between the MPEA and the UK government in March 1948 was for a combination of numerical quotas and high limits on the export of earning from Britain. Although at least one anti-government British newspaper painted the deal as a sellout to Hollywood, the members of the MPEA appear to have regarded the agreement reluctantly as all they could obtain at that time.[195]

This pattern continued of the MPEA taking over responsibility from the US administration for negotiating market access in Europe. However, trade association negotiating power was not equivalent to that of a government. In Italy, for instance, screen quotas had reduced access of American films to around 400 films per year in 195.[196] In 1951, the MPEA signed an agreement with its Italian counterpart, ANICA, reducing its exports to 225 per year, with a further 60 American films allocated to Italian distributors.[197] In 1954, the combined quota was cut to 245 films.[198] By 1959, the MPEA quota was down to 185 films.[199] However, these declines coincided with a steady fall in production in Hollywood. Under various pressures, including rising costs, falling attendances, the break-up of the long-established structure of the studio system and the arrival of television, US film production fell from 383 films in 1950 to 154 in 1960. By contrast, filmmaking in the UK and France remained fairly stable over the decade, while in Italy, it actually rose.[200] Even though Italian quotas were abolished altogether in 1962, the total number of American films (MPEA and independent) screened in Italy in the three years 1964-1966 was 463, an average of just over 154 films per year,[201] and lower than the lowest negotiated quota figure.

In France, too, the MPEA had taken over negotiations of film quotas from the US government. The 1948 regime, originally a four-year arrangement, remained in force for a decade, however, as the French government declined to increase the MPEA's allocation. In 1959, the MPEA's licenses were increased to the equivalent of 127 per year, and in 1960 to 140. More significantly, barriers to repatriating film earnings were removed.[202] It seems unlikely, as was suggested at the time, that France liberalized its regime to improve access for its films to foreign markets:[203] the US, the main beneficiary of the move, had erected no official barriers to the importation of foreign films. More likely, France was concerned with improving its overall trading conditions, and the easing of quotas was a symbolic act to ease one particular area of difference with the US. There were other means of limiting access to national marketplaces, notably through censorship. Of 174 films banned in France from 1945 on, and remaining so in the 1980s, some 67 were American. However, judging by their titles, at least, most had violent and/or erotic content.[204] By contrast, before the Second World War, films suffered censorship in France for shocking religious sensibilities, containing national propaganda or reflecting ill upon the army or national defense. But the relaxation of the quota regime was nonetheless mainly symbolic, all the same: as with Italy, the threat of Hollywood had receded as production fell.

---

1   Kristin Thompson, *Exporting Entertainment: America in the World Film Market 1907-34* (1985), 213. London: British Film Institute.

2   *Exporting Entertainment*, 4-5.

3   *Exporting Entertainment*, 1.

4   *Exporting Entertainment*, 2.

5   *Exporting Entertainment*, 3-4.

6   Susan Hayward, *French National Cinema* (1993), 20. London: Routledge.

7   *Exporting Entertainment*, 4.

8   *Exporting Entertainment*, 4.

9   *Exporting Entertainment*, 10-11.

10   *Exporting Entertainment*, 15.

11   See, eg, *Edison v. American Mutoscope Co.*, 114 F. 926 (2d Cir. 1902), *cert. denied*, 186 US 486 (1902) (patent claims describing process but without specifying functions to be employed, except functionally, are void, as broader than the actual invention of the patentee); *Edison v. American Mutoscope & Biograph Co.*, 151 F. 767 (2d Cir. 1907) (no infringement of reissue patent where film moved in camera by frictional contact alone, not sprocket wheels); *Motion Picture Patents Co. v. Champion Film Co.*, 183 F. 986 (C.C.S.D.N.Y. 1910) (French cameras using sprocket wheels and not purely frictional system infringed Edison reissue patent); *Motion*

Picture Patents Co. v. Indep. Moving Pictures Co. of Am., 200 F. 411 (2d Cir. 1912) (patent covering Latham loop film projector could not apply to similar mechanism to move film in a camera); *Motion Picture Patents Co. v. Calehuff Supply Co. Inc.*, 251 F. 598 (3d. Cir. 1918) (Latham loop patent taken from prior art without developing new functions and thus invalid for want of patentable invention); *Motion Picture Patent Co. v. Laemmle*, 178 F. 104 (C.C.S.D.N.Y. 1910) (complainant's membership of combination in violation of federal anti-trust statute does not make available defense in action for infringement of patent); *United States v. Motion Picture Patents Co.*, 225 F. 800 (E.D. Pa. 1915), *appeal dismissed per stipulation*, 247 US 524 (1918) (patents cannot be acquired or combined for purpose of unlawful restraining of trade).

12   *Exporting Entertainment*, 17-18.

13   *Exporting Entertainment*, 17.

14   *Exporting Entertainment*, 19.

15   *Exporting Entertainment*, 20.

16   *Exporting Entertainment*, 19-26.

17   *Exporting Entertainment*, 18-19.

18   *Exporting Entertainment*, 20-21.

19   *Exporting Entertainment*, 213-14.

20   *Exporting Entertainment*, 57-61.

21   *Scientific American* (Aug. 20, 1921), 132.

22   *Exporting Entertainment*, 35.

23   *Exporting Entertainment*, 37.

24   *Exporting Entertainment*, 37-38.

25   *Exporting Entertainment*, 38-39.

26   *Exporting Entertainment*, 71-74.

27   *Exporting Entertainment*, 83.

28   *Exporting Entertainment*, 88.

29   *Exporting Entertainment*, 91.

30   In 1913, the director Cecil B. De Mille stumbled upon the Los Angeles district of Hollywood as a place to film beyond the reach of the eastern-based MPPC. Other producers followed, and, after the MPPC's breakup, remained. By 1920, Hollywood was synonymous with the film business. *The Macmillan International Film Encyclopedia*, 640.

31   *French Cinema*, 35.

32   Siegfried Kracauer *From Caligari to Hitler* (1947), 35-36. London, New York: Dennis Dobson.

33   Thomas J. Saunders, *Hollywood In Berlin: American Cinema and Weimar Germany* (1994), 24-25. Berkeley, London: University of California Press.

34   *Exporting Entertainment*, 104-05.

35   *Exporting Entertainment*, 105.

36   *French National Cinema*, 22.

37   *French National Cinema*, 22.

38   Robert Murphy, "Under the Shadow of Hollywood" in *All Our Yesterdays: 90 Years of British Cinema* (Charles Barr ed. 1986), 51. London: British Film Institute.

39   A Danish company, Nordisk, was exempted from the 1916 ban, because of its "commanding position" in the German market, including distribution, production and exhibition (theater) facilities. *Hollywood In Berlin*, 22-23.

40   *Exporting Entertainment*, 106.

41   Adapted from *Exporting Entertainment*, 211-12.

42   *Hollywood In Berlin*, 56.

43   *Hollywood In Berlin*, 57-58.

44   Bruce Murray, *Film and the German Left in the Weimar Republic* (1990), 60. Austin: University of Texas Press.

45   *Hollywood In Berlin*, 58-60.

46   *Hollywood In Berlin*, 58.

47   *From Caligari to Hitler*, 206.

48   Raymond Moley, *The Hays Office* (1945), 172-73. Indianopolis, New York: Bobbs-Merrill Co.

49   *Exporting Entertainment*, 106-07.

50   *Exporting Entertainment*, 107.

51   *The Hays Office*, 172.

52   *Exporting Entertainment*, 107.

53   *Exporting Entertainment*, 107

54   *Exporting Entertainment*, 108.

55   *Exporting Entertainment*, 125.

56   *Exporting Entertainment*, 107.

57   *From Caligari to Hitler*, 133.

58   *Exporting Entertainment*, 128.

59   *Hollywood In Berlin*, 54.

60   *Exporting Entertainment*, 67.

61   *Exporting Entertainment*, 83.

62   *Exporting Entertainment*, 125.

63   "Dollars and Ideology," 211.

64   The electoral franchise was extended to men over 21 in 1918 and women of the same age in 1928. For a discussion of this fear, see Ian C. Jarvie, *Hollywood's Overseas Campaign*, (1992), 103-06. Cambridge, New York: Cambridge University Press.

65   Letter, *Morning Post*, June 20, 1925, quoted in *Hollywood's Overseas Campaign*, 106.

66   *Hollywood's Overseas Campaign*, 109.

67   Speech by Viscount Peel in 61 Parl. Deb., H.L. (5th ser.) (1925), 288-89, quoted in *Hollywood's Overseas Campaign*, 112.

68   *Hollywood's Overseas Campaign*, 110.

69   Speech by Lord Newton in 61 Parl. Deb., H.L. (5th ser.) (1925), 273-76 , quoted in *Hollywood's Overseas Campaign*, 111.

70   *Hollywood's Overseas Campaign*, 126.

71   *Hollywood's Overseas Campaign*, 126-27.

72   Margaret Dickinson and Sarah Street, *Cinema and State: The Film Industry and the British Government* 1927-84 (1985), 40. London: British Film Institute.

73   *Hollywood's Overseas Campaign*, 151.

74   *Exporting Entertainment*, 125.

75   Georges Sadoul, *Le Cinéma Français* (1962), 144

76   *Exporting Entertainment*, 126.

77   *Exporting Entertainment*, 126.

78   Paul Leglise, *Histoire de la Politique du Cinéma Français* (1969), 1:45-49. Paris: Film Éditions.

79   *Histoire de la Politique du Cinéma Français* , 1:262. See also *Exporting Entertainment*, 119-20.

80   *Histoire de la Politique du Cinéma Français* 1:262.

81   *Exporting Entertainment*, 119. The French quotas were constantly reorganized and refined: ten different systems were announced between 1927 and 1934: see Table 3. In 1936, following a trade agreement with the US, the system was changed once more, with further modifications decreed in 1937, 1938 and 1939. *Histoire de la Politique du Cinéma Français* , 1:266-67.

82   Edouard Herriot, statement to *L'Oeuvre*, Feb. 19, 1928, quoted in *Histoire de la Politique du Cinéma Français* , 1:262.

83   *French National Cinema*, 24.

84   Charles Pomaret, *L'Amérique à la conquête de l'Europe* (1931), 24. Paris: Librarie Armand Colin.

85   "England" in the original.

86   *L'Amérique à la conquête de l'Europe*,100-01.

87   WESTI/Société Générale de Films, 1927.

88   *L'Amérique à la conquête de l'Europe* , 103-04. To Pomaret's list should be added another allegation that would return in years to come, that the US systematically boycotted European films and remained "hermetically sealed to French production." René Jeanne, "L'Invasion Cinématographique Américaine," *Revue des Deux Mondes* (Feb. 15, 1930), 860-61

89   *Variety*, Jan. 23, 1929, in *Variety Film Reviews* (1983), vol. 3. The same newspaper's France correspondent had hailed *Napoleon* as "a splendid achievement" on its Paris opening nearly two years earlier. *Variety*, Apr. 4, 1927, in *Variety Film Reviews* vol. 3

90   *L'Amérique à la conquête de l'Europe*, 104.

91   See *Hollywood's Overseas Campaign*, 321.

92   Margaret Dickinson and Sarah Street, *Cinema and State: The Film Industry and the British Government 1927-84* (1985), 34-39. London: British Film Institute.

93   *Le Cinéma Français*, 25.

94   *Le Cinéma Français*, 25.

95   *Le Cinéma Français*, 139.

96   *Exporting Entertainment*, 125.

97   It might be more accurate to say that sound brought strength to the German cinema alone, since a German company, Tobis-Klangfilm-Kuchenmeister, owned the only viable European patent for talking pictures. Oddly, the attempts of Tobis to use its patent leverage to dominate the European film sector has been viewed as a last-ditch stand by Europe bargaining for the wide entry of its films into the US market. See, eg, R.L., "L'Europe contre l'Amérique: la lutte pour le film parlant," in *Europe-Hollywood et retour* (Michel Boujut & Jules Chancel, eds. 1992), 95. Paris: "Autremont". As far as the French were concerned, the arrival of sound increased costs and forced industry consolidation, leading some companies to bankruptcy. *French Cinema*, 67-68. A substantial part of the increase in French production is due to both Hollywood and German producers making multi-language films including French versions. *French Cinema*, 71-77. Nevertheless, this development appears to have been a market-driven response to the possibilities created by the arrival of sound, rather than a realizing of French creative energy caused by the introduction of quotas.

98   *Hollywood's Overseas Campaign*, 276.

99   *Hollywood's Overseas Campaign*, 79-80.

100   *Hollywood's Overseas Campaign*, 82-83.

101   O.R. Geyer, "Winning Foreign Film Markets," *Scientific American* (Aug. 20, 1921), 132.

102   *Hollywood's Overseas Campaign*, 279-92.

103   Edward G. Lowry, "Trade Follows The Film," *Saturday Evening Post* (Nov. 7, 1925), 12.

104   Frank J. Marion, head of the Kalem film company had used the phrase in 1918 in the context of educational and instructional films: "Trade follows the film. The projection of industrial pictures, backed by distribution of the product advertised, will create an immediate outlet for goods of American manufacture." *Exporting Entertainment*, 122.

105   "Trade Follows The Film," 12.

106   "Trade Follows The Film," 13.

107   "Trade Follows The Film," 12-13, 151.

108   "Trade Follows The Film," 13, 151.

109   *Hollywood's Overseas Campaign*, 303-05.

110   "Trade Follows The Film," 12.

111   *Exporting Entertainment*, 122. On North, see *Hollywood's Overseas Campaign*, 309-20.

112   *Hollywood's Overseas Campaign*, 309-10.

113   *Hollywood's Overseas Campaign*, 310-11; Thompson, *Exporting Entertainment*, 117.

114   *Exporting Entertainment*, 118.

115   *Exporting Entertainment*, 107-110. See also *From Caligari to Hitler*, 133.

116   Will H. Hays, *Memoirs* (1955), 509 quoted in *Hollywood's Overseas Campaign*, 308. Garden City, N.Y: Doubleday.

117   *L'Amérique à la conquête de l'Europe*, 103.

118   Notably, Lubitsch's *Passion* (Union-UFA, 1919) [known in the US as *Madame Dubarry*], and

Wiene's *Das Cabinet des Dr. Caligari* (Decla-Bioscop, 1919).

119   *Exporting Entertainment*, 105.

120   *Exporting Entertainment*, 62-63.

121   *Exporting Entertainment*, 63.

122   *The Hays Office*, 32-35.

123   *The Hays Office*, 30. On Landis, see Harold Seymour, *Baseball 2* (1971) 367-99.

124   Ian Jarvie, "Dollars and Ideology: Will Hays' Economic Foreign Policy 1922-1945," *Film History 2* (1988), 210. New York, London: Taylor & Francis.

125   *Hollywood's Overseas Campaign*, 290.

126   *Hollywood's Overseas Campaign*, 279.

127   *The Hays Office*, 227.

128   *Hollywood's Overseas Campaign*, 294.

129   Will H. Hays, *Memoirs* (1955), 333-34, quoted in *Hollywood's Overseas Campaign*, 295.

130   *Hollywood's Overseas Campaign*, 314

131   *The Hays Office*, 171.

132   *Exporting Entertainment*, 112.

133   *Hollywood's Overseas Campaign*, 307-08.

134   *Hollywood's Overseas Campaign*, 308-09.

135   Adapted from data in John Eugene Harley, *World-Wide Influences of the Cinema* (1940), 254. Los Angeles: The University of Southern California Press.

136   *Hollywood's Overseas Campaign*, 311.

137   *Hollywood's Overseas Campaign*, 316.

138   *Hollywood's Overseas Campaign*, 315.

139   *Hollywood's Overseas Campaign*, 316.

140   According to Jarvie, Lowry was not appointed MPPDA representative abroad until May 1927. *Hollywood's Overseas Campaign*, 317.

141   *Exporting Entertainment*, 118-19

142   *Exporting Entertainment*, 118-19.

143   *Hollywood's Overseas Campaign*, 21-22.

144   Jean-Pierre Jeancolas, "L'arrangement Blum-Byrnes à l'épreuve des faits," *1895* (Dec. 1993), 7.

145   Figures taken from United States Senate, "The Motion Picture Industry – A Pattern of Control," Temporary National Economic Committee, Investigation of Concentration of Economic Power, Monograph No. 43, (1941), cited in *Hollywood's Overseas Campaign*, 218. The MPPDA members concerned were Paramount, Loew's, Fox, Warner Brothers, RKO, Columbia, Universal and United Artists.

146   André Paulvé 1942. Released in English as *The Devil's Envoys*.

147   Pathé 1945. Released in English as *Children of Paradise*.

148   U.T.C. 1942.

149   André Paulvé 1943. Released in English as *Love Eternal*.

150   Robert Paul 1943. Released in English as *Angels of the Streets*.

151   Synops/Consortium du Film 1946. Released in English as *Ladies of the Park*.

152   Eg, André Bazin, *Le Cinéma de l'occupation et de la résistance* (1975); Paris: Henri Veyrier. Jacques Siclier, *La France de Pétain et son cinéma* (1981), François Garçon, *De Blum à Pétain; cinéma et société française (1936-1944)* (1984). Paris: Cerf. *Histoire de la Politique du Cinéma Français*, lists all films produced under the Vichy régime, together with details of the regulatory regime under which they were produced.

153   *French Cinema*, 111 ff.

154   Lévy/Strauss/Sigma 1937. Released in English as *Life Dances On*.

155   Paris Film 1936

156   Réalisations d'Art Cinématographique 1937

157   Janet Flanner, *Paris Was Yesterday 1925-1939* (1972), 169-70. New York: Viking Press.

158   Richard F. Kuisel, *Seducing the French: The Dilemma of Americanization* (1993), 19. Berkeley, London: University of California Press.

159   *Foreign Relations of the United States* (1969) 5:399 et seq. .

160   *Foreign Relations of the United States*, 5:409, 411.

161   "Understanding Between the Government of the United States of America and the Provisional Government of the French Republic With Respect to the Exhibition of American Motion Pictures in France," *Department of State Bulletin* (June 9, 1946), 999.

162   Even normally judicious historians have shared this characterization of events, or at least allowed it to color their analysis, as in this account from the excellent Cambridge *History of Modern France*:
       Significantly, the Blum-Byrnes agreements opened the way for a massive diffusion of American films, thus delighting the long-deprived cinema enthusiasts, and accelerating – at the time of the 'Série Noire' and *Reader's Digest* – the Americanization of the nascent mass culture.
       Jean-Pierre Rioux, *The Fourth Republic, 1944-1958* (trans. Godfrey Rogers, 1987) 479 n.8. Cambridge: Cambridge University Press.

163   Jacques Thibau, *La France colonisée* (1980), 66. Paris: Flammarion.

164   See, eg, Michel Margairaz, "Autour des accords Blum-Byrnes: Jean Monnet entre le consensus national et le consensus atlantique, "*Histoire, Économie, Société* (1982), 439; Patricia Hubert-Lacombe, "L'acceuil des films américains en France pendant la guerre froide (1946-1953)," *Revue d'histoire moderne et contemporaine* 33 (1986), 301; Jacques Portes, "Les origines de la légende noire des accords Blum-Byrnes sur le cinéma, "*Revue d'histoire moderne et contemporaine* 33 (1986), 314; Jean-Pierre Jeancolas, "L'arrangement Blum-Byrnes à l'épreuve des faits: les relations (cinématographiques) franco-américaines de 1944 à 1948," *1895* (Dec. 1993), 3.

165   "L'arrangement Blum-Byrnes", 16.

166   "Autour des accords Blum-Byrnes," 453.

167   "L'arrangement Blum-Byrnes," 7-8.

168   Thomas Guback, *The International Film Industry* (1969), 21 & note. Bloomington: Indiana University Press.

169   Jean Lacouture, *Léon Blum* (1977), 530. Paris: Seuil.

170 See generally, David Robertson, *Sly and Able, A Political Biography of James F. Byrnes* (1994), especially 490, 493, 503. New York, London: Norton.

171 "L'arrangement Blum-Byrnes," 33.

172 "L'arrangement Blum-Byrnes," 33.

173 "Joint Declaration of the Government of the United States of America and the Government of the French Republic on Motion Pictures," *T.I.A.S.* no. 1841, at 1.

174 "L'arrangement Blum-Byrnes," 23

175 Pascal Ory, "Mister Blum goes to Hollywood," *Europe-Hollywood et retour* 104.

176 "L'arrangement Blum-Byrnes," 6.

177 Ronald Brownstein, *The Power and the Glitter: The Hollywood-Washington Connection* (1990), 121-123. New York: Pantheon.

178 MGM/Selznick International 1939.

179 *The International Film Industry*, 19.

180 *The International Film Industry*, 92.

181 15 U.S.C. §§ 61-65.

182 Wilbur L. Fugate & Lee H. Simowitz, *Foreign Commerce & the Antitrust Laws* (4th ed. 1991) 1:§7.18 . The European Court of Justice, for one, has also denied comity to Webb-Pomerene associations. Case 89/85, *Re Wood Pulp Cartel*, 1988 E.C.R. 5193, 4 C.M.L.R. 901 (1988).

183 Dennis Unkovic et al., *International Opportunities and the Export Trading Company Act of 1982* (1984) A-37.

184 *International Opportunities*, A-7 n. 29.

185 "Mass Culture and Sovereignty," 59.

186 "L'arrangement Blum-Byrnes," 15.

187 *The International Film Industry*, 91-92.

188 *The International Film Industry*, 18.

189 Paul Swann, *The Hollywood Feature Film in Postwar Britain* (1987), 86. London, Sydney: Croom Helm.

190 *The International Film Industry*, 18.

191 *The Hollywood Feature Film*, 87, 90-91.

192 *The Hollywood Feature Film*, 90.

193 *The Hollywood Feature Film*, 91.

194 *The International Film Industry*, 129.

195 *The Hollywood Feature Film*, 101.

196 *The International Film Industry*, 25.

197 *The International Film Industry*, 26.

198 *The International Film Industry*, 26.

199 *The International Film Industry*, 26-27.

200 *The International Film Industry*, 35.

201   *The International Film Industry*, 39.

202   *The International Film Industry*, 23-24.

203   *The International Film Industry*, 23.

204   Philippe J. Maarek, *La Censure Cinématographique* (1982), 131-37. Paris: Litec.

205   *World-Wide Influences of the Cinema*, 126-129.

2

The development of the international television program economy

The birth of the international television business

The earliest television experiments were, intentionally or not, international. When atmospheric conditions were right it was possible, in the 1930s, for television broadcasts from London to be received in Paris. However, the technical standards finally adopted by most countries precluded substantial transfrontier broadcasting, such transmissions being mainly limited to unintended and unavoidable spillover in border areas.[1] This ethos of purely national broadcasting was sealed in international treaties.

In the 1950s, the invention of videotape recording produced a major change in the economics of television through the introduction of easy and relatively inexpensive repeats. (Prior to tape, only filmed programs – notably feature films – could be repeated by television channels. Sometimes, studio-based live television dramas would be "repeated" in the same way live theater is repeated: by doing the whole production again on another day.) Videotape further drew attention to an unusual economic feature of television: programs are substantially paid for at the time they are first broadcast. A videotaped program may therefore present an opportunity to exploit in other markets an asset whose costs have already been recouped. There is thus no pressure on the owner of the tape to charge a price to the secondary market that is consistent with the cost of creating the original program: indeed, in order to compete effectively with the market for new (and therefore expensive) programs, the secondary exploiter has an incentive to charge lower prices. Further, the national nature of television markets, as described above, entails a multiplicity of largely discrete markets, in which the program can be exploited separately. The accumulated revenues from many program sales can thus be substantial, even if the price charged in any single market is relatively low in comparison with the unit cost of the original program. (See Table 4.)

[Television programs may be sold on a country-by-country basis, or regionally (ie, to Western Europe or Central America), or to combined geographical-linguistic markets (German-speaking Europe or Francophone Africa), or to linguistically-defined sub-regions within national markets (such as Anglophone Canada or Catalan-language Spain). Outside the United States, it is less usual – but by no means unknown – for program rights to be sold for a single-language version in different regions of the same country, Programs may also be sold into different *media*, such as television or video, and for different forms of *exploitation within a given medium* for instance, "free" (or broadcast) television, cable, satellite, pay-television, pay-per-view, etc.]

Table 4: Representative television program acquisition prices in European Union countries[2]

	US $ minimum	US $ maximum
Austria	2,000	10,000
Belgium	2,500	6,500
Denmark	2,500	5,000
Finland	2,500	5,500
France	13,000	66,000
Germany	25,000	165,000
Greece	1,600	5,000
Ireland	1,000	2,000
Italy	6,500	58,000
Luxembourg	1,300	4,000
Netherlands	4,000	9,000
Portugal	2,500	6,700
Spain	1,600	25,000
Sweden	3,000	8,000
United Kingdom	10,000	116,000

Most purchasers of television programs – broadcasters – are also program makers – producers. They thus find themselves in the unusual position of being able to acquire their raw materials for considerably less than the cost of making them themselves. Because acquired television programs tend to be foreign made, the choice of cheaper bought programs is sometimes viewed as a decision made at the expense of the national television production sector where the broadcaster is based. For several reasons, discussed later, this is not strictly true. But the huge price disparities – $50,000 to "buy" a program that has cost $1.5 million to make – has led to accusations that program sellers engage in practices akin to dumping. Two ways of dealing with this question have been suggested. One is to point out that the price of programs sold to foreign markets should be compared with the *incremental* price of preparing such a sale – which is to say, the tiny additional cost of making new tapes of the original program. Another approach has been to say that if dumping is characterized as the selling of a product in foreign markets more cheaply than its price in the home market, then *all* sellers of programs, and not just those in the US, are guilty of dumping.[3]

By the mid-to-late 1950s, an international television business was developing: by 1963, this business was large enough to create its own trade fair, the Marché International des Programmes de Télévision, of MIP-TV, in Cannes, France. Some public broadcasters, particularly in Europe, sought to resist the commercialization of the program markets – and the encroachment of American programming – by creating no-cash exchange schemes. The European Broadcasting Union, the "club" of western European public broadcasters. organized an exchange system for news footage among its various members. The former Warsaw pact countries exchanged programs among themselves as did the Nordic states of northern Europe. Despite these efforts, the volume of shows bought and sold internationally continued to grow rapidly.

The role of US television suppliers in the international television program market

From the outset, US program suppliers played a substantial role in this international market. This was for a number of reasons. First, US production was spearheaded by large, mature entertainment conglomerates. Three radio networks had become wealthy and dominant forces in broadcasting – CBS and NBC since the 1920s and ABC by regulatory fiat in the 1940s . The Hollywood studios, some in existence since before the First World War, were vast production machines with a virtual lock on creative and technical talent. After initial reticence, Hollywood embraced television in the 1950s, becoming the major independent supplier to the three dominant networks ABC, CBS and NBC.

In 1970, the Nixon administration effectively barred the networks both from owning most programs, and from selling them in domestic and international markets. (The "financial interest and syndication" or "finsyn" rule, which sought to curb the oligopoly powers of the networks over program production and distribution has been effectively abolished.) The result was to increase Hollywood's position as both producer and distributor. Armed with substantial capital, lengthy experience in creating mass entertainment, and a long tradition of international distribution, the major studios grew to dominate the market for the two main staples of television program sales – one-hour series and half-hour situation comedies. And because Hollywood ruled the international program sales business, its trade association, the Motion Picture Association of America (MPAA), effectively became the mouthpiece of US television abroad.

The second factor in the United States' success in selling television programs internationally was the size of the domestic market. The most affluent country in the world, with the largest population of any western, industrialized nation, the US generated much higher revenues, principally from advertising, than anyone else. In 1996, US television advertisers (including on cable and satellite) spent $42.5 billion. In Japan, they spent $19.5 billion and in the third-ranked country, the United Kingdom, they spent $5.3 billion. In terms of dollars per household with television, US advertisers spent $443, Japanese $336. Australians $254 and the British $239. This allowed for much larger production budgets than anyone else.[4] Although some of this money went to higher comparative operating costs – more expensive stars, writers, directors, technicians and so on – much of it went into "production values," the on-screen sheen that gives a program allure. With the price advantages generally associated with the sale of second-hand programming and described above, American shows represented particularly good value for money.

Further, the American market could accommodate high volumes of production. This contributed not only to a large number of different programs, but also to substantial numbers of episodes of each program. Where a typical European series might last only six or 10 episodes, American shows, cranked out 22, 26 or 39 times a year, were available in attractive quantities, particularly when they were popular with audiences.

In addition, American programming had wide appeal. The reasons for this are not absolutely clear, but many suggestions have been made. Hollywood had large experience, through its feature film business, in reaching mass audiences across the world. The US television system, highly sensitive to advertising revenues and strongly influenced by audience research, strove to refine its programs so as to maximize their appeal.

Of the hegemony of ratings in the American television system, little needs to be said, except to underline that the success (or failure) of a given program tends to have a direct impact on its financial yield to the network that broadcasts it. Networks offer advertisers guarantees of ratings performance: if the program fails to meet the guaranteed audience level, refunds may be made to advertisers, either in cash or in make-good advertising in other programs. Ratings success, on the other hand, allows the network to raise advertising spot rates for the program concerned. Ratings also have a big impact on the types of programs offered. Advertisers generally seek not simply big numbers, but particular demographic categories of viewer programs are accordingly tailored to such categories On the heels of demographics have come other, qualitative measures, such as "psychographics", seeking to tailor program content to audience taste.[5] To this end, programs, in particular fiction series and situation comedies, became highly formulaic, following clear rules – explicit or otherwise – about subject matter, plot, pacing, characters and the like. Some people believed, Europeans in particular, that there was also something intrinsic to the US, a cultural pooling contingent to the melting pot, that had given American entertainment the ability to penetrate all the many communities from which the nation had once drawn its people.

The one check on the extent of US television program sales was the structure of the buying market. Outside the United States, for-profit commercial television was comparatively rare. In Europe until the 1980s just two countries – the United Kingdom and Finland – had privately owned broadcasters that competed with public television services funded wholly or in part by the state. In Britain, the Independent Television (ITV) network established in the 1950s was a for-profit system widely regarded as being subjected to public service goal and content rules. This was particularly so after its first years of operation, where its success in gaining audiences from the established public broadcaster, BBC, was so spectacular, that a government-commissioned report led to reorganization of ITV to keep it under greater regulatory control. In Finland, a for-profit station, Mainos TV, shared airtime with the national public broadcaster, YLE, until it finally received its own frequency it the late 1980s.

One consequence of this absence of competition was monopsony, a market in which only a single buyer existed. Where there was no pure monopsony, market collusion achieved the same effect. For instance, in Britain, the BBC and ITV networks for many years operated what was termed a "gentleman's agreement" not to engage in price competition for American programs they bought. The two networks colluded as to the highest price they would be willing to pay for top series. The system broke down in the mid-1980s, when a member company of the ITV network, Thames Television, "poached" the then hugely popular series *Dallas* from the BBC, which has previously aired it. The almost talismanic force of the "gentleman's agreement" was such that Thames found itself obliged by its fellow ITV companies to return *Dallas* to the BBC. With greater competition now present in the British market, such collusion appears to have abated: certainly price paid by the networks have risen considerably in the past decade.

In purely economic terms, this absence of buyer competition placed a brake on the ability of the program suppliers to raise prices. A UNESCO study suggested that monopsony might achieve price savings for buyers of around 55 per cent,[6] although others have argued that when monopsony breaks down, program prices may rise, depending on the level of competitive frenzy, by anything from a rapid 40 per cent to 1,000 per cent over a number of years.[7] Further, monopsony buyers, not vulnerable to the consequences of the program choices made by competitors, may make buying decisions based on non-economic criteria, such as the desire to limit particular types of programs, to police content, or to reduce the amounts of programs bought from particular countries.

The transformation of the international television program market in the 1980s

In the 1980s, both the American and European television markets changed in important ways. In the US, cable television had developed from a method of boosting the signals from broadcast networks to an alternative source of television programs for viewers. Home Box Office (HBO), a pay-television service began in 1975 and led the way in boosting the typical television watcher's choice of service from a handful to several score. Within 15 years of HBO's launch, nearly three-fifths of US homes received multichannel cable. In 1975, 9.8 million US household received basic cable services. In 1989, the figure was 47.5 million.[8] By 1997, the leading basic cable network, ESPN, reached 71 million US homes.[9] One consequence of this growth was a dramatic decrease in the audiences of the main networks. In the twenty years following the introduction of the new cable services, the networks' share of total audiences fell to below 70 per cent of their heyday in the 1950s and 1960s. In 1980, when there were 79.9 million US households, the three networks ABC, CBS and NBC took an 85 per cent share of prime time viewing. By 1996, there were 96.9 million television households, but network primetime share (including that of the lately-arrived Fox network) had fallen to a little over 60 per cent.[10]

The fall in audiences caused a fall in advertising revenues. The advertising revenue fall was not in proportion to the loss of audience, however, because the networks were able to continue to charge a premium for their ability to reach people in greater numbers than anybody else, even if the percentage audiences continued to fall. Thus, network television advertising revenues in 1975 were $2.306 billion, or 44 per cent of the total. In 1995, the revenues of the four networks (including Fox) were 503 per cent of their 1975 level, at $11.6 billion; however, this figure was just 31 per cent of the national total. (These revenue figures do not however include the substantial income the networks gained as television station owners).[11] This, in turn, led to smaller program budgets. The networks met this new problem in two main ways. They shifted production to some extent from expensive series and situation comedies to cheaper magazine and "reality" shows that nevertheless attracted substantial audiences. Secondly, they began to pay producers less money for the traditionally high-cost programs. (Under the now-defunct "finsyn" rules, networks did not own many of their programs, but instead obtained licenses from producers to broadcast them. It was thus the producer who bore the responsibility for raising production finance, but who was able to keep all the profits that might accrue from a successful show.) This latter move increasingly left the producer having to make programs through deficit financing, as production budgets for network shows proved difficult to reduce. Indeed, throughout the 1980s, producers both in the US and elsewhere persistently claimed that inflation in production costs consistently outstripped inflation in the rest of the economy, variously pointing to the costs of introducing new technologies, escalating demands from talent and the introduction of ever-glossier production values. Further, network production cost more because of certain rigidities imposed on producers, such as collective bargaining agreements combining high wages with elevated staffing levels.

Both in the film and television businesses, the producer receives a fee for making the movie of program, as well as a cut of the net profits. In television, the fee may be as much as 15 per cent of the production budget, allowing the producer to earn substantial moneys even if the program is not profitable. Indeed, in the film business, "the producer's fee is the only compensation a feature film producer will receive for the production of a film, since net profits are rarely generated."[12]

(Where television program budgets are squeezed, producers may defer payment of their fees to make up for shortfalls in cash needed to make the show.) Essentially a producer could make good the production deficit – and increase profits – through a combination of two ways. The program can be sold in the secondary, so-called "syndication" market in the United States. This market, of non-network independent television stations, grew up in the 1980s.[13] Syndicated programs need first to have been successful on the networks, and to have run for at least three years so that there are sufficient shows to allow their "stripping" at the same time each day over a number of months.[14] In other words, the producer will have to bear the costs of financing its production deficit for some time after the program is first made.

The second way of making up the deficit, through sales in the international market, allows cash to flow much more quickly, because few foreign television services buy programs to strip: instead, they usually acquire network shows to run in their own prime first-run scheduling slots (principally because they want the newest shows as soon as possible). The following table shows how these various costs and earnings might apply to a successful one-hour network television program:[15]

Table 5: Television program production costs and sales revenues (US$)

Production costs

Cost per episode	1,200,000	
No. of episodes in series	22	
Total cost of series	26,400,000	
Network license fee @ 80 per cent of cash outlay	21,120,000	
Deficit per season	5,280,000	
Additional overhead and interest	220,000	
Accrued deficit per season		5,500,000

Syndication and distribution costs

Residuals per series	1,980,000	
Distribution costs	1,430,000	
Total syndication and distribution costs		3,410,000
Total accrued deficit + syndication and distribution costs		8,910,000

Domestic syndication and foreign sales revenues

Domestic gross income per episode	500,000	
% fee paid to distributor	35	
Domestic net per episode	325,000	
Domestic net for series	7,150,000	
Foreign gross income per episode	500,000	
% fee paid to distributor	50	
Foreign net per episode	250,000	
Foreign net for series	5,500,000	
Total sales revenues		12,650,000
Profit (revenues less accrued deficit and syndication and distribution costs)		3,740,000

As can be seen from these figures, net income from foreign sales, at more than $5 million per series, may represent the difference between profit and loss on even a successful television program. By the end of the 1980s, these foreign sales were essential for American producers.

At the same time, major changes were taking place in Europe. At the beginning of the 1980s, the European television landscape had not altered much in two decades. But the transformation of the American market and, in particular, the development of multichannel cable television has not gone unnoticed, particularly in those countries, notably in Scandinavia and the Benelux countries, where cable, as a means of improving broadcast reception, was viewed as a public utility and was thus already widespread. The climate of change in Europe was also influenced by bizarre goings-on in Italy. In 1975, the constitutional court had struck down the monopoly of the state broadcaster, RAI, with respect to local broadcasting. What in other countries might have been treated as an unforeseen judicial anomaly, quickly treated by parliamentary action, became, in the uncertain Italian political environment, a legislative void. In the more than ten years it took Italy to pass a new media law, entrepreneurial commercial television operators sprung into action, notably a future Italian prime minister, Silvio Berlusconi.[16] Within a decade, Berlusconi controlled three national private television networks, in direct competition for audiences and advertising revenues with the three public networks operated by RAI. As a student, Berlusconi had been fascinated by the advertising revenues of American television. As a television entrepreneur with no previous experience (he had made his first fortune in the Milanese construction business), his instinct was to turn to the most successful private television system he could find – that of the US – and to buy its programs voraciously.

Berlusconi's success was viewed in many parts of Europe in the early 1980s as a terrible warning of what might occur if the continent's television were to be deregulated. (One British television station, Television South, even took advertisements in the press claiming that planned regulatory change in the UK would result in television screens being swamped by "stripping housewives" all'Italiana.) Yet, at the same time, two forces were combining to make radical change – if not outright deregulation – inevitable. The first force was technological. Communications satellites had been the key to the success of cable television in the US: thanks to them, the new services gnawing away at network hegemony were delivered cheaply to cable systems across the entire country. In Europe, it seemed clear that similar satellite could be used to do the same thing. And in 1982, precisely this happened. A London-based company, Satellite Television plc, rented a transponder on a European communications satellite and launched a television channel. (On a communications satellite, a transponder at this time was the functional equivalent of a channel, although it was possible to use transponder's subcarriers to transmit other material, such as alternative sound channels, text, radio stations or data. Recent advances in digital compression have now made it possible for several channels to be transmitted from certain types of single transponder.) Within a couple of years, the channel had been taken over by News Corporation, the Australian-based vehicle of media entrepreneur Rupert Murdoch, who already had extensive newspaper holdings in the United Kingdom.

News Corporation, via a subsidiary, News International, owns (and owned at the time of the satellite takeover) the highest selling daily newspaper in Britain (*The Sun*), the top selling Sunday newspaper (*The News of the World*), *The Times* of London and its sister paper *The Sunday Times*. Although he had briefly controlled a London television station, London Weekend Television, he was expelled from this position through regulatory action – a decision, many said, gave Murdoch a festering sense of grievance against the British television establishment. Renamed Sky Television, the channel never made Murdoch very much money, and never gained substantial audiences, but it had a substantial impact on European television. Sky was conceived as a pan-European channel in the English language. By its very nature, it offended against the deeply-ingrained European principle of broadcasting limited to national borders. Further, in an environment where all communications and broadcasting were tightly regulated by national agencies, there was no overarching, crossborder regulator to deal with an overarching, crossborder television service: instead, Sky painstakingly negotiated terms for access to cable systems country by country. (The international apparatus regulating communications satellites calls for regulation of the uplink – the delivery of the service to the satellite – and of the downlink – the redelivery from the satellite to the end user. Countries are allocated orbital position for their satellites by the World Administrative Radio Conference of the Geneva-based International Telecommunications Union. The arrival of communication satellites in the 1960s caused great anxiety to some governments, who – correctly – saw their control over the airways at risk of erosion from crossborder broadcasting beyond their control.)

Sky's move, quickly followed by other services, demonstrated three things to European governments. The first was that it was possible for an operator to enter the market at a far lower cost than ever before and, for the first time, without anybody's permission. The second was that an international regulatory framework would be needed to police television services that originated in one country but were aimed at others. The third was that such an operator, with virtually no production facilities, limited studio space and a small staff, could launch satisfactorily thanks to the presence of one key commodity: tens of thousands of hours of cheap, well-made, highly-palatable American programming.

The second force, in additional to technological change, that was due to transform European broadcasting in the 1980s was political. The resurgence of market economics and neo-liberalism in the western democracies throughout the decade brought with it a strong distrust of the public broadcasting establishments that were, in most countries, the sole source of television viewing. This mood was most strongly felt in the United Kingdom, where the government of Margaret Thatcher was particularly antagonistic both to the public British Broadcasting Corporation (too liberal) and the private Independent Television network companies (massively profitable state-protected monopolies). However, Britain was not alone in its restlessness to change the television system. The center-right administration that came to power in France in 1986 combined a strong dash of neo-liberalism mixed in with the *dirigisme* more characteristic of French governance.[17] In other countries, too, the general rollback of the postwar principles of statism and central regulation – whether rhetorical or practical – inevitably subjected the national television structures to political questioning. While it is notorious that politicians rarely watch television – principally because they do not have time, and find their evenings taken up with other matters – they could not be unaware that their constituents seemed restless for other forms of television entertainment, as evidenced, for instance, by the burgeoning market for videocassettes in virtually every country in the world.[18] Growing philosophical distrust of state monopolies combined with a populist belief that voters wanted both change and choice. For the first time since television began in Europe in the 1930s, governments were inclined to give the people that choice. But what if this choice extended to widespread demand for American programs? One response was to use a long-standing remedy, import quotas. Only this time, on a pan-European level through the rapidly-expanding and developing institutions of pan-European cooperation, notably the European Community.

The first television quotas

The growth of television in Europe in the 1950s created a new market for American entertainment. Yet, as can be seen from Table 6, this market was small, and increased only gradually from the late 1950s to the early 1970s, when the impact of the arrival of color television began to boost revenues. Although income growth 1958-1975 was more than 1,000 per cent, foreign television sales only accounted for a small fraction of Hollywood's theatrical and television distribution revenues, which by 1975 were in the region of $2 billion.[19]

Table 6: US foreign television program sales, 1958-1975, in $ million[20]

Year	Value
1958	15
1960	25
1961	45
1963	66
1964	70
1965	76
1966	60
1967	78
1968	95
1969	99
1970	97
1971	85
1972	93
1973	130
1974	85
1975	175

As has been seen already, the European television market until the 1980s was principally comprised of public broadcasters. Although the degree of direct state control of these services varied, the near-total absence of for-profit competition that might have had an impact on audiences meant that programming philosophies could be implemented that took into account criteria other than popular taste. Public service broadcasting has been described as "a prime instance of the rejection of the subordination of cultural politics to economic forces."[21] One French view defines the public service mission thus:

> The existence of a public sector of television is legitimate, given the essential cultural role that the small screen plays in the life of French people, through the need to make it assume tasks of general interest contrasted with the purely economic preoccupations of the private sector. These tasks which ought to be subject to Parliamentary debate and a certain consensus among all currents of opinion could be: the socio-educational development of the public, the defense of pluralism, the objectivity of news and the good functioning of democracy, protection of the French language and of the national heritage, the protection of minorities, support for creativity, religious services, etc.[22]

This essentially ideological function can be achieved in publicly-owned broadcasting services through the basic operation framework they are placed under and the people who are installed to run them. A preference for national production over foreign television programs need not necessarily be written into any law or regulation if the governing ethos of public broadcasting has already been instilled structurally. In other words, the acquisition of American programming could operate in the context of a kind of auto-censorship: a self-generating, institutional quota that exists silently, uncodified, unbroached.

Even where there were explicit quotas, their operation was similarly tactful and inarticulate. One example for which information is available occurred in the United Kingdom. In 1954, a new for-profit network, Independent Television (ITV) was authorized, under the regulatory control of an Independent Television Authority (ITA). The implementing legislation stated:

> It shall be the duty of the [ITA] to satisfy themselves that, so far as possible, the programmes broadcast by the Authority comply with the following requirements, that is to say –

> (d) that proper proportions of the recorded and other matter included in the programmes are of British origins and of British performance.[23]

The ITA announced that it had "entered into early discussions on this matter with the bodies representing British artistes, writers and composers ..."[24] It turned out that these bodies numbered fourteen, and their speaking together with one voice was unprecedented in the British entertainment profession.[25] These consultations, which also included the various contractors awarded franchises to run ITV network stations, produced a secret, never published agreement that remained in force, with slight changes, for two decades and imposed a foreign program quota of 14 per cent of available airtime.[26] This arrangement was termed the "Gentleman's Agreement." – This is to be distinguished from that other British arrangement of the same name, discussed previously, that fixed prices for purchased foreign programs. (By 1982-83, the year before the publication of the EC's first 'Television Without Frontiers' green paper, the ITA's successor body, the Independent Broadcasting Authority (IBA) published the fact that programming on ITV and on Channel 4 (a new network under its regulatory control) was governed by an 86 per cent quota, subject to some exemptions, including EEC programs, those of special cultural or education value, documentary material, programs of archival interest and those originating in countries from which British ethnic minorities were drawn.)[27]

The argument in favor of quotas came from two principal sources. There were those who opposed the commercial television project altogether, who believed that the public service mission of the BBC would be fatally compromised by exposure to naked competition from unfettered market forces. Although the pro-commercial lobby's argument against the monopoly position of the BBC had been powerfully made,[28] it was vulnerable on the question of program quality, where "Americanization" could be – and was – used as a code word for the crass excesses of unbridled commercial entertainment.[29] Indeed, one way in which the BBC's role had been defined at its inception in the 1920s was as a bulwark against creeping Americanization of British life.[30] Added to this cultural argument was the industrial lobby of producers and artists, which believed that they should benefit to the maximum from any extension to the supply of programming. (A third reason was more directly commercial: the desire to build a British program export business.)[31] Both these approaches would have found comfort in the recent history of the Hollywood film boycott which had taken place only seven years previously – indeed, the Hungarian (but British by adoption) film maker Alexander Korda did just that in a public campaign to advance the case for a commercial television system that was exclusively British.[32] The principal resisters of quotas were the companies that would have to implement them – the ITV license-holders. It was they who opposed the 25 per cent quotas advanced by commercial television's opponents in Parliament, and the 20 per cent quota put forward by the artists' representatives.[33] However, their principal ground for opposition was administrative and bureaucratic: they disliked the idea of a statutory limit and the need to police it. Hence, the preference for an informal arrangement, even one with a stricter quota than had been proposed at any time during the legislative enactment of the commercial television system.

These two factors in implementing television quotas – the institutional bias of public broadcasters and the deliberate secrecy of some quota arrangements – may have been factors in the relative silence of Hollywood in the face of such market-limiting methods (although, as will be seen, the issue was raised to some extent at the GATT). The fact of quotas was not lost on America however, where by the mid-1960s, it was being acknowledged that they existed "nearly everywhere."[34]

A further reason may concern the small size of the foreign television market, alluded to earlier: Hollywood in the 1960s was enjoying the benefits of near-free entry to theatrical markets, thanks to the progressive alleviation of screen quotas: in such circumstances, it may not have seemed the right moment to launch an all-out attack on television arrangements.

Finally, American television's foreign lobbying efforts were divided. The MPEA had set up its own television committee to represent Hollywood's interests. However, the networks ABC, CBS and NBC, alongside some other production and distribution companies established a separate organization, the Television Program Export Association in 1959.[35] As the production power of the Hollywood studios grew – and the networks, operating under public licenses, grew anxious about possible fallout from the kind of activity a Webb-Pomerene association might legally engage in – the TPEA began to wither, finally disappearing at the end of the 1960s.[36]

The European market for American television programs began to expand rapidly in the 1980s, reaching a value of $1.3 billion for the EC alone by 1991, an increase of nearly 9,000 per cent since 1958. With such astonishing expansion, apparently unhindered by the presence of the existing quota regimes, it might have been supposed that Hollywood would have been largely indifferent to any new proposals that did not threaten to change the existing dynamic. Further, given Hollywood's longtime posture of only half-hearted opposition to television quotas, Europeans had good reason to believe that the American television sector would not be greatly exercised by any new moves that were made. Both these views, of course, turned out to be wrong.

1   Conventional VHF television broadcasting signals extend only for about 100 miles, beyond which the signal must be boosted by relay stations. Harold L. Vogel, *Entertainment Industry Economics* (4th ed. 1998), 156. Cambridge: Cambridge University Press.

2   Prices are for all types of programs (excluding feature films) and are based on the rate for a single commercial hour.Figures are adapted from *Television Business International* (April 1999), 161-63 and (October 1995),122. The cost of actually producing a single hour of US network fiction programming may cost $1.5 million or, in the case of highly successful shows with expensive stars, much more.

3   See C. Hoskins, et al., "US Television Programs in the International Market: Unfair Pricing?, *Journal of Communications* 39 (Spring 1989), 55.

4   *Entertainment Industry Economics*, (4th ed.) 164.

5   See Barry Gunter, "On the Future of Television Ratings," *Journal of Broadcasting & Electronic Media* 37 (1993), 359 ; Lawrence W. Lichty, "Ratings in the Real World: A Reply to Gunter," *Journal of Broadcasting & Electronic Media* 37 (1993), 483.

6   Peter Larsen (ed), *Import/Export: International Flow of Television Fiction*, 87. Paris: UNESCO.

7   "US Television Programs in the International Market: Unfair Pricing?" 64-65.

8   Harold L. Vogel, *Entertainment Industry Economics*, (2d ed., 1990), 377. Cambridge, New York: Cambridge University Press.

9   *Entertainment Industry Economics* (4th ed.), 186.

10   *Entertainment Industry Economics* (4th ed.), 166, 427.

11   *Entertainment Industry Economics* (4th ed.),162.

12   John W. Cones, *Film Finance & Distribution*, (1992), 397. Los Angeles: Silman-James Press.

13   In 1980, the syndication market drew $50 million in advertising revenues. By 1995, that figure rose to $2.016 billion. *Entertainment Industry Economics* (4th ed.), 162.

14   *Entertainment Industry Economics* (4th ed.),120.

15   Figures are in 1995 dollars, and are adapted from *Entertainment Industry Economics* (4th ed.), 121. They assume that 100 hours are available for the syndication market, indicating a program sufficiently successful to have run for five seasons on network television.

16   Most of this description is drawn from Jay Stuart, "The Emperor Comes Home," *Television Business International* (April 1988), 50; and Bill Grantham, *Moguls vs. Managers,"* *Television Business International* (October 1991), 24.

17   See generally, Philippe Kieffer & Marie-Eve Chamard, *La Télé: dix ans d'histoires sécrètes*, (1993), 45. Paris: Flammarion.

18   In the US alone, the major film entertainment companies saw home video revenues grow from $280 million in 1980 (7 per cent of total revenues) to $7.3 *billion* in 1995 (40.6 per cent of revenues). *Entertainment Industry Economics* (4th ed.), 51. For attacks on public broadcasting during the 1980s, see Kenneth Dyson & Peter Humphreys, *Broadcasting and New Media Policies in Western Europe* (1988), ix. London: Routledge.

19   Figures taken from data in Thomas Guback & Tapio Varis, *Transnational Communication and Cultural Industries* (1982)17. Bloomington: Indiana University Press.

20   *Transnational Communication and Cultural Industries*, 9.

21   Ien Ang *Desperately Seeking the Audience*, (1991) 101. London: Routledge.

22   René Bonnell, *La vingt-cinquième image* (1989), 350. Paris: Gallimard.

23   *Television Act*, 1954, 2 & 3 Eliz. 2, ch. 55, § 3(1) (UK).

24   Independent Television Authority, *Annual Reports and Accounts for the period 4 August 1954 - 31 March 1955* (1955), 7.

25   Bernard Sendall, *Independent Television in Britain*, (1982-1990) 1:106. London: Macmillan.

26   *Independent Television in Britain*, 1:108.

27   *Independent Television in Britain* , 1:107

28   See, eg, R.H. Coase, *British Broadcasting: a Study in Monopoly* (1950). Longmans, Green & Co.

29   *Independent Television in Britain*, 1:51.

30   Ien Ang *Desperately Seeking the Audience*, (1991) 108. London: Routledge.

31   *Independent Television in Britain* (1982-1990), 1:51.

32   Asa Briggs, *History of Broadcasting in the UK* (1979), 4:893-894. Oxford: Oxford University Press.

33   *Independent Television in Britain*, 1:51, 106.

34   John Tebbel, "US Television Abroad: Big New Business," in *Problems and controversies in Television and Radio* (Harry J. Skorma & Jack William Kitson eds., 1968), 437.

35   *Transnational Communication and Cultural Industries*, 30.

36   *Transnational Communication and Cultural Industries*, 30.

3
The quota dispute

The events of the 1980s and 1990s regarding television program quotas were underpinned by the bodies involved both in provoking and – to an extent – resolving them. Two international institutions are principally implicated in this story: the European Union (EU), heavily influenced by France, and the General Agreement on Tariffs and Trade (GATT). (GATT has now been transformed into a new body, the World Trade Organization, or WTO.) These two bodies found themselves in conflict with the third main player in the dispute, the United States.

The GATT, film quotas and television programs

The General Agreement on Tariffs and Trade was the child of postwar attempts to create a world economic order in the capitalist economies, which attempts in their turn were rooted in a global desire to avoid a return to the depressed conditions of the 1920s and 1930s.[1] The GATT was created in parallel with such other features of the post-1945 order as the International Monetary Fund,[2] but was of a more limited form. It was the remnant of attempts to create an international agency, the International Trade Organization (ITO). When the Havana Charter establishing the ITO failed to be ratified by potential member-states, the GATT, originally merely "a temporary agreement containing most of the ITO's trade policy rules" was the sole survivor of the negotiators' efforts.[3]

Accepted initially by 23 countries, the GATT came into force on Jan 1. 1948.[4] Its aim was to lower tariffs and reduce trade restrictions among signatory nations while they awaited – vainly, as it turned out – the creation of the ITO.[5] The early GATT conferences, at Geneva in 1947, Annecy (France) in 1949 and Torquay (England) in 1951, dealt principally with tariff reductions, with some success.[6] However, the GATT also included significant provisions on trade liberalization, on most-favored nation status, on transit trade, anti-dumping duties, customs provisions, quantitative restrictions on imports and exports, and balance-of-payments questions.[7] The agreement also provided for settlement of complaints of breach of the GATT, first by meetings of the contracting parties, and then through formal investigation and rulings.[8]

Article IV of the GATT allowed members to impose quotas on imported films exhibited in cinemas It stated:

Special Provisions relating to Cinematograph Films

If any contracting party establishes or maintains internal quantitative regulations relating to exposed cinematograph films, such regulations shall take the form of screen quotas which shall conform to the following requirements:

(a)   Screen quotas may require the exhibition of cinematograph films of national origin during a specified minimum proportion of the total screen time actually utilized, over a specified period of not less than one year, in the commercial exhibition of all films of whatever origin, and shall be computed on the basis of screen time per theatre per year or the equivalent thereof;

(b)   With the exception of screen time reserved for films of national origin under a screen quota, screen time including that released by administrative action from screen time reserved for films of national origin, shall not be allocated formally or in effect among sources of supply;

(c)   Notwithstanding the provisions of sub-paragraph (b) of this Article, and contracting party may maintain screen quotas conforming to the requirements of sub-paragraph (a) of this Article which reserve a minimum proportion of screen time for films of a specified origin other than that of the contracting party imposing such screen quotas; Provided that no such minimum proportion of screen time shall be increased above the level in effect on April 10, 1947;

(d)   Screen quotas shall be subject to negotiation for their limitation, liberalization or elimination.[9]

Such quotas were to be based on "screen time" rather than a target number of films. Further, they were not to be allocated "among sources of supply" (although existing arrangements to this effect were allowed to remain in place).

Despite the fact that the principal victim of Article IV was Hollywood, the United States remained largely quiet over screen quotas. However, in the early 1960s, the US raised for the first time the issue of quotas against *television programs*, claiming that these violated Article III:4 of the GATT (on non-discrimination against imports).[10] Even so, the US accepted that some provisions of Article IV might apply to the television quota question.[11] Others, notably France, argued that television programs represented a service, not a good, and were thus not covered by the GATT.[12] Further, a working party convened by the GATT to consider the issue failed to agree, and several draft resolutions proposed in 1962/63 failed to be adopted.[13]

As part of its progressive mission to liberalize world trade, the GATT proceeded through a number of negotiating "rounds". A preliminary conference to establish the parameters of a particular round would then be followed by several years of negotiation, arriving at a new agreement in the form of a modified GATT treaty. Thus, the Kennedy Round of 1964-67 (reducing tariffs on manufactured goods and introducing rules against dumping) was followed by the Tokyo Round on 1973-79 (more tariff reductions and curbs on various non-tariff barriers).[14] Then, in 1986, in Punta del Este, Uruguay, a new round was launched. The Uruguay Round, as it came to be called, involved a significant expansion of the GATT, through extension of its coverage from trade in goods to that in services.[15] The importance of this was that the audiovisual sector,[16] arguably not involved in trade as a good, was certainly a service, and as such, would be covered by the outcome of the Uruguay Round. Indeed, at a meeting of member-state ministers in Montreal in 1988, it was affirmed that no sector would be excluded from the new service document, the General Agreement on Trade in Services, or GATS.[17] Yet, despite such apparent accord, moves were already afoot that would make inclusion of the audiovisual sector in the GATS an impossibility.

The European Union and television programs

The European Union was not conceived as a body likely to interest itself much in television programs. Indeed, it was originally viewed, after 1945, as a way of preventing further wars among the great powers of Europe, notably between France and Germany and of creating a barrier to Soviet expansion.[18] Thus the first institution of what would become the EU was the European Coal and Steel Community (ECSC), concerned with the crucial raw materials of the armaments industry, and established by six western European states (France, Germany, Italy and the Benelux countries) under the Treaty of Paris of 18 April 1951.[19] Subsequent efforts at common European institutions were also aimed at reducing the potential for conflict: a European Defense Community and a European Political Community, neither of which could overcome domestic opposition among potential member-states, and which were abandoned.[20] The same six nations succeeded, however, in establishing, in the same spirit, a European Atomic Energy Community (known as Euratom) by a treaty signed in Rome on 25 March, 1957. More significantly, however, these countries signed another treaty in the same place on the same day: that establishing the European Economic Community (EEC).[21]

The EEC's institutional structure mirrored that of the original ECSC: a Council, made up of ministers delegated by member-governments; a Commission (known as the High Authority under the ECSC) to provide a secretariat with some quasi-executive powers; an Assembly with parliamentary functions; and a European Court of Justice (ECJ) to rule on the implementation of the treaty. From the outset the ECJ was a body common to the ECSC, Euratom and EEC treaties: following the Merger Treaty of 8 April 1965, a single Council and single Commission were created for all three treaties.[22] Similarly the Council and Assembly (now the European Parliament) are common to all three regimes.[23]

The EEC's principal goal from its inception was to create a common market among its members and to ensure the introduction of certain concrete reforms: the elimination of tariff and customs barriers and the creation of free movement of workers, goods, services and capital within the six member-states.[24] To this end, the ECJ became a significant tool for overcoming domestic political resistance to EEC reforms, turning to the founding treaties for expansive readings of the EEC's powers and ultimately claiming the authority to review legislative decisions of European institutions.[25] The ECJ interpreted the EEC's powers expansively, as well. In 1974, the court held that the transmission of television signals was governed by Treaty of Rome's provisions relating to the free flow of services. Trade in television programs, the ECJ decided, was subject to the treaty's provisions for the free movement of goods.[26] Six years later, in the *Coditel* case, the same court upheld the right of copyright owners to prevent the prohibit the exhibition of a film through the retransmission on cable television in one member-state of a broadcast television signal that had spilled over from an adjacent state.[27]

After *Coditel*, there was thus tension between the principle of free flow of goods and services across national borders and the ability of copyright holders to use monopoly powers to obstruct such a flow. This issue was later crystallized in the *Magill* case, where the ECJ held that in some circumstances, exercise of copyright could breach the Treaty of Rome provisions on the flow of goods and services.[28] More broadly, it had become clear that European law would move television's traditional form of national regulation into a wider sphere wherein national preferences might be trumped by European imperatives.

Thus, in March 1982, the European Parliament (the renamed Assembly) called, in a resolution for the drafting of rules on European radio and television broadcasting.[29] At this stage, no concerns were expressed formally about imports of foreign television programs; indeed, when, in June 1984, the Commission published its Green Paper, or consultative document, in response to the parliamentary resolution, the question was not addressed. Instead, the Green Paper's aims were: (1) to "demonstrate the importance of broadcasting to European integration"; (2) to "illustrate the importance of the Treaty [of Rome]" for producers and broadcasters; and (3) to open discussion about member-states' national broadcasting and copyright laws.[30]

Indeed, the ultimate aim of European Community policy, as stated in the Green Paper – "the step-by-step establishment of a common market for broadcasters and audiences"[31] – was a sufficiently difficult task that other, arguably extraneous issues did not arise at that stage. The aim of the Commission was to create an *internal* market in television through general provisions covering advertising, copyright and public order and safety. Describing this as a "limited approach," the Commission noted that television was "an undoubtedly sensitive activity, the organization of which varies from State to State."[32] The relationship of such a market with *external* markets, such as that of the US was not a matter for concern in this context.

However, if the Commission had hoped that its "step-by-step" approach would satisfy its political masters, it miscalculated. Within six weeks of the publication of the Green Paper, the issue of quotas on foreign television programs had been placed on the agenda by the politicians. The prime mover behind this development was Jack Lang, a law professor and theatrical impresario who had become Minister for Culture and Communications in France's socialist-communist coalition government.[33]

Lang was already famous, if not notorious. At a UNESCO meeting in Mexico City in 1982, in his official capacity, he had attacked the United States and the global dominance of its television. American cultural domination would turn us into "men-sandwiches," the meat between the influence, on the one hand, of transnational corporations and, on the other, of US television.[34] In his Mexico speech, Lang also attacked "the intellectual and financial imperialism" of the United States in "cultural and artistic areas".[35] Intelligent and handsome, Lang was that classic revolutionary combination, an anti-establishment puritan. As a theater administrator, he had built the annual festival in the city of Nancy into the "capital of the counter-culture".[36] With a collaborator in austerity, Michel Guy, he sought to "attack the roots of evil that undermine French theater: frivolity, the taste for amiable and superficial elegance".[37] As an activist, he distrusted the bureaucratic cultural mind that endlessly turned out sectoral policies for museums, libraries, the cinema and so on. Instead, he believed in radical action, "above all in the audacious and lucid determination of those responsible [for making culture] and in the mobilizing utopias of the popular imagination."[38] Lang set out to mobilize a utopia of his own. Within weeks of the Mexico speech, Lang called a meeting of the EC's culture ministers, primarily to discuss American domination of film and television markets.[39] Within two years, by the time of the publication of the Green Paper, the culture ministers' meeting had become a formal one, within the EC institutional apparatus.[40] Lang went to this meeting, in Luxembourg, telling the press that he was "not pleading for restrictions but development" of the European audiovisual sector.[41] However, the end-of-meeting resolution called blandly only for the encouragement of measures to ensure, in all audiovisual media, an "appropriate place" for European-origin works and programs.[42] Lang told the German publication *EZ Magazin*:

> It's a first stage: bravo! But at the same time, what timidity! What caution in conceiving common policies! Why can we not do for culture, for those fragile goods that are immaterial assets, what is done for agriculture and industry?[43]

According to Ivo Schwartz, a senior European Commission officer responsible, among other things, for the freedom to provide services, it was France that first proposed Europe-wide television quotas in Brussels.[44] One reason for this may have been that Lang was not gaining the same sympathetic audience within his own government than he received among France's European partners. In late 1985, the socialist government of President François Mitterrand announced the creation of two new television networks, each to be launched as for-profit ventures by private interests. One network was attributed to an Italian, Silvio Berlusconi, already a hugely successful television magnate in his home country but whose success had been founded on his skill in scheduling American programs. Mitterrand chose Berlusconi for political reasons, largely because of the mogul's closeness to the Italian prime minister and socialist party leader, Bettino Craxi. Most galling to Lang was Mitterrand's agreement that only 25 per cent of programs aired on the new network would have to be of French origin.[45] Lang stepped back from resignation, it is claimed, only because of personal loyalty to Mitterrand and the fact that just three months remained of the term of a government facing almost certain electoral defeat.[46] Sure enough, Lang's colorful reign as culture minister ended – for the time being – early in 1986.

By then, however, those in favor of quotas had seized the initiative. In April 1986, the European Commission submitted its draft proposal for a Council Directive – essentially a binding instruction to member-states to bring their national law into conformity with the Directive's provisions – on broadcasting activities.[47]

Lang had nevertheless succeeded in putting the quota question on the agenda, both in his own country and in Europe. The incoming French government of conservative prime minister Jacques Chirac, embraced Lang's idea with an expedient fervor, doubtless in part to embarrass Mitterrand who remained president in "cohabitation" with the new administration. In September 1986, the government imposed a requirement that television channels broadcast a majority of feature films both of French and EC origin.[48] An implementing decree the following January fixed quotas for both feature films and other programs: 60 per cent had to be of EC origin and 50 per cent of "French expression". (French programs themselves were, of course, of EC origin within the meaning of the law.)[49]

Lang's – and France's – support for quotas, and the pressure both exerted on the EC, produced results. In April 1986, the Green Paper was transformed into a proposal from the Commission for a Council Directive on broadcasting activities.[50] (Article 189 of the Treaty Establishing the European Community – the Treaty of Rome – states that a directive "shall be binding, as to the result to be achieved, upon each Member State to which it is addressed, but shall leave to the national authorities the choice of form and methods."[51]) The lengthy opening recitals to the proposed Directive set out the official rationale for the quota on non-EC television programs it now contained:

> Whereas minimum requirements in respect of all public or private Community television programmes for audiovisual productions originating in the Community are an effective means to promote production, independent production and distribution in the above-mentioned [audiovisual] industries and are complementary to other instruments which are already or will be proposed to pursue the same objective;
>
> Whereas the vulnerability of European cultural industries is not due to

lack of creative talent, but to fragmented production and distribution systems and whereas it is therefore necessary to promote markets of sufficient size for television productions in the Member States to recover necessary investments not only by establishing common rules opening up national markets but also by offering productions from the Community of each kind an adequate part in television programmes of all Member States, which will at the same time promote the presence of other European cultures in the television programmes of each Member State;[52]

The proposed Directive itself provided that 30 per cent of program time, excluding news, sport, game shows and advertising should be "Community works",[53] rising to 60 per cent within three years of the entry into force of the Directive.[54] (Most of the excluded categories of programming would usually be locally-produced even without regulation.)

The concentration in the recitals and Directive on an industrial and structural rationale for the quota was for two reasons. First, the EC at that time did not have power under its establishing treaty to intervene on a purely cultural level: it needed to express its goals within its existing powers. (The present article 128 of the EU Treaty provides for EU intervention at the cultural level: it was inserted by the 1992 Maastricht Treat on European Union, and did not apply at the time of the Proposed Directive.)[55] Secondly, the idea that the EC's powers should be extended at all was a controversial one in certain countries such as the UK whose then prime minister, Margaret Thatcher, had gained consistent political capital from being seen to "stand up to Europe." The practical reality, however, was that the Commission at least had been converted to the cause of quotas.

Some caution was in the air, nevertheless. The Economic and Social Committee of the EC, a consultative body,[56] warned that the aim of a quota system should be to boost European production, and should "not be viewed so much in terms of the national identity of the program.[57]

Despite such reservations, the prevailing mood favored the Lang strategy of favoring culture and introducing strong quotas. The European Parliament suggested strengthening amendments to the proposed Directive. (The European Parliament did not function at that time as a legislature *per se*, but had rights of non-binding consultation granted by the EU Treaty.)[58] The Parliament explicitly inserted language about culture into the opening recitals:

Whereas additional Community measures to promote the international competitiveness of European cinema and television production are needed, in view of the strength of the non-European media industry, not only in order to achieve the economic objectives of the Community but also to counteract any loss of linguistic and cultural identity.[59]

A further sign of the cultural mission of the amendments was the Parliament's suggestion extending the concept of a European work beyond the borders of the EC and to the whole of Western Europe.[60] On the other hand, the Parliament proposed that the 60 per cent quota be introduced less quickly, "gradually through appropriate criteria" and *after* the three-year introduction period of the proposed Directive. Further, the 30 per cent initial quota of the proposed Directive was deleted.[61]

The rationale for quotas at the time of the Directive and the GATT

We have seen that the two previous quota "crises" in Europe came at times of particular turmoil. In the aftermath of two great wars, the weakened European economies were being required to rebuild and transform themselves. Many traditional markets had been lost. At the same time, despite having also participated in those wars, the US economy emerged on both occasions as the strongest in the world, dynamic and – crucially – with much greater access to capital than anybody else. In these senses, Hollywood's international strength in the 1920s and 1940s was merely a mirror of the overall power of the US Other, more specific factors in its history – proprietary technology, vertical integration, the size of the home market, among others – may have given Hollywood and even greater advantage, but the essential ingredient was the way its existing strengths became greatly magnified in the extreme conditions of the times. To this was added Hollywood's unique cultural position in European consciousness, giving a particular emotional force to the attack on its economic power. When the crises passed – as most notably occurred in the late 1950s and 1960s, the Hollywood "threat" ebbed.

In the 1980s, there was no world war. But there was comparable turmoil in the limited field of broadcasting. As has been seen, rapid technological change was undoing the classic means at governments' disposal to regulate television. Political and social pressure was leading to the authorization of unprecedented numbers of new channels, mainly for-profit and unenamored of the public service ethos that had dominated European broadcasting for 60 years. At the same time, the European program market was seriously under-capitalized: new broadcasters had limited resources, and the advertising market had not yet reached the maturity and affluence of that of the US. Without money to make programs, there would be just one place to turn to buy them cheaply and "off the shelf": Hollywood. Yet, as in the 1920s and 1940s, the fear was that once Hollywood had occupied these vulnerable markets, it would never be ousted; a short-term crisis would become a situation of permanent subjection.

Nevertheless, the empirical basis on which quotas might be justified was never clear. For instance, there was little evidence of significant shifts in the proportions of programs bought from different sources among the established channels in western European countries in the 1980s (See Table 7). In other words, even without quotas, the television establishment did not appear to succumb to a Gresham's Law of television, where bad programs drove out good.

Table 7: Sources of European television programs, 1982 and 1988[62]
(figures as per cent of total programs broadcast)

Country	EC		US		Other W. Europe		Other	
	1982	1988	1982	1988	1982	1988	1982	1988
Great Britain	79	84	13	13	3	2	5	1
West Germany	81	81	10	6	5	13	4	0
Spain	58	67	25	21	11	12	6	0
Netherlands	70	70	9	13	14	11	7	16
Portugal	57	63	14	13	16	19	13	15
Sweden	60	56	11	11	20	29	9	4

The new commercial channels certainly did show more imported programs. In 1987, two private channels in Germany showed 57 per cent American programs and just 12 per cent domestic output. Their two long-established public rivals showed 32 per cent American and 49 per cent domestic.[63] Yet, as Table 8 shows, these new commercial channels had a powerful incentive to provide domestic programs to their viewers: that is what they preferred watching.

Table 8: Weekly average viewing on multichannel cable system, Denmark 1987[64]
(figures as per cent of total viewing)

Type of channel	Per cent
Domestic public	51
Domestic private	14
Nordic public	9
German private	6
Pay-TV[65]	4
US private[66]	7
UK private	3
Sports channel	5
Community TV	1

Of course, there is a distinction between watching national channels and watching national programs. But these figures are typical of European multichannel environments where viewers have a wide choice of national and non-national services. Naturally, these viewer preferences display a language bias, although it is noticeable that the three Nordic public channels – two from Sweden and one from Norway – broadcast in languages highly comprehensible to most Danes, are also scantily watched. However, the idea that the national character of the most popular channels is significant is supported by research showing that in the period 1983-87, some 15 per cent of national television consumption was of US programs, while domestic programs totaled 62 per cent. In competitive conditions, such as pertained when new private channels entered the market, it was necessary to create a supply of attractive national programs as quickly as possible.[67] This was most possible for the new national broadcast channels, which could reach large portions of national populations with few language barriers. Table 9 presents data from a 44-channel study to show how quickly the new private channels switched from imported to national programs:

Table 9: Sources of programs in Western Europe, 1986 and 1987[68]

(figures as per cent of total programs)

	1986		1987	
	US	**National**	**US**	**National**
National private broadcast channels	43	47	56	34
National public broadcast channels	72-75	10-15	75-78	10-15
Private satellite channels	58	22	68	19
All channels	66	20	68	21

Between 1986 and 1987, private broadcasters stepped up national production aggressively, and the overall percentage of domestic production remained stable. (The satellite television figures are less dramatic than they appear, since they are distorted by the way the original sampling was done. The broadcast figures are more representative of the state of the market in 1986-87.)

The importance of these data from the 1980s is that they represent the time immediately before Europe-wide quotas were introduced. The picture remains fairly constant from country to country: more than 50 per cent domestic production, 70-94 per cent European programming, viewer preference for home-grown programs and competitive pressure on new entrants to switch from imports to national production. Hollywood was maintaining its share of a fast expanding market, and yet Europe held on to as many of its viewers as before.

In March 1988, the Commission produced its amended proposal for a Council Directive, incorporating some of the suggestions of both the Economic and Social Committee and the European Parliament.[69] The additional recital on culture adopted by the Parliament was retained,[70] as was the amended form of the quota.[71] The proposal to extend the scope of the quota to Western Europe was accepted, albeit in a different form from that suggested by Parliament.[72] However, this proved to be the high water mark for the tide of cultural intervention in television program imports. There was opposition to quotas, and it began to make itself felt.

The United States fails to react

In the four years since the publication of the *Television Without Frontiers* Green Paper, the United States – publicly at least – had been curiously quiet about the quota issue. Indeed, American concerns towards European trade policies were, by 1988, focused much more on the EC's attempt to create a single internal market by the end of 1992 – as mandated by the Single European Act of 1986[73] – and consequent fears that such a move might create a "Fortress Europe".[74] Further, despite clear signals to the contrary, it is possible that Jack Lang's absence from government calmed American fears about European intentions: one newspaper interviewer believed the more moderate declarations of François Léotard, Lang's successor as culture minister, represented a "dramatic departure" from Lang's position, even though, just four weeks previously, the *loi Léotard* had signaled steeper quotas on non-European television programs in France.[75]

By the spring of 1988, however, the draft Directive had embraced quotas, and Jack Lang was back as culture minister in a new socialist government in France. Even so, the return of Lang was portrayed in America as that of a flamboyant yet mature, declamatory yet contemplative figure, a man who did not even mention, in the course of one long interview, the proposed quotas that were due to be adopted in Europe in the coming year.[76] In addition, the Uruguay Round was becoming bogged down by its huge agenda. The big issue for the US administration was not trade in television programs, but trade itself. In December 1988, GATT member-state trade ministers – rather than the usual senior officials – were forced to meet in order to give political impetus to the near-stalled process.[77] Farm subsidies, the creation of the new GATS framework on services and intellectual property protection were the key areas of contention, according to the US trade representative, Clayton K. Yeutter, at a pre-Montreal briefing. With these problems to surmount, Yeutter warned, no agreement would be better than a bad one.[78] Prophetically, the New York Times correspondent noted that Yeutter's advance bombast conformed to the "well-accepted pattern" of international trade negotiations: "governments often stake out tough initial positions, only to compromise in the final hour."[79]

The Montreal meeting which, as noted earlier, decided not to exempt any sector from the GATS agreement, was the last time the Reagan administration participated in the Uruguay Round.[80] In the US, as in France, a new government was to introduce new personalities to the trade talks who would have an important impact on their outcome. Replacing Yeutter as US trade representative was Carla Anderson Hills, a Californian lawyer and seasoned politician.[81]

American officials clamed that Hills' arrival in her new post in the middle of this delicate moment in the GATT negotiations would have no impact on the discussions; further, they insisted that Hills' appointment did not signal any shift in US policy between the Reagan and Bush administrations.[82] Nevertheless, it took two months for Hills' appointment to be confirmed, first by a unanimous vote of the Senate Finance committee, in advance of confirmation by the full Senate shortly afterwards.[83] These possibly inevitable changes and delays led to Hills' taking office at the time when the EC's television Directive was taking its final shape, and may have impeded her from fully mastering this aspect of her brief.

In addition, virtually from the day she was named to her job, there were aspects of Carla Hills' temperament and skills which would quickly make themselves felt in the trade negotiations. She was very smart. She was very aggressive. She knew virtually nothing about trade. Hills' intelligence was gushingly documented in the *New York Times* the day after her appointment. Even her four children were described as "overachievers, all fascinating." One unusual indirect connection with Hollywood was noted: the exterior of her father's Beverly Hills home was used as the setting for Gloria Swanson's house in Billy Wilder's 1950 film *Sunset Boulevard* – one of whose themes was (arguably) the crushing of European film culture by Hollywood crassness.[84] Hill's reputation for being "tough" and "aggressive" was commented on approvingly even by those who were initially doubtful about her nomination.[85] Her relative lack of trade experience, particularly in agriculture was also noted early, although it was claimed she was well versed in exports. One lobbyist believed the fact she was a lawyer would overcome her lack of direct knowledge of her brief.[86]

All these qualities of Hills showed themselves early on, at the Senate Finance Committee confirmation hearings. Hills showed a lawyer's mastery of the trade brief, moving effortlessly from committee questions about Japanese semiconductors to the European single market, from Canadian plywood to Hong Kong textiles, from Airbus subsidies to agricultural subsidies, from the flow of rice to the tide of Soviet emigration.[87] Hills showed her aggression, too, in telling the committee:

> You know, I would like to have you think of me as the USTR with a crowbar where we are prying open markets, keeping them open so that our private sector can take advantage of them. ... We must use the retaliatory tools that we have, not because we want to, but because they are the leverage that make credible a bilateral or a multilateral arrangement with the United States.[88]

(At her swearing in, President George Bush presented Hills with a crowbar. He wrote on the photograph recording the scene, "To Carla, I know you'll use this with finesse and strength.")[89]

Hill gave a brilliant performance that disarmed the committee. But it was nonetheless a performance, by a skilled lawyer and an experienced politician,[90] an elegantly-wrought and trenchant statement of the trade policies of the new administration. In terms of Hills' operational readiness to embark immediately on the many-faceted and complex trade brief, there was a hint of organizational difficulties. The chairman of the committee, Lloyd Bentsen, noted that he had hoped to hold the confirmation hearing earlier, to allow Hills to get started on her job, "but the paperwork was not done on the administration's side".[91]

For the administration, as articulated by Hills before the committee, the priority for the GATT talks, "our severe task" would be to address "agriculture, intellectual property, textiles, and safeguards. And we feel very strongly about all of these items."[92] As for Europe, she expressed only a general and cautious warning about the creation of the single market:

We need to monitor other nations' undertakings such as the European community's 1992 internal integration project, The creation of a single market of 320 million people can present a substantial opportunity for US exporters and investors. We must be vigilant, however, to ensure that the process of lowering barrier inside Europe does not lead to the erection of new barriers to those outside of Europe.[93]

At this stage, there was no hint that the television issue itself might be an obstacle either to the GATT itself or to US-Europe trade relations. One other aspect of the hearings incites a little speculation on this point. Two California senators, Pete Wilson and Alan Cranston, gave testimony in Hills' behalf before the committee.[94] Unlike their colleagues who were actually members of the committee, they may have felt that their role was purely ceremonial and laudatory. Yet these representatives of the state from which films and television programs were a major export, did not even hint at the apparent threat to their home state industry posed by the imminent arrival of European quotas. (Their fellow-Senators serving on the committee did not scruple to raise with Hills the problems faced in world markets by rice or timber producers back home.)

Taken together, it would not have been unreasonable for Europe to believe that the United States was not strongly exercised by the threat of television program quotas, that the new administration was still trying to pull its trade act together, that its clearly-enunciated priorities lay elsewhere, that there was little political interest in the quota question, and that the influence of Hollywood had not manifested itself by sparking the interest in the problem of California's own political representatives. As the Directive began to take its final shape throughout 1989, few can have suspected the hue and cry that was about to go up.

Towards a final television Directive

A European Directive is ultimately a political decision, made by members of governments meeting in the EC's Council. For a Directive to pass, it must achieve a majority of votes in Council, usually using a weighting formula giving a larger number of votes to the more populous member states. This formula of so-called "qualified majority voting" is one of the ways in which the EC diverges from the classic public international law regime of unanimity and consent, as it can be used to bind a member-state to a legislative provision to which it is opposed. It was used in the Council for decisions in the core areas of EC activities, such as the creation of the common market.[95] Under the 12-member EC that existed at this time, 54 votes were required out of 76 to obtain such a qualified majority.[96] Germany, France, Italy, the UK each had 10 votes, Spain eight, Belgium Greece, the Netherlands and Portugal five each, Denmark and Ireland three each and Luxembourg two.[97] In practical terms, then, any opponent of a policy had to assemble a block of 23 votes to defeat it. The smallest number of countries that could do this was three: two large countries and any one of the small states apart from Luxembourg. On contentious matters, compromise is essential. In early 1988, the television quota issue began to prove contentious.

For a number of reasons, Britain had reservations about the amended draft Directive. Some proposals, notably concerning regulation of advertising, would entail tougher standards than those currently in existence. Other ideas, such as quotas, were more offensive to British ideas of what Europe should be regulating. (Britain, as has been seen, had had television quotas, tougher than anything Europe would propose, since the 1950s.)

Britain was also interested in a parallel attempt at European television regulation. This was being proposed by the Council of Europe, a non-EC body with much wider membership, whose functions include drafting conventions on matters such as human rights and judicial co-operation. The drafters of a proposed convention on transfrontier television were also contemplating quotas. However, Britain and other states still hoped that within the Council of Europe, where French influence was more diluted, and unanimity was required, a more moderate plan might be adopted. The convention route had constitutional attractions as well. An executory treaty might not be incorporated into national statutes after ratification; further, negotiations might allow reservations to be entered over disfavored provisions. An EC Directive, on the other hand, required incorporation into national laws. Further, the reservation provision did not exist within the EC framework: national exceptions, while possible, were difficult to obtain.

The British strategy, then, was to criticize all proposals it did not like, such as advertising curbs and program quotas, but to favor the Council of Europe convention over the EC Directive. In February 1988, three weeks after the European Parliament approved its toughened, amended text of the draft Directive, the British government publicly criticized both the draft Directive and the council of Europe proposals. The Home Secretary, Douglas Hurd, told a conference that his government opposed minimum quotas for EC programming.[98]

In March 1988, EC trade and industry ministers met for the first time to agree on the Directive. Six countries, on different sides of the debates – Germany, France, the Netherlands, Britain, Ireland and Belgium – all raised objections to aspects of the amended text. The British Minster present, Alan Clark, said the quotas constituted "unnecessary government control."[99] Other difficulties arose, not directly related to the quotas. Germany, which chaired the ministers' meeting, was said to have been unenthusiastic about pushing forward the Directive because of difficulties about the sharing of power over broadcasting within its federal system. Nevertheless, the Commission's post-meeting draft Directive made few changes to the text amended in January by the European Parliament.[100]

Throughout 1988, it became clear that the Council of Europe convention had become a stalking horse for the Directive, that its negotiations were where many of the contentious issues among EC members would be resolved. By March, the Council of Europe was considering three contradictory formulas for quotas. One would have required television channels to carry a "reasonable proportion" of European programs; another called for a majority of European shows; yet another obliged channels whose signals crossed national frontiers to invest in the audiovisual sector of the receiving state.[101] By October, France was still pushing for a majority European content quota in place of the "reasonable proportion" language – and still facing resistance from others, notably Britain.[102] In November 1988, compromise was agreed, as the various parties accepted a quota formula that, in its final form, was to make much of the ensuing row incomprehensible:

> Cultural objectives
> 1.   Each transmitting Party shall ensure, where practicable and by appropriate means, that broadcasters reserve for European works a majority proportion of their transmission time, excluding the time appointed to news, sports events, games, advertising and teletext services. This proportion, having regard to the broadcaster's informational, educational, cultural and entertainment responsibilities to its viewing public, should be achieved progressively, on the basis of suitable criteria.[103]

The words "where practicable" were not defined, but clearly left signatories wide discretion over which circumstances might or might not render implementation practicable. The reference to "by appropriate means" absolved signatories from the need to pass laws to implement the quotas. Further, whatever quotas were introduced were to be "achieved progressively" – with no schedule attached – and on the basis of "suitable criteria" – which could be anything and everything. Article 10 allowed any signatory to do more or less anything it wanted. It was thus chilling to supporters of tough quotas to hear British minister Tim Renton, present at the convention negotiations, hoping that this agreed text "would form the natural basis for the EC Directive."[104] Despite warnings from Commission officials, the EC heads of government, meeting shortly afterwards in Rhodes, agreed that "the Community's efforts should be deployed in a manner consistent with the Council of Europe convention."[105]

Despite this resolution, France made one further attempt to toughen the quota rules. In March 1989, on the eve of signature of the Council of Europe convention, France tried unsuccessfully to insist, at an EC trade and industry ministers' meeting, on protections for European content in television programs.[106] The following month, amid some grumbling on a number of issues, the trade and industry ministers' meeting adopted the amended draft Directive with the "where practicable" language from the Council of Europe convention.[107] Edith Cresson, then French trade minister, was instrumental in overcoming Jack Lang's opposition to the agreed text.[108] Indeed, Article 4(1) of the common position of the Council, as agreed by the ministers, was virtually identical to Article 10.1 of the convention.[109] American trade briefings would later identify this meeting as the moment when the US became alarmed by quotas.[110] According to this view, once it became clear that France would accept a diluted quota formula it then became likely that the Directive would pass. But the April 1989 meeting was just one more affirmation that the EC had accepted the Council of Europe formulation. Further, it is unlikely that France would have rejected any quota formula if the alternative was to have no quota at all. Hollywood had misread what was happening in Europe and thus waited until the last minute to launch its lobbying effort against the quotas.

One further aspect of the April 1989 meeting which may have contributed to the mobilization of trade and political opinion, was that it was reported in the American press, by the *Wall Street Journal*.[111] EC minister were quoted declaring that the quotas represented only "a political commitment" and were not a legally binding requirement for broadcasters.[112] Bush administration reaction was tentative, not trenchant. The government spokesman requested anonymity and said, "We're concerned with some elements in that directive," suggesting that parts of it might contravene the GATT.[113]

Nevertheless, it appears to be here, as Europe inched towards this loophole-ridden political accommodation, that the US, finally, became alarmed. In May, the European Parliament attempted one last time to toughen the quota proposals by removing the "where practicable" language, and by imposing legal enforcement and a timetable for implementation.[114] By now, however, it was clear what the political solution would be: the EC was going to adopt the watered-down compromise of the Council of Europe convention.

The United States administration reacts at last

The radical switch in the United States posture on the question can be seen by the appearances of trade officials before the trade subcommittee of the House of Representatives' Ways and Means committee in the spring of 1989. In March, just after the EC trade ministers had resisted France's last-ditch attempt to toughen the quotas – but before the April meeting which apparently wrought the change in position – the US administration seem publicly unaware that there was a potential quota problem. The subcommittee held hearings on the creation of the single market in Europe where James M. Murphy, assistant US trade representative with responsibility for Europe and the Mediterranean, outlined wide-range administration concerns without once mentioning the television issue.[115] According to Murphy, new European quotas in general were concerning his office:

> There are some sectors in which the EC doesn't feel competitive and there is movement toward creation of new EC-wide barriers. ...

We have told the Community quite firmly that any creation of new EC-wide quotas as a part of 1992 would be in violation of their GATT obligations.[116]

However, this general warning over quotas turned out, upon questioning by the committee, to refer to sectors other than television: notably, automobiles, consumer electronics, footwear, urea and bananas.[117] Other areas raised during the hearings included agriculture, meat hormones, semiconductors and financial services.[118] These priority areas were being addressed by a special task force, ACTPN EC-92 [for Advisory Committee on Trade Policy and Negotiations].[119]

The United States appeared to have identified the principal areas of concern as far as European market integration and the Uruguay Round were concerned. There was some suggestion that because of the importance of European support over the GATT, the Bush administration was less strident towards alleged unfair practices by European states than it was against similar practices in Asia and Latin

America.[120] Nevertheless, the US appeared to have signaled both its interests and its seriousness in wanting them addressed by the Europeans.

On June 8, 1989, this enunciated policy took on a new and – for the Europeans – somewhat unexpected dimension. Carla Hills appeared before the same subcommittee to discuss her priorities under the so-called "Super 301" and "Special 301" provisions for retaliating against countries judged to be trading unfairly. No European countries were concerned at this stage, and television quotas were not on the agenda. In the middle of the hearing, the subcommittee chairman, Rep. Sam Gibbons made the following intervention during Hills' testimony:

> *Chairman Gibbons.* I would like to have your comment on two things that recently came to my attention while I was visiting Europe. I ran into the problem of domestic content in an act related to EC-1992 entitled *Television Without Frontiers*.
>
> They are talking about television without frontiers. I am not worried about television. I think the American television people can take care of themselves. But if the Europeans adopt their proposal for television without frontiers and we do not strongly object to it, they will analogize their television without frontiers to everything else that they are doing over there.
>
> Their television without frontiers, as you know, requires that the vast majority of it be European content. To me, nothing could be further from target than that. We have no restraint upon content in this country. It is one of our great traditions.
>
> Our Constitution guarantees that no one shall control content. It looks like the Europeans are set upon a course of excluding American content and entering into censorship so as to prescribe what this television without frontiers is going to do in Europe.
>
> As I say, I am not too worried about the television industry. Some of it over there is very good, like BBC, and some of it is not very good. I won't try to characterize the television in those countries I think is not very good.
>
> But I worry about the whole principle of freedom. We are talking about free trade, the free flow of products. Certainly you can't have a free flow of products if you are going to have control of intellectual material that flows across the borders and to the public.
>
> And I worry about how that can be analogized into everything else. If you can control ideas, if you can control content, if you can control the media, then it is just a short, short step in one's thinking to control everything else.
>
> I wonder how you feel about that.
>
> *Ambassador Hills.* I agree with you Mr Chairman. We have registered a very sharp and strong objection to local content in the broadcast Directive. I have talked to a number of trade ministers in the countries that make up the European Community.

We are strongly opposed. They have made arguments that the quantity of television will expand as they move toward their single market. But I think your underlying thesis of a restriction on thought and in effect censorship of fine programs that are developed in this country is simply unacceptable.[121]

This appears to be the first time that political voices are publicly raised in the United States against the quotas, nearly five years after they were first proposed in Jack Lang's initiative. What is striking about this intervention is that its rationale is not entirely clear. Rep. Gibbons appears to have two objections. One is that quotas on television programs are the thin end of the wedge: if not opposed, other quotas on more important goods will follow. The other is that content control is inherently repugnant, because it imposes a form of censorship.

Carla Hills' reply is also not entirely clear. She acknowledges, apparently for the first time, that the administration has made strong representations to the EC on the quota question. She endorses Gibbons' idea of "a restriction on thought". But she also misstates the EC position. It is not that the single market would of itself create greater volume in available television programming: as will be seen in the section on the economic of television, the enormous rise in the number of available channels in Europe in the 1980s had *already* greatly increased demand for programs; at the same time, competition had forced up prices. With or without quotas, American program suppliers were selling more shows and earning more money than ever before.

Nevertheless, this exchange essentially set the tone for the United States objections to the Directive. Quotas were wrong in principle, regardless of the economic damage they caused – or did not cause – and their mere presence should be challenged at all costs. Quotas on television programs were an attack on the free flow of ideas, and were per se repugnant. Until the bitter end of the GATT negotiations, these positions scarcely wavered.

These public declarations in a forum dealing with other matters give rise to the suspicion that this first volley was stage managed, a suspicion reinforced by the appearance the next day of a long article in the *New York Times* that mainly ignored the rest of the Super 301 issues raised at the hearing and concentrated on Hills' statements.[122] According to figures cited in the article from Hollywood's trade body, the Motion Picture Association of America (MPAA), US television earnings in the EC reached $630 million in 1988, up from $100 million in 1980.[123] The article did not discuss to what extent these revenues were threatened by the introduction of quotas.

Hollywood stirs

Throughout the summer of 1989, exchanges between the US and Europe intensified. European Commission president Jacques Delors, on a visit to Washington, tried to downplay fears of "Fortress Europe" while defending quotas.[124] The United States Ambassador to the GATT, acknowledging the relative newness of his country's position, announced that the administration's concerns about the Directive had grown "significantly" as other trade fears diminished.[125] In parallel, Hollywood, in the person of the colorful President of the MPAA, Jack Valenti, began publicly to campaign against the quotas.

For more than 23 years, Valenti had been Hollywood's voice in Washington and elsewhere. A former special assistant and advisor to President Lyndon B. Johnson, he became known early as a master of the florid and sometimes inopportune phrase, notably his declaration that "I sleep each night a little better, a little more confidently, because Lyndon Johnson is my President."[126] (Valenti may have been mocked for this, but he was rarely underestimated: Lew Wasserman, the legendary head of MCA, later said, "I sleep a little more soundly at night knowing that Jack Valenti is head of the motion picture association.")[127] Valenti was a lobbyist in the Texan mold, a glad-hander, party-giver and inveterate booster, tireless, ceaseless, exhausting. Over the years, he had consistently delivered results for Hollywood in Washington. But his brief had become much wider over the years, as he admitted himself. "[A]ll of a sudden," he told an interviewer in 1990, "I'm being assaulted by problems and issues that never existed before."[128] This may be why the MPAA was so late off the mark on the Directive question. Valenti's style created another problem as far as the quotas were concerned: like Hills, he had a gift for rubbing the Europeans up the wrong way. After the April EC ministers' meeting, he had issued a press release saying that "The European Community, today, in my judgment, took a step backward in time."[129] In August 1989, as he began his efforts to persuade Europe to abandon quotas, he told the Commission that it was "throwing a grenade with the pin pulled out at US film makers."[130] (Of course, Jack Lang in his turn rubbed Americans up the wrong way. The stridency of party declarations when set against the intrinsic issues at stake was one of the important factors distorting and disrupting the resolution of this question.)

The Directive is completed

France renewed its demands for a tougher quota, apparently both because of rising calls for protection from its domestic production sector and as a hardening of attitude following the public airing of the US objections.[131] The Directive was facing its own political difficulties, for reasons unconnected with the quota. Germany still worried about its federal-state division of powers in broadcasting policy. Denmark believed the Directive itself was beyond the powers of the EC. Belgium and the Netherlands were under pressure from their local broadcasters and producers to reject the Directive.[132] Further, Greece and Portugal had concerns about the timetable for introducing the quota (this would later be resolved by granting these countries greater time for implementation). Under EC rules, the Directive had to be approved by October 1989, and there was still a fear that a blocking minority to defeat it could be found among these various interests.[133]

In September, Carla Hills came to Europe on a visit originally intended to boost the Uruguay Round, but which had become mired in specific issues, notably television.[134] Hills' seriousness in attacking the quotas appeared to be shown by her schedule, which included meetings with ministers such as Jack Lang and Britain's Douglas Hurd, whose governmental responsibilities included television, but not trade.[135] However, at the same time, Commission officials were briefing journalists that they did not take the US objections to quotas too seriously, since they had been raised so late in the day, after they had had years in which to respond.[136] In other words, if the US had been slow to understand Europe's intentions in creating the quotas, Europe was itself tardy in realizing there had been a genuine policy shift that required attention. At the end of her trip, which had also addressed other important trade issues, such as the US "voluntary" quota on European steel and European content rules on manufactured goods, Hills told a press conference that she was "more positive" on Europe's 1992 plans.[137] But she underlined her continuing opposition to quotas in "fields of thought", comparing a quota on television programs to one on books.[138]

One reason that Hills and the EC governments may have misread each other is because they did not appreciate the depth of feeling behind each others' positions. One newspaper editorial, opposed to quotas, nonetheless remarked that, "the stridency of the US protests looks out of proportion to the threat,"[139] pointing to the vague and non-binding nature of the Directive's provisions. Europe pressed ahead in the same spirit. Although the US continued to lobby fiercely against the Directive,[140] the main goal within the EC was to iron out those other political differences that had threatened the Directive during the summer.[141]

On October 3, the foreign ministers of the EC approved the directive, with just Denmark and Belgium voting against.[142] The quota language of Article 4(1) was identical to that agreed in April and thus functionally equivalent to the language of the Council of Europe convention.[143] West Germany, on the eve of the meeting, decided to back the Directive on receipt of assurances that the quota requirements were politically but not legally binding.[144] One German commissioner, Martin Bangemann, responsible for the internal market, underlined this by confirming that failure to reach the content goal "would not be sufficient for the Commission to bring member states to court" for breach.[145] Thus, the quota itself was non-specific, non-binding and non-enforceable. After four-and-a-half years, Europe had its television Directive.

The aftermath of the Directive

It will be recalled that the claim that European curbs on imports of television programs from the United States violated Article IV of the GATT agreement first surfaced in the early 1960s, and was never resolved. In the months between first attacking the quotas and the final promulgation of the Directive, the US administration periodically claimed Europe was contravening Article IV and were rebuffed by the Commission, echoing the European position of the 1960s, that television programs were services and not good subject to the GATT.

The US invokes the GATT

The US had already claimed that the Council of Europe convention contravened the GATT;[146] further, during the runup to its adoption, Hills and others had repeatedly stated that the Directive's quota provisions also violated the GATT.[147] One week after the adoption of the Directive, the US said it would seek GATT adjudication of the quota question if bilateral talks with the EC failed to resolve the dispute.[148]

It was clear that, from the American perspective, the passing of the Directive was not merely a diplomatic defeat. Carla Hills was affronted by the idea of local content curbs "in the province of thoughts."[149] An American broadcasting official, echoing Sam Gibbons' original fear, reiterated the slippery slope argument, while dismissing the riposte that the quotas were merely aspirational and non-binding:

> If it's just rhetoric this time, it might not be next time....We think it's better to fight now, because if you say it's all right as they move down the road toward quotas, then reversing that trend will be difficult.[150]

This was the strongest argument against quotas. It did not account for the American failure to challenge the Directive much sooner, but it provided a good rationale for continuing to fight. France, after all, had consistently pushed for the Directive to be tougher: there was no reason to suppose that it would not continue to encourage Europe to introduce more stringent quotas, as it had done itself. Yet it was equally clear that, with Britain and West Germany in favor only of non-binding and deliberately vague provisions, only one further small country's vote was needed to ensure a blocking minority against any future change. In principle, the slippery slope fear was valid: in practice, it was not heavily supported by the state of the political terrain.

Nonetheless, politics can always change quickly, and the US was resolved to fight. It also chose to take on Europe rhetorically, challenging the EC's central position, that culture was different. This view had been expressed on the eve of the adoption of the Directive, by European Commission president Jacques Delors, a Frenchman, addressing a Paris audience:

> Culture is not a piece of merchandise, like other things. ... There will not be protection of the European market [under the Directive], but nor will there be laissez-faire. I say to the United States, 'Have we the right to exist, to perpetuate our traditions?'[151]

Carla Hills, a week later, declared such arguments "fallacious" and appeared to suggest that European culture – as opposed to that of the individual EC member-states – did not exist at all:

> We don't understand why the Spanish culture is more protected by a film produced in German by 'Europeans' than by a Spanish film of Mexican origin. Or why the English culture is more promoted by a film in France by 'Europeans' than by a film of New Zealand origin.[152]

The extremity of Hill's remarks – rather more tactfully termed "excessive" by an EC official[153] – may have been connected to confusion within the Bush administration about how to proceed: a recourse to bluster where policy had not been fully formulated. (On the other hand, it would be wrong to see Hills as a loose cannon. To the contrary, she regarded herself as a team player, and insisted that it was her "style to consult" the "upper reaches" of the administration about policies and pronouncements, and not to "surprise" it.[154] If she blustered, it was collective bluster.) For some time, the Commerce Department had been feuding with the State Department over who had responsibility for Europe and the 1992 integration of the single market.[155] In May 1989, the month after the final shape of the Directive had become clear, Hills had just one official based in Brussels tracking developments within the EC.[156] Just days before the Directive was promulgated, Commerce Secretary Robert A. Mosbacher admitted to the House Foreign Affairs Committee's Subcommittee on International Economic Policy and Trade that his department did not have a single specialist in Brussels following 1992-linked developments.[157] One result of this was that the Bush Administration had difficulty creating a cogent policy concerning the EC's single market plans, which it had originally strongly supported, but certain of whose details it came equally strongly to oppose.[158] In this environment of underdeveloped policies and overstretched resources, it made sense for the US to seek the help of GATT, which had established dispute resolution machinery, acknowledged expertise, and a general bias in favor of freeing markets, not curbing them.

There was a problem, however. GATT arbitration panels had consistently ruled against the United States in a number of long-running disputes, notably over intellectual property, but also customs fees and payments to clean up waste.[159] However, successive administrations had resisted amending federal law to conform to GATT findings: in the case of one patent law provision that discriminated against foreign goods, the United States had resisted no fewer than eight formal requests from GATT to make the necessary statutory changes.[160] Yet, the US was now proposing to use GATT machinery to attack not merely the television Directive, but other aspects of EC single market integration that it found displeasing. Given the value of the trade the administration felt was at stake, the decision was taken to stop impeding implementation of GATT rulings. "We're signaling that the United States is interested in promoting effective dispute settlement in GATT in large part because we view ourselves more as a plaintiff than a defendant in the future," admitted John Bolten, general counsel at Carla Hills' office.[161]

The United States' chances under the then-current GATT regime of winning its challenged to the quotas were not at all clear. On the other hand, the 1988 Montreal agreement, through rejecting exceptions to the forthcoming GATS agreement, would appear to bring the audiovisual sector into the framework of international trade regulation. If the quotas did not infringe the GATT in 1989, it was likely that, once the Uruguay Round was complete, they would.

Europe was the first to signal publicly that there could be a problem with the GATS. In June 1990, the EC served notice that it wanted special treatment for the audiovisual sector in the Uruguay Round, the first indication of Europe's hope of obtaining what would come to be called the "cultural exception" to the GATT[162].

Despite this GATT activity, the Uruguay Round would not become the main battlefield between the US and Europe over quotas for another couple of years.

An illustrative digression: the abortive boycott

Generally in this book, I have avoided personal anecdotes, preferring to rely on tangible sources to support the arguments to be found here. As I was however peripherally a participant in one small series of events symptomatic of the Franco-American rift described here, I offer this "war story". Between 1989 and 1991, I was Publications and Press Director of Midem Organisation (now Reed-Midem Organisation), a Paris-based company staging professional exhibitions, notably for the television and music industries. Two international television exhibitions were held annually, both in Cannes: MIP-TV each April and MIPCOM every October. Although these exhibitions attracted many hundreds of companies and many thousands of participants, the presence of the international television program sales subsidiaries of the Hollywood "majors" was significant in terms of revenues (booth space, advertising, etc), attracting other participants (to do business with the majors) and general prestige. At the beginning of 1990, it came to our attention that the heads of these divisions, angry at the quotas (which were aimed principally at the activities of their divisions) were considering asking us to relocate our exhibitions from Cannes, where they had been held since the second MIP-TV in 1965, to an unspecified location in another, presumably European country. It did not matter that any other country to which the exhibitions moved would be subject to the same quota regime: France was symbolically associated with the enactment of this (to Hollywood) hateful policy, and should be punished for it. The implicit threat was that if the request was made, and we did not accede to it, our events would be boycotted by the majors.

The request never materialized, for reasons that may shed some light on the difficulty both Hollywood and successive US administrations had in formulating policies that rose above the declamatory. The prime mover behind the call was the head of a television program sales division at one of the majors who had obtained his job through the purchase by the major of the independent (ie, non-major) distribution company he had founded and built into a sectoral leader. He was regarded by his fellow division heads within the MPAA companies as a brash parvenu. He had also enraged the more diplomatically-inclined of his colleagues by haranguing Jack Lang in public at MIPCOM in October 1989, calling him, among other things, "ignorant". The other companies were thus disinclined to support any measure proposed by this particular executive.

The other reason for the majors' lack of unity was that, despite being tarred by Europeans as part of a single phalanx assault by Hollywood, they each had different economic interests. Companies with substantial archives of feature films and children's animation had a lot of programs that, to an extent "sold themselves". If they chose to boycott international trade gatherings, the world's buyers would probably beat a path to their door in any case. Similarly , companies that were lucky enough to be selling the current prime time ratings winning programs on the US networks, would find high buyer demand for their shows, regardless of their marketing strategy. But those companies that were selling the middle-ranked programs, squeezing the last sales out of largely sold-out archives, unable to rely on "cushions" of high-demand programs to even out the highs and lows of the selling cycle — these companies were less keen to make grand symbolic gestures that might hit their business.

For whatever reason, the request never came. The majors continued to hate the quotas, but could not agree on detailed policies to combat them.

Instead, France was. The quotas may have been a Europe-wide policy, implemented by both the EC and the Council of Europe, but France was viewed as the culprit, with Jack Lang as the personification of the attack on Hollywood.

The impact of the Directive in France

France, of course, did not hesitate to play up to its image. The Directive left EC member-states to decide on how it should be implemented within their own territories. France, thanks to the *loi Léotard*, had already imposed a stricter quotas than that required by the Directive. It now decided to make its quota provisions even tougher, through a prime ministerial decree following a report by Jack Lang and his subordinate, communications minister Catherine Tasca.[163] The decree kept the *loi Leotard*'s percentage quota of 60 per cent European and 50 per cent French works. But it redefined the term "works" (*oeuvres*) so that, essentially, it applied only to feature films, television drama and documentaries.[164] The decree then required that European and French versions of such works constitute the required percentage of *all* broadcasts. It further imposed the quota equally in a widely-defined, officially-designated prime time,[165] although this last provision would not enter into force until Jan. 1, 1992. (Prime time was defined as 6.00pm - 1.00pm, with an additional block on Wednesdays from 2.00pm - 6.00pm, when school children are usually at home).[166]

The target of the more stringent quotas was France's three private networks, TF1, La Cinq and M6, which had attempted to circumvent the spirit of the *loi Léotard* by airing low-quality (but French-made) games and studio-based variety shows in prime time, and cheap soap-like dramas broadcast after midnight to free up prime time slots for top American series.[167] It was by no means unusual for European governments to place content restrictions on television networks to impose state-defined norms of diversity and quality of programming.[168] But the combination of content restrictions and quotas was designed to be particularly limiting on American programs, since the principal US television exports were feature films, telefilms, one-hour dramas and half-hour situation comedies. Nevertheless, as will be seen when the Europe-wide impact of the quotas is examined, it is by no means clear that France's more stringent limits materially increased the proportion of local and European programming shown on French television: in fact, instead of damaging Hollywood, France's quotas likely inflicted greater harm on its own television economy.

Indeed, it was from within France – and Europe – that the loudest protests came in the two years immediately following the "Tasca decrees" of January 1990. France's pay-television channel, Canal Plus, pointed out that the country did not make enough feature films to satisfy the quota requirements for French production.[169] Television services beamed into France from neighboring EC countries complained that, despite respecting both the Directive and their host nation's implementation of it, they were required to meet the more stringent French standard to gain legal access to the French market – in apparent contravention of EC law on the free movement of goods and services.[170] Jacques Rigaud, a senior figure in both Luxembourg and French broadcasting, denounced the Tasca decrees as "unrealistic and unsustainable" and accused the government of "Chernobylizing the audiovisual landscape."[171] A trade association of broadcast networks and producers railed against "the accumulation of contradictory and counter-productive regulations."[172] Even Jacques Boutet, government-appointed chairman of the television regulatory body, the Conseil supérieur de l'audiovisuel (CSA), called for the quota to be reduced (while introducing a stricter definition of French works, thereby avoiding production under, as it were, flags of convenience).[173]

French producers believed there were insufficient resources to make the French programs required by the quotas. They further believed that the Tasca decrees would lock them out of the increasingly lucrative international coproduction market where, in the nature of things, the jointly venture programs might not be made in French, but in English. Jack Lang thought these objections were ridiculous. "Where are the European coproduction projects that the [television industry] professionals could not produce because of regulation?" he said. "Helping coproductions in English can not in any case be considered as a cultural objective."[174]

Nevertheless, if domestic pressure could be ignored, the view of the EC in Brussels was less easily brushed aside. Both the French network TF1 and the German producers' trade association made complaints about the Tasca decrees, and the European Commissioner responsible for audiovisual questions, Jean Dondelinger, promised that Brussels would "do its duty if the French regulations are not modified."[175] France had a new prime minister, Edith Cresson – who, as trade minister in 1989, had forced Jack Lang to accept the watered-down quota language in the Directive – and following several months of negotiation between Lang and Catherine Tasca's Cresson-appointed successor as communications minister, Georges, Kiejman, the Tasca decrees were modified.[176] The changes were of no comfort to Hollywood: the 60 per cent European works quota was unchanged. Instead, the 50 per cent French works quota was reduced to 40 per cent, and the special application of the quota for French works to prime time was extended to cover European works.[177] The provenance of a European work was extended yet further to include Eastern Europe and Turkey.[178] Further changes would allow French-language screenwriters from other countries, such as Belgium and Luxembourg, contribute their screenplays to productions designated as French works.[179] By the time the agreed formula had passed into law, one further innovation was made: the CSA was allowed to apply the quotas not in primetime, but during "hours of significant viewing".[180] This was viewed as giving the CSA flexibility to enforce the quotas according to the special needs of particular channels.[181] In fact, the changes had something for everyone – except Hollywood. Even with something for everyone, however, the new quota law was not welcomed by everyone: indeed, it was "attacked on all sides: economically unworkable for some, unacceptable because too dirigiste for others."[182]

If anything, these sectional attacks on quotas seemed to comfort French governments, who never seemed to regard their cultural policies as less than a moral crusade. Indeed, for them, the response both within and outside Europe could be taken to prove that big money had had its way in the television industry for too long. Further, France – and Europe – had one good reason to believe that American opposition, which began to subdue somewhat after the promulgation of the Tasca decrees, might eventually evaporate altogether: Canada. The United States and Canada had successfully negotiated free trade agreements despite the presence of quotas on foreign television programs similarly restrictive to those imposed in Europe. France was inspired by Canada, whose vulnerable borders, hugely distended along thousands of miles of frontier, was peculiarly vulnerable to US televisual culture. Particularly inspiring to the French was Quebec, whose tiny population nevertheless produced more television drama than France, Belgium and Switzerland combined.[183] All of this had taken place without the kind of polemic engendered by the EC Directive. If the US could put up with Canada, it could tolerate Europe; the Canadian experience gave France encouragement that the quota row would simply blow over.

(The differences between Canada and the US over trade and cultural questions are beyond the scope of this book. Suffice it so say, the "Canada is different" argument, used to justify that country's substantial audiovisual protections, appears to have been accepted with greater equanimity in the US and Hollywood than similar measures in Europe. The first so-called "CanCon" (Canadian content) quotas were set in the 1950s. From a 55 per cent CanCon quota for "primetime" (6pm to midnight), the quotas were progressively raised on the public CBC network to 85 per cent, remaining at 55 per cent on commercial networks. Despite allegations that CanCon programs were systematically slotted into the least viewed parts of the schedule, a government task force report in 1986 said that 71 per cent of viewing on English-language stations, and 68 per cent on French languages stations was CanCon. By comparison, the US accounted for 75 per cent of book market imports in 1979, 84 per cent of recording revenues paid to foreign firms in 1978, 93 per cent of all film distribution rentals in 1976 and 73 per cent of all periodical sales in 1978.)[184]

The GATT process accelerates

In fact, the Bush administration – as has been seen, stretched to the limit by the demands of Europe and the Uruguay Round – was preoccupied with a much more directly menacing issue, the phasing out of agricultural subsidies, over which the US and Europe – ironically, notably France – had sharp differences. The wrangles over this and other matters had begun to sap the administration's confidence in its push for free trade. At the same time, the MPAA began to see opposition to the GATT in general as a way of mobilizing specific opposition to the Directive.[185]

The MPAA's own target had widened as well, to include the degree of protection the GATT would include for intellectual property under new provisions contained in the Uruguay Round. As the GATT talks came close to foundering on European and American differences over agriculture policy in December 1991, Jack Valenti was lobbying Congress for a rejection of a compromise solution proposed by GATT's secretary-general, Arthur Dunkel.[186]

Dunkel's report made no mention of the audiovisual sector. EC members had mandated their GATT negotiators to seek an explicit exception for the audiovisual sector.[187] According to Dominique Wallon, a senior French official, and director of the state-run cinema regulator, the Centre National de la Cinématographie (CNC), it was impossible for Europe to grant the United States most favored nation status for its audiovisual exports when there was a US-EC trade imbalance in this sector of $1.65 billion.[188] As so often on both sides of this affair, Wallon took pains to present his case emotively:

> In the end, [the Americans] are aiming for absolute domination (even with capital of Japanese or other origin);[189] it is an imperialist monopoly policy tending towards a substantial growth in profits. For Europe and in particular France, as elsewhere for the other countries of the world, it is not financial growth that is in place, but a problem of survival pure and simple.[190]

Wallon's plaint came at a strangely-charged moment in Franco-American cultural relations: just before the opening in France of the exemplar of all that was admired and detested in Hollywood: the Euro Disneyland theme park (now called Disneyland Paris) in Marne la Vallée to the east of Paris. France's attitude to this symbol of American plutocracy – and Plutocracy – was paradoxical. The country supplied Disney, at discount rates, with the sugar beet fields on which the park was constructed.[191] State banks negotiated long-term credits for the project.[192] High-speed and suburban railway lines were extended to the site, at public expense.[193] According to one estimate, total French state support for Euro Disneyland, including tax breaks, amounted to FFr 13 billion, or around $2.5 billion.[194]

Jack Lang sniffed at the finished project. "one might have hoped that the attractions made more space for the cultures of the different countries of Europe," he said. (In fact, there had been a single special concession to European culture: the Tomorrowland exhibit from Disney World in Florida, judged too out of date, had been replaced by a specially-created Discoveryland, based on the works of the French writer Jules Verne, and conceived by the French screenwriter Jean-Claude Carrière.)[195] Reinforcing the traditional language of cultural defensiveness, Lang accused Disneyland of being "an enclave of the American leisure industry in Europe."[196] He declared he was too busy to attend the opening of the park. (Lang was positively restrained alongside those French intellectuals who described Euro Disneyland as "a cultural Chernobyl," "a construction of hardened chewing gum and idiotic folklore taken straight out of comic books written for obese Americans," "a terrifying giant's step towards world homogenization," and "a world that will have all the appearance of civilization and all the savage reality of barbarism." Nor did he go as far as the May 1968 nostalgist who hoped "with all my heart for a May 1992 that will set fire to Euro Disneyland.")[197] Lang's snub to Disney was presumably calculated. It is interesting to wonder whether this calculation included the knowledge that the then president of the Walt Disney Co., Frank Wells, was also a member of a committee advising the US government on trade policy matters, including the issue of television quotas and the GATT.[198]

Indeed, Hollywood's lobbying efforts continued to be directed against the GATT. In November 1992, the Uruguay Round nearly foundered on the issue of oilseed subsidies, when France withheld support for a joint EC-US solution.[199] France was eventually forced into a humiliating climbdown over the agriculture issue.[200] The affair illustrated an important truth about the GATT: despite their huge differences, both the US and the EC wanted a successful Uruguay Round that would ease their way into other markets, notably in Asia. Consequently, and under sufficient pressure, they would always eventually make the necessary concessions to each other to achieve this end. This trend alarmed Hollywood. "We're afraid we're going to be sold out," Jack Valenti said after the agriculture deal.[201] The committee on which Disney's Frank Wells served convened to complain that a GATT agreement risked leaving the television quotas intact. We're on the verge of real damage being done," Valenti declared.[202]

If, as had been hoped, the remaining Uruguay Round issues had been resolved by December 1992, then perhaps the quota issue might have quietly gone away, as Valenti feared. But France was determined to get the EC to reverse its policy on farm subsidies and vowed to press on.[203] Its strategy was to seek to reopen all the previously negotiated GATT issues and to stand firm on those not yet settled – including television quotas, a question which, one year before the it nearly caused the GATT talks to collapse, some believed had the potential to create a "real blockage" in the Uruguay Round.[204]

A new administration: the same policy

At the same time, there was a new administration in Washington. Bill Clinton was a Democratic Party president, as had been Jack Valenti's mentor, Lyndon Johnson. He was also closer much closer to Hollywood than had been George Bush, deliberately attempting to cultivate glamour and youth in contrast to Bush's hokier set-dancing and horseshoe-tossing image. More importantly, Hollywood contributed around two million dollars to Clinton and the Democrats during the presidential campaign.[205] Hollywood even had its own direct line to the White House through David Geffen, a hugely successful music entrepreneur, reportedly the richest man in Hollywood, and a major fundraiser for Clinton.[206] Geffen formed a close working relationship with White House chief of staff Mike McLarty, became a frequent visitor to Clinton, and had a long-standing friendship with the new US Trade Representative, Mickey Kantor.[207] Kantor, like his predecessor Carla Hills (who, like many an unemployed cabinet officer, became a consultant advising businesses on the global economy and US trade policy)[208] was a Los Angeles lawyer and who knew next to nothing about trade when he embarked on his job. Given the intense engagement of the United States at that time in both the GATT and the North American Free Trade Agreement, this was a cause for concern and some comment.[209] When the GATT crisis reached its height, Kantor would routinely be referred to, in journalistic shorthand, as "a Hollywood lawyer."[210] This was not strictly true: Kantor's major law clients had been big corporations in other fields, such as Lockheed,

Occidental Petroleum, Philip Morris and NEC.[211] His Hollywood connections were mainly political, through his years of activism in LA, state and finally national elections. He had one other perhaps over-prized quality in common with Carla Hills: aggressiveness. "I can't stand to lose," he said in an interview. "I am the worst loser you even met in your life. I get mad."[212]

The slowing-down in the GATT process took some of the lobbying pressure off the incoming US administration.[213] Indeed, one French official signaled his government's willingness to keep talk going for another six months or a year, rather than arrive at an unsatisfactory early deal.[214] This breathing space was fine for France as concerned the GATT issues it wanted movement on; unfortunately, it was also advantageous to those gathering their forces for one final onslaught on the quotas.

Jack Valenti, stepping into his accustomed position in the spotlight, told *Le Monde* that the United States would not sign a GATT agreement which included a cultural exception for the audiovisual sector. (Because there is a tendency in France to regard Hollywood and Washington DC as part of the same power nexus, a statement such as this from Jack Valenti would have been widely read as containing some kind of quasi-official authority. Nevertheless, Valenti spoke with the confidence of one who had successfully moved his issue higher up the agenda of the US administration – which, as will be seen, he had.) Valenti claimed that US television imports to Europe – and in particular to France – had fallen since the adoption of the Directive, but moderated his demands over the quotas by calling for them to be "lightened progressively" according to a timetable "subject to negotiation."[215] He also raised an issue that would provide another stumbling-block in the Uruguay Round talks later that year: French subsidies to its audiovisual production sector. Insisting that he was not opposed to such subventions, he nonetheless argued that they could have a "certain effect on the closure of the market."[216]

Valenti's intervention provoked fury in France, as politicians, officials, producers and artists flocked to the pages of *Le Monde* to denounce him. "We are at war," declared Jean-Claude Carrière, the man who worked for Disney to conceive Discoveryworld.[217] Ever fastidious, Jack Lang reproached Valenti, who had differentiated commercial television from the world of culture, for "this very personal and somewhat sinister description of a cosmogony."[218] Valenti's claim that television program exports to France had failed was treated with particular scorn: according to Alain Modot of the producers' association USPA, 500 more hours of American drama programs had been sold to France in 1991 than in 1990, the US proportion of the whole having *risen* to 45 per cent.[219] The CNC pointed out that in terms of money, the Franco-American trade gap in television programs had widened in 1991 from FFr 367 million to FFr 768 million (roughly from $73 million to $153 million).[220]

The significance of this exchange was that, in the year the Uruguay Round was due to be completed, there was absolutely no common ground between France and the US over quotas. But this flare-up was also part of a phony war, empty sparring going on in the time before the GATT talks began. These had been slowed in part by the arrival of the Clinton Administration and by the engagement of its trade team in the North American Free Trade Agreement negotiations.[221] France, too, had a new government, under conservative prime minister Edouard Balladur, which vowed to continue the policies of the outgoing administration and remain tough over the GATT.[222] In particular, and even without Jack Lang, the Balladur government declared its support for television quotas and the cultural exception to the GATT.[223] Nevertheless, the new communications minister, Alain Carignon,[224] said he planned to review broadcasting quotas which "may have isolated France."[225] The new culture minister, Jacques Toubon, who retained responsibility for the cinema, also spoke publicly in favor of retention of the quotas while signaling a general policy shift away from Langian support for producers towards concern with the industrial and technical needs of the film sector.[226]

The phony war was soon at an end. President Clinton's "fast track" authority to conclude a GATT agreement without risking amendment by Congress was due to expire on December 15. The US and the EC had succeeded in agreeing on a new GATT secretary-general, Peter Sutherland, who took the job on the understanding that his sponsors intended to achieve an agreement before the fast track authority expired.[227] The plan was for the group of leading industrialized nations, the G-7, to meet in Tokyo in June and July, hammer out their differences, and present a fait accompli on the major GATT issues which the rest of the world would have no choice but to follow. Despite the more moderate tone of the Balladur government, France and Europe continued to take a hard line on the cultural exception. The June meeting of G-7 trade ministers foundered acrimoniously, the main discord coming over textiles, shipping and television programs.[228] However, even at this impasse, the EC held out a deal: in return for a more flexible US approach to aluminum, electronics and television quotas, France might withdraw its opposition to the farm subsidies deal.[229] At the full G-7 meeting in July, however, the various leaders chose to give the Uruguay Round a boost by agreeing on a large package of outstanding differences while leaving a number, including the television quotas, unsolved.[230] Five months remained until the expiry of Clinton's fast-track authority, and the culture question was still obstinately present.

France renews the offensive

The would be five bad-tempered months, the tone of which was captured by this anonymous US view of the talks:

> "We say entertainment and motion pictures are a service industry and must be the object of trade negotiations aimed at eliminating quotas," said an American official who insisted on anonymity "The French say: 'Nope Sorry. Movies are a cultural issue and we don't negotiate.'"[231]

As before, the conflict spilled out of the negotiating room and into public debate, where it was crystallized by a Hollywood invasion as controversial as that of Euro Disneyland the previous year: the French release, in October 1993, of Steven Spielberg's *Jurassic Park*.[233] The polemic over GATT and that over the all-conquering dinosaur blockbuster became inseparable in France in late 1993. This was partly calculated. The Balladur government had decided not to budge on the quota issue. After the humbling isolation of France over farm subsidies, Carignon decided to ensure that the position over quotas would be more solid. He appointed Bernard Miyet, a highly experienced career diplomat, as roving ambassador for the audiovisual aspects of GATT, with the mission "to determine the quality of our community partners' attachment to the cultural exception and to assure himself that the member states are on the same wavelength."[233]

While Miyet worked the back rooms, Carignon mobilized public opinion, traveling to a meeting of the European Parliament to plead for the cultural exception with a roadshow of actors, directors and producers, including Gérard Depardieu and Isabelle Huppert.[234] The director Bertrand Tavernier (a champion of American cinema and co-author of the standard French reference work on the subject) exemplified the evaporation of all moderate discourse at this stage of the debate:

> The Americans want to treat us like they treated the redskins ... If we're very good, they will give us a reservation; they will give us the Dakota hills; and if we stay nice, perhaps we'll get one more hill ...[235]

The third element of the French government's offensive was aimed directly at Hollywood. Two American channels belonging to Turner Broadcasting System (TBS), TNT and The Cartoon Network, had been given licenses by the British television regulator, the ITC, to transmit via satellite from a base in the UK. The British authorization illustrated the problem with the loose wording of Article 4(1) of the Directive. It was at least arguable that if a channel's mission was to show American programs, it was not "practicable" to demand that it broadcast a majority of European shows. (Indeed, this very hypothesis of how the Directive might work in practice was explained to me by a senior responsible EC official at the time it was promulgated in 1989. On the other hand, there was a view that the penumbra of the Directive included the principle that member states should not allow the proportion of European works fall below what it was in 1988.)[236] TNT and The Cartoon Network were designed to draw on TBS' huge archives of Hollywood films and animation. Carignon threatened to bring a complaint against the UK for non-respect of the Directive (which, it will be recalled, was non-binding and contained no legal enforcement mechanism).[237] More seriously, he acted to prevent cable systems from carrying the two Turner services.[238] France was not isolated in acting against TBS: on Sept. 17, Belgium blocked TNT and The Cartoon Network on Brussels cable systems, citing cultural reasons.[239]

The government's strategy built consensus within France. Even the displaced Jack Lang issued a trenchant statement backing Carignon's action against Turner. (Bear in mind while reading it, that all Turner did was to obtain proper legal clearance to launch his service and then attempt to exploit his license):

In this domain vital to our national identity, France must speak with a single voice. And all responsible political bodies must form a bloc to contain this American aggression. These incidents demonstrate more than ever that we must say twice "no" to the cultural GATT. In the face of such unfair behavior on the part of certain American industrialists, one might go so far as to ask if, quite simply, we must not call the entire GATT into question.[240]

That this degree of unanimity in France was exceptional did not go unnoticed. The reason in French eyes? Jack Valenti and his strident campaign against the quotas, as described by one commentator:

Jack Valenti, eminent advocate for cultural free trade, has involuntarily succeeded in what nobody has managed to achieve in France since the Battle of Verdun: the sacred union of all the [political] parties.[241]

Having pulled together its campaign, France could now develop its GATT offensive. Ambassador Miyet's groundwork produced results in early October, when the EC's broadcasting ministers, meeting in Mons, Belgium, agreed a common position on the cultural exception, based on six points:

1. The maintenance and development of all national or Community financial aid policies in the television sector;

2. Exemption of these aid programs from the Most Favored Nations provisions of the GATT;

3. The maintenance of powers to regulate image transmission technologies;

4. Freedom in the future to develop policies for aiding the audiovisual sector;

5. Maintenance of the Directive; and

6. Assurances that these gains will not be placed in question by future negotiations.[242]

France obtained support for the principles of what came to be known as the Mons Declaration from Italy, Spain, Belgium, Greece, Portugal and Ireland. However, Germany, the UK, the Netherlands, Denmark and Luxembourg supported the communiqué outlining the six points despite reservations about the cultural exception.[243] This was a considerable victory for the French position. Nevertheless, France still felt isolated, fearful that it would be betrayed by the less culturally-enthusiastic countries of Northern Europe. Particular suspicion fell on the EC's chief trade negotiator, Sir Leon Brittan, whose fundamental unsoundness in French eyes was evidenced by his being (a) English; (b) English-speaking; and (c) a former minister in the cabinet of the nemesis of European cooperation, Margaret Thatcher. (Brittan was in Brussels because he had been the loser in a nasty – and public – bit of British cabinet infighting over a helicopter contract. Few in France ever seemed to realize that Brittan resented both Thatcher and his party for ruining his chances of becoming prime minister. He was instead generally regarded – quite wrongly – as some kind of Thatcherite catspaw.) Brittan advanced the idea of "cultural specificity" as a GATT term of art, rather than the preferred "cultural exception" at a meeting of EC foreign ministers in early October.[244] To the French, this spelled sellout. The Commission president, Jacques Delors, attempted to resolve the problem by redefining both terms so that they meant the same thing, only that "cultural specificity" was safer in legal terms, and less susceptible to future retaliation if adopted.[245] In doing so, Delors also adopted the demand for the exception, and agreed that the broadcasting ministers' six points should be regarded as a package, and not as various points to be bargained over by the GATT negotiators.[246]

The filmmakers start to feud

As European political attitudes hardened, the cultural air finally became completely poisoned when the film community itself – rather than trough its political and trade representatives – began mutual hostilities. At the major film industry gathering of the fall of 1993, the Venice Film Festival, two leading US directors arrived with major films, Steven Spielberg with *Jurassic Park*, and Martin Scorsese with *The Age of Innocence*.[247] Having experienced the heat of the quota debate in Europe at first hand, they waited until after the festival to issue personal statements opposing restrictions on audiovisual imports. the statements were subdued and respectful of other opinions, with which, Spielberg said, "I must reluctantly beg to differ."[248]

Spielberg was not just any American director. He was the most successful director, in box office terms, in cinema history, but had come to Venice to pay homage to one of Europe's own heroes. Gillo Pontecorvo had won the Festival's top prize, the Golden Lion, in 1966, for his film *The Battle of Algiers*.[249] Later, Pontecorvo donated his statuette to a Los Angeles auction in support of the moral rights of film makers and, in particular, American directors' demands for the final cut of their films.[250] Spielberg, as a young filmmaker, bought the statuette at the auction and, in a ceremony in Venice, returned it to Pontecorvo as a mark of solidarity between Hollywood's creators and those in Europe, and an expression of their common concern for artists' rights.[251] The sense of betrayal some Europeans felt at Spielberg's statement was acute.

European filmmakers (including Pedro Almodovar, Bernardo Bertolucci, David Puttnam and Wim Wenders) responded to the Spielberg and Scorsese statements by taking an advertisement in the Hollywood trade press warning that the MPAA's demand for an end to quotas – implicitly supported by the statements – would result in the "complete annihilation" of the European film industry.[252]

The row took on particular force in France, where *Jurassic Park* was due to be released at the same time as the most expensive French film ever made. *Germinal*, adapted from the novel by Emile Zola, was budgeted at $30 million and was the latest offering from producer-writer-director Claude Berri, previously responsible for such internationally successful films as *Jean de Florette*[253] and *Manon des sources.*[254] With his worldwide acclaim and strong track record, Berri might have seemed peculiarly invulnerable to even the biggest American blockbuster. Instead, the *Jurassic Park-Germinal* conjunction was built by politicians, intellectuals, journalists, filmmakers and marketers into the most potent peacetime confrontation between representatives of incompatible systems since Joe Louis fought Max Schmelling for the heavyweight championship of the world.

Jurassic Park was released on 450 cinema screens or around one-tenth of the French total, backed by an enormous marketing and merchandising campaign. (UIP, the film's Hollywood-owned distributor, claimed that it could have released 700 prints of the film – covering around 16 per cent of all screens – had it met all requests for prints from theater owners.)[255] *Germinal*'s release was on 350 screens. To counter the *Jurassic Park*'s threat, the culture minister, Jacques Toubon, announced that the government would pay for a further 90 prints of *Germinal* to be struck.[256] This manufactured battle was transformed into a touchstone of cultural correctness. The French press revealed that Clinton's trade representative, Mickey Kantor, had seen *Jurassic Park* three times, while Sir Leon Brittan, ever the object of suspicion, did not have time to go to the cinema, but had "heard about" both *Jurassic Park* and *Germinal.*[257] (The prime minister, Edouard Balladur, was bearded by a reporter in a train, where he confessed to having seen neither film, to preferring comedies, and to having liked *Love Story* [Paramount 1970][258]). Some voices protested an all this forced "cultural patriotism," where *Germinal* became the "new special sign of Frenchness,[259] after the beret and the baguette."[260] In the end, both films did good business, although *Jurassic Park* did better.[261] (Spielberg was quickly forgiven: the following year, when his somber drama about the Holocaust, *Schindler's List* [Universal/Amblin 1993], was released, he was feted in Europe and even invited to meet French president François Mitterrand, apparently the first American director ever to do so.)[262]

The GATT countdown

It was in this highly-charged state that the EC and US GATT negotiators met to attempt to resolve their remaining differences. The US administration had remained publicly quiet in the face of the previous months' ire, leaving the field to Jack Valenti to confront the European position. By mid-October, however, just two months remained until the fast track authority expired. It had also become absolutely clear that failure to conclude the GATT by December 15 would make any agreement impossible, a position accepted on the European side.[263] The new GATT secretary-general, Peter Sutherland, also began to sound the alarm, writing in the *Wall Street Journal*:

> [T]he Uruguay Round is about a lot more than farm subsidies, antidumping duties and TV film quotas. It is about more than a boost to economic growth – which it undoubtedly would be – and it is about more than the fight to create new jobs – which it would undoubtedly assist....

The Uruguay Round is the most comprehensive and complex multilateral economic negotiation ever undertaken. There are many reasons why it was launched, but the most persuasive and frank one is that the multilateral system that had held create so much prosperity in the '50s, '60s and '70s was, and is, collapsing...

Failure means we lose everything. There will be no intellectual property agreement to be salvaged from the wreck. Services companies will have to forget the new opportunities they had hoped for, and manufacturers seeking new markets will be left trying to hang on to what they have. That is probably the up side of a failure. The down side is a rapid erosion of the existing system, a gathering storm of unresolvable trade disputes, a vicious circle of new protectionist actions by governments, and a down turn in global economic prospects.[264]

But Valenti's efforts had succeeded in making the television quota issue a major priority for the Clinton administration. On October 15, Valenti organized a one-hour meeting at the White House between the President and 16 leading Hollywood figures, including studio heads and representatives of talent and labor. The meeting was an apparent triumph for Valenti and the MPAA. In a statement released afterwards, Clinton appeared to rule out a cultural exception. "Audiovisual services must be included in any GATT accord," he declared, adding that the US could not "accept that audiovisual products be singled out for unacceptable restrictions."[265] However, figures released by Jack Valenti put the issue into clearer perspective: he gave the example of one major US producer who had apparently lost $5-12 million per year because of the Directive.[266] Even if this degree of loss was equal for all MPAA members,[267] the worst possible impact of quotas would be around $35-84 million per year (or around 3-6 per cent of the total television revenues earned by the studios in the EC market. The MPAA drew one quarter of its foreign revenues from EC markets, suggesting that the maximum worldwide impact of the quotas was around 0.75-1.5 per cent of television income (and thus an even lower proportion of all foreign income, including theatrical and home video revenues). If these figures were real, they nonetheless represented significant cash losses. But an $80 million worst-case impact was infinitesimal compared to the multi-billion dollar benefits expected from a successful conclusion to the Uruguay Round.

Clinton's intervention was badly received. François Mitterrand attacked it the next day,[268] while others commented unfavorably on the US' willingness to allow cultural specificity in the North American Free Trade Agreement, but apparently not in the GATT.[269] However, cracks were developing once more in the common EC position. Jacques Toubon accused the Commission of "skidding" through choosing to negotiate on the basis of "cultural specificity" and not the "cultural exception."[270] He produced an internal report by Commission legal experts who concluded that the exception, rather than specificity, afforded better protection to the audiovisual sector. The Commission retorted that these lawyers were experts in EU[271] law, not that of the GATT, and that after long discussions they "recognized" that specificity was better adapted to the world trade context.[272]

At the same time, the tide was turning in favor of concluding the Uruguay Round by December 16. The narrow passage of the North American Free Trade Agreement by the House of Representatives on November 17 gave new impetus to the flagging GATT talks and convinced non-Americans that the US, despite a strong Congressional counter-current, was still in favor of liberalizing trade. But the close vote also underscored, if such were necessary, the finality of the December 15 fast track deadline. "There'll be no Dec. 16," the US Secretary of State, Warren Christopher, announced. "That's the message I want to go from here to Europe."[273]

Meanwhile, a glimpse of the ultimate outcome surfaced. Yves Mamou, a *Le Monde* journalist particularly well-briefed on the French position, floated the idea that the audiovisual sector might be excluded altogether from the Uruguay Round.[274] There were good reasons why this should not happen, as Mamou pointed out. It was contrary to the Montreal agreement, which reflected US insistence on a comprehensive services accord; and it would deny the Europeans an explicit legal framework for protecting their audiovisual sector.[275] Nevertheless, exclusion had been the approach adopted in the Canada-US trade agreement, and now it appeared to have been raised in the GATT.

However, just as a possible way out had manifested itself, the US upped the stakes. It began to attack not merely the quotas, but also the European system of support for audiovisual production, including French taxes on cinema tickets, whose yields were used to support the local film industry.[276] The Clinton administration's aggressive stand on the audiovisual quota was attributed to the success of the lobby mounted by the Democrat-supporting (and -funding) Hollywood community, including, of course, Valenti's MPAA.[277] Opening these new fronts, which also included an attack on taxes on blank audio and video cassettes, the receipts from which went to EU artists, may also have been a tactic to delimit the field that would be covered by an exclusion of the audiovisual sector from the GATT.[278] One other reason for the tougher tone on the audiovisual issue was that the US was preparing to yield ground on the farm subsidies problem which, it was believed, would lend weight to the post-NAFTA optimism that a GATT agreement could be had.[279] Agreement with Europe served another key aim for the US: enlisting the EU as allies against other countries, notably in Asia, to ensure the outcome most favorable to Western interests in the talks. However, the expected agriculture deal, reached eight days before the expiration of Clinton's fast track authority, failed to settle the question of aircraft subsidies and television quotas.[280]

Did the US nearly win?

It is at this point that the negotiations appear to have taken a strange turn. The following account is taken entirely from the French camp, having been recorded by the ever well-informed Yves Mamou.[281] The principal Anglo-American reporters covering the talks do not seem to have been aware of these events, if in fact they took place. The French version centers on the ever-questionable Sir Leon Brittan. Brittan was engaged in face-to-face negotiations on all US-EU differences with Mickey Kantor. According to the French account, Brittan had conceded all six points of the Mons Declaration, in particular diluting the quotas yet further so that they would be simply a "desirable" base.[282] Brittan also allegedly agreed to prior consultation with the US if any EU member-state wanted to amend its audiovisual regulations. EU states would similarly consult Washington over any future extension of their subsidy regimes. Brittan also apparently gained US agreement for the exemption of bilateral co-production accords from most-favored nation provisions on the GATT.[283]

If this account is true, such a surrender would have represented a huge breakthrough for Kantor. Yet, according to Mamou, at this point the US snatched defeat from the jaws of victory. Kantor allegedly demanded that the US should received "national treatment" via a share of tax revenues on blank video cassettes.[284] These revenues – not levied by the EU, but by national governments, and therefore not strictly negotiable by Brittan – were considerable: in France alone, they reached FFr 650 million, or $100 million, per year.[285] Brittan's response was to offer discussions on black cassettes, but on condition Kantor agreed to open the question of patents on US military technology. The talks broke down, and Brittan's prior concessions evaporated.[286]

What to make of this story? Did Europe nearly cave in? It is difficult to believe Brittan would have made such an offer unless, in doing so, he believed that France could be isolated within the EU, in particular by the UK and Germany. On the other hand, the story of US over-reaching is not inconsistent with the way its negotiations strategy had been developing, under the influence of Valenti and the MPAA. On 8 December, the day the Kantor-Brittan talks broke down, President Clinton himself once more asserted that the audiovisual row was a "very big issue for the US."[287] At the same time, Valenti was being lionized in the press as "Washington's premier lobbyist," the man who had extracted a pledge from Clinton that there would be no GATT if Hollywood were treated "shabbily" and whose efforts had led Mickey Kantor to declare that the EU quotas were "deal-breakers."[288] Valenti had come a long way from those days in 1989 when it appeared that neither the MPAA nor Washington had mastered the television quota issue. The weekend before Clinton made his statement in the GATT, he attended a $25,000-a couple Hollywood dinner that raised $2 million for his Democratic Party.[289] Valenti had also mobilized 233 members of Congress to urge Kantor to "insist" on GATT curbs on quotas and for intellectual property protection.[290]

Valenti had apparently even agreed a "common position" with Kantor's office on a compromise offer: that the EU maintain its current quotas, but not apply them to new satellite or cable technologies.[291] The details of the "common position" were revealed in the French press by *Le Monde*, using leaked EU documents, on the day after the GATT agreement was concluded. According to *Le Monde*, Kantor made the following demands:

- The quotas should be limited to "free" (non-subscription) broadcast (not cable or satellite) television channels.

- For cable, satellite and all other new technologies, quotas would be applied only to the total number of available channels, with 100 per cent non-European content allowed on pay-television services.

- Services using new payment technologies, such as pay-per-view, would not be subject to quotas.

- The GATT would lead negotiations to create structures that would suppress the market-distorting effect of subsidies.

- The EU would invite the US to participate in preparatory discussions for the forthcoming Green Paper on the audiovisual sector, as well as further discussions afterwards.

- The US would also have the right to participate in all proposals to adapt the Directive to new technologies.

- Income from blank video cassette levies would be shared with the US.

Leon Brittan's response to Kantor was to offer, in return, for "exceptional treatment" for the audiovisual sector in the GATT, a permanent EU-US working group to consider mutual problems, and an undertaking that "quantitative" restrictions would not be applied to pay-per-view. Even this modest proposal, however, was rejected by Brittan's colleagues.[292] Valenti was also said to support the US position on film subsidies.[293]

"A great and beautiful victory for Europe and French culture"

With four days to go until the expiry of Clinton's fast track authority, and doubtless emboldened by the political impossibility of accepting Kantor's new set of demands, EU leaders publicly backed maintenance of both the quota and subsidy systems, thereby putting an end to any further temptations Leon Brittan might have had to yield ground.[294] The French foreign minister, Alain Juppé, publicly aired the possibility that the audiovisual sector might be excluded altogether from the final agreement.[295] As the deadline approached, Clinton began phoning European leaders, and succeeded in removing obstacles over such remaining issues as anti-dumping rules, rice and textiles.[296] But the audiovisual question remained intractable; with two days to go, and with all other issues either settled, nearly settled or dropped, one of the leading negotiators – it was Brittan – used, for the first time, the word "crisis."[297]

On 13 December, Brittan formally rejected the US-MPAA "common position" offer.[298] At the same time, more contentious issues, including maritime provisions, aircraft subsidies and semiconductors continued to be resolved, either by exclusion from the agreement or through compromise.[299] Only the audiovisual issue appeared incapable of resolution. But as the fast track deadline approached, the advantage was moving in the French direction. "When the Americans settled agriculture early," said one German official, "they left the door wide open for the French to raise hell with audio-visual."[300]

On 14 December, at 4.00am, having negotiated for 20 hours, Mickey Kantor came to a conclusion. At 6.00am Geneva time (3.00pm in Washington), he telephoned President Clinton, with Leon Brittan waiting in an adjoining room. The phone call over, Kantor and Brittan negotiated for three more hours, showered, changed clothes and held a press conference. Mickey Kantor called Leon Brittan a "master diplomat;" Leon Brittan called Mickey Kantor a "friend." Agreement had been reached: the audiovisual sector would be excluded from the Uruguay Round. There would be a GATT, after all.[301]

Jack Valenti, defeated, wretchedly repeated his well-practiced mantra for the press: "[T]his is just protectionism, It has nothing to do with culture."[302] Alain Carignon, the French communications Minster, was as triumphant as Valenti was despondent. "This is a great and beautiful victory for Europe and French culture," he declared. "We got what we wanted from the beginning."[303]

It was indeed a triumph of diplomacy. Valenti warned that, by excluding the quotas from the GATT, the US would be able to take unilateral retaliatory measures against the EU.[304] But there was no conviction behind this claim and, indeed, no retaliation was ever taken. Indeed, the administration's own advisory committee, the ACTPN, on which Valenti sat, could only recommend, in its review of GATT, that the Trade Representative pursue the creation of a committee under the GATS to review the ultimate applicability of the agreement on services to the audiovisual sector. The ACTPN further wanted the US to ensure that adherence to the GATS did not prejudice pre-existing rights under the GATT. Published exactly one month after the conclusion of the Uruguay Round, it represented a subdued acceptance of the realities of the situation.[305] For in the end, the quota issue represented, at best, a minuscule American interest compared to the estimated $100-200 billion per year the Clinton administration calculated the new GATT was worth to the US economy.[306]

In Hollywood, the administration was spared serious criticism. Valenti was not directly attacked, but was sniped at as a high-profile uncompromising figure who had antagonized Europe and narrowed the room for settlement. And this industry of negotiators and dealmakers noticed one serious flaw in the US approach to the audiovisual debate. "How did we end up as the last piece on the table?" asked Sidney Sheinberg, then president of MCA, echoing the German official who saw the advantage swinging to France. "That's never a good place to be."[307]

Could the outcome have been different?

If you want to win, not winning is a defeat. The audiovisual issue in GATT only became a dealing point for the US on 13 December, 1993, when the entire world trade agreement was on the brink of collapse. Although the EU wobbled on occasions, its essential position, that the only way audiovisual would appear in the Uruguay Round would be as an exception, never changed. Looking at the way the two sides went about their negotiations, one important difference emerges. The European position was always politically-led. At key moments in the long years of argument and negotiation, France ensured that it had sufficient support among other EU member-states to proceed. When that support did not materialize, such as at the time the Directive was adopted, the French regrouped, continued to push, and rebuilt their coalition. In retrospect, the key success for France in the final months of the GATT negotiations was the Mons Declaration, where the silence of France's major partners, notably the UK and Germany, was sufficient to cement an agreed EU position which could not be bargained away in later dealings. France used the paraphernalia of public opinion building – enlisting professional support, using well-known figures as window-dressing, repeatedly declaiming its positions for the maximum emotive impact – but always from the perspective of a government pulling the reins of policy. The achievement of Jack Lang was to build a wide multilateral consensus, inside politics and without, that France was on the side of right and the US and its culture were the enemy. Most remarkably, this was achieved during a time when the *behavior* of the French belied this claim: they kept on going to see American films in the cinemas, and watched American series on television. But the *emotional* appeal of the argument was sufficient to sustain the all-party political will to succeed with the policy, even in the face of tremendous pressure, both from the US and, on occasions, from its EU partners.

The United States position, on the other hand, was developed from the ground up. It was Hollywood pressure that got the quota issue on to the agenda at all. Indeed, it appears to have been Hollywood's lack of pressure in the years before 1989 that led the administration to have been so slow to what was developing in Europe. Competing government departments, often short-staffed, failed to monitor the development of the Directive until it had nearly been promulgated. Further, when the administration attempted to mount a campaign against the Directive, it appeared for a long time to substitute bluster for argument as it failed to get a tight grasp on the real economic issues and the extent to which fundamental US issues were implicated. Right up to the end, the MPAA was feeding the Clinton administration its detailed policy on the audiovisual issue, with seemingly no voice contributing a view of the political possibility or desirability of adopting these postures. Kantor's decision, under MPAA pressure, to increase American demands as the finale of the Uruguay Round approached, entirely misread which side had its back to the wall. This mistake made the US climbdown all the more humiliating.

What makes this particularly unfortunate is that the conclusion of the Uruguay Round, in the same year as the passage of the NAFTA through Congress, was an outstanding achievement of Clinton's first year in office. As he was being elected, US officials were in Montreal, mired in the details of an agreement on which they could find little common ground with their negotiating partners. One year later –

helped greatly, of course, by the mind-concentrating force of the approach fast track authority expiry – a deal had been struck which guaranteed the US hugely more than had been yielded up. It seems extraordinary that so much could have been put at risk by so little.

Why did this happen? As has already been pointed out, Canada succeeded, in two trade agreements with the United States, to ensure itself a cultural exception for its audiovisual industry. However tough the negotiation of these terms may have been there was none of the sheer acrimony that passed between the EU and US during the GATT negotiations. Further, there does not have been the abyss of incomprehension between the two sides as existed during the Uruguay Round, the iron conviction that, on the one side, this was simply a question of culture in fear for its very existence, and, on the other side, this was simply a question of protectionism, barely masked by a humbug cultural rationale.

1   Robert E. Hudec, *The GATT Legal System and World Trade Diplomacy* (Second ed. 1990), 5. Salem N.H. Butterworth Legal Publishers.

2   *The GATT Legal System and World Trade Diplomacy*, 13.

3   *The GATT Legal System and World Trade Diplomacy*, 49.

4   GATT Secretariat, *The General Agreement on Tariffs and Trade (GATT), What It Is and What It Has Done*, Document MGT/3/54 (2nd ed., Feb. 1954), 2. Geneva: GATT.

5   *The General Agreement on Tariffs and Trade (GATT), What It Is and What It Has Done*, 1-2.

6   *The General Agreement on Tariffs and Trade (GATT), What It Is and What It Has Done*, 2-3.

7   *The General Agreement on Tariffs and Trade (GATT), What It Is and What It Has Done*, 3.

8   *The General Agreement on Tariffs and Trade (GATT), What It Is and What It Has Done*, 3.

9   *Guide to GATT Law and Practice* (6th ed. 1994), 191. Lonham, M.D: World Trade Organization Berman Press.

10   *Guide to GATT Law and Practice*, 192. Article III:4 states:

     The products of the territory of any contracting party imported into the territory of any other contracting party shall be accorded treatment no less favorable than that accorded to like products of national origin in respect of all laws, regulations and requirements affecting their internal sale, offering for sale, purchase, transportation, distribution or use. The provisions of this paragraph shall not prevent the application of differential internal transportation charges which are based exclusively on the economic operation of the means of transport and not on the nationality of the product.

11   *Guide to GATT Law and Practice*, 192.

12   Clint N. Smith, "International Trade in Television Programming and GATT: An Analysis of Why the European Community's Local Program Requirement Violates the General Agreement on Tariffs and Trade," *International Tax & Business Lawyer* 10 (1993), 117.

13   *Guide to GATT Law and Practice*, 192.

14   "The World Trade Picture," *Wall Street Journal* (Dec. 16, 1993), A12.

15   "Background Note on the Audiovisual Sector," GATT press release NUR 069 (Oct. 14, 1993), 4.

16   The term "audiovisual" covers the cinema, television, home video and allied sectors. It is a word disliked by many native English speakers, since, in this sense, it effectively supplants the original English sense of the word, as in "audiovisual aid". Its use to describe a sector of economic activity is derived from the French term *audiovisuel*. It has also been recognized in the US in the Copyright Act, where "audiovisual works" are defined as:

> ... works that consist of a series of related images which are intrinsically intended to be shown by the use of machines or devices such a projectors, viewers, or electronic equipment, together with accompanying sounds, if any, regardless of the nature of the material objects, such as films or tapes, in which the works are embodied. 17 U.S.C. § 101.

Through increased use in this sense in English language jurisdictions, as well as in international bodies such as the EU and GATT, the English word has now largely taken on the French meaning, and is used thus in this book.

17   "Background Note," 5.

18   Derrick Wyatt and Alan Dashwood, *Wyatt & Dashwood's European Community Law* (5th. ed. 1994), 3. London: Sweet & Maxwell. Jean Boulouis, *Droit Institutionnel de l'Union European* (6th ed. 1996), 9-10. Paris: Éditions Montchrestien.

19   *Wyatt & Dashwood*, 3.

20   *Wyatt & Dashwood*, 4-7.

21   *Wyatt & Dashwood*, 7.

22   *Wyatt & Dashwood*, 9; *Droit Institutionnel*, 22.

23   *Wyatt & Dashwood*, 9.

24   *Wyatt & Dashwood*, 8.

25   Case 22/70, *Commission v. Council* [the E.R.T.A. case], 1971 E.C.R. 273, 1971 C.M.L.R. 335 (1971).

26   Case 155/73, *Guiseppe Sacchi*, 1974 E.C.R. 409, 2 C.M.L.R. 177 (1974).

27   Case 62/79, *Coditel v. Cine Vog Films*, 1980 ECR 881, 2 C.M.L.R. 362 (1980).

28   *Radio Téléfis Eireann and another v European Commission*, Joined cases Nos. C-241-242/91 P (Court Of Justice Of The European Communities, April 6, 1995) (LEXIS, Intlaw library, ECcase file).

29   *Television Without Frontiers Green Paper from the Commission to the Council*, COM(84)300 final, 1.

30   *Television Without Frontiers*, 1.

31   *Television Without Frontiers*, 4.

32   Bulletin of the European Communities, 5-1984, 14.

33   Other work that attempts to trace the history of EU policy on television program quotas either fails to notice this policy-shift, fails to account for it, or both. See, eg, Rebecca Wallace and David Goldberg, "The EEC Directive on Television Broadcasting," *Yearbook of European Law*, 9 (1989), 175. Oxford: Clarendon Press. N.C.M. Peck, "Transfrontier Television and Europe 1992: A Common Position, *Temple International & Comparative Law Journal* 4 (1990), 307; Brian L. Ross, "'I Love Lucy,' But the European Community Doesn't: Apparent Protectionism in the European Community's Broadcast Market," *Brooklyn Journal of International Law* 16 (1990), 529; Timothy L. Lupinacci, "The Pursuit of Television Broadcasting Activities in the European Community: Cultural Preservation or Economic Protectionism?" *Vanderbilt Journal of Transnational Law* 24 (1991), 112; Kelly L. Wilkins,

"*Television Without Frontiers*: An EEC Broadcasting Premiere," *Boston College International & Comparative Law Review* 14 (1991), 112; John Filipek, "'Culture Quotas': The Trade Controversy over the European Community's Broadcasting Directive," *Stanford Journal of International Law* 28 (1994), 323; Janet L. Conley, "Hollywood's Last Hurrah? *Television Without Frontiers'* Directive May Close Borders to the European Community's Broadcast Market, " *University of Pennsylvania Journal of International Business Law* 14 (1993), 87; Lisa L. Garrett, "Commerce versus Culture: The Battle Between the United States and the European Union Over Audiovisual Trade Policies," *North Carolina Journal of International Law & Comparative Regulation*, 19 (1994), 553; Laurence G. C. Kaplan, "The European Community's *'Television Without Frontiers'* Directive: Stimulating Europe to Regulate Culture," *Emory International Law Review* 8 (1994), 255.

34   Bruno Lopez Kupitsky, report, UPI, July 27, 1982, available in LEXIS, Nexis Library, UPI File.

35   "The culture war," *The Economist* (Sept. 18, 1982), 54.

36   Jack Lang & Jean-Denis Bredin, *Éclats* (1978), 98. Paris: J.-C. Simoen.

37   *Éclats*, 187.

38   *Éclats*, 215.

39   "The culture war," 54.

40   Mary Ellen Bortin, "France Launches American-Style Drive to Save European Cinema," Reuter, June 21, 1984, available in LEXIS, Nexis library, Reuter file.

41   "France Launches American-Style Drive to Save European Cinema."

42   *Resolution of the Representatives of the Governments of the Member-States*, 1984 Official Journal (C 204), 2.

43   Cited in Ivo Schwartz, "La politique de la Commission en matière de télévision," *Revue du marché commun* (1985), 496.

44   "La politique de la Commission en matière de télévision," 496.

45   Philippe Kieffer & Marie-Eve Chamard, *La Télé: Dix ans d'histoires sécrètes* (1992), 270. Paris: Flammarion.

46   *La Télé*, 270.

47   *Commission Proposal for a Council Directive on the coordination of certain provisions laid down by law, regulation or administrative action in Member States concerning the pursuit of broadcasting activities*, 1986 Official Journal (86/C 179/05),1.

48   Loi No. 86-1067 du 30 septembre 1986 relative à la liberté de communication, art. 70, *J.O.* (Oct. 1. 1986); *G.P.* (Oct. 8-9 1986), 504.

49   Decret no. 87-36 du 26 janvier 1987, art. 5, *J.O.* (Jan. 27, 1986), 946.

50   Proposal for a Council Directive on the coordination of certain provisions laid down by law, regulation or administrative action in Member States concerning the pursuit of broadcasting activities: submitted by the Commission to the Council, 1986 O.J. (C 179/05), 4.

51   Bernard Rudden and Derrick Wyatt, *Basic Community Laws* (6th ed. 1996), 120. Oxford: Oxford University Press.

52   *Proposed Directive*, 6.

53   Community works were defined as either produced or coproduced entirely within member-states, or where coproduction took place with producers from non-member states, 70 per cent financed within the Community. *Proposed Directive*, art. 4.

54   *Proposed Directive*, art. 2.

55   See *Basic Community Laws*, 89-90.

56   Art. 193 of the EC Treaty provides for the committee to consist of "representatives of the various categories of economic and social activity, in particular, representative of producers, farmers, carriers, workers, dealers, craftsmen, professional occupations and representative of the general public." Art. 198 provides for the committee to consider questions referred to it either mandatorily through provisions of the Treaty, or at the discretion of the Council or Commission. *Basic Community Laws*, 124-26.

57   *Opinion of the Economic and Social Committee on the proposal for a Council Directive on the coordination of certain provisions laid down by law, regulation or administrative action in Member States concerning the pursuit of broadcasting activities*, 1987 O.J. (C 232/16), 31.

58   *Wyatt & Dashwood*, 37. Since the Maastricht Treaty, the Parliament's powers have been expanded considerably from what they were in 1988. See *Droit Institutionnel*, 151-153.

59   *Proposal for a directive* COM (86) 146 final, 1988 O.J. (C 49) 53, 54.

60   Proposed amended art. 3. *Proposal for a directive*, 56.

61   Proposed amended art. 2. *Proposal for a directive*, 56.

62   Data adapted from Preben Sepstrup, *Transnationalization of Television in Western Europe*, 28, 122, citing E[uropean] B[roadcasting] U[nion] Statistics 10, pt. 3 (1989). London: John Libbey; and A. Pragnell, *Television in Europe: Quality and Value in a Time of Change* (1985). Manchester: European Institute for the Media. These figures do not cover all channels in these countries and certainly either understate or omit the significance of new channels.

63   *Transnationalization of Television*, 52.

64   Adapted from data in *Transnationalization of Television*, at 54.

65   One premium subscription film channel.

66   The Discovery Channel and MTV.

67   *Transnationalization of Television*, 131.

68   *Transnationalization of Television*, 49. Figures based on one week in each year.

69   *Amended Proposal for a Council Directive on the coordination of certain provisions laid down by law, regulation or administrative action in Member States concerning the pursuit of broadcasting activities: submitted by the Commission to the Council pursuant to Article 149(3) of the EEC Treaty*, COM(88) 154 final - SYN 52., I

70   *Amended Proposal*, III.

71   *Amended Proposal*, 22.

72   *Amended Proposal*, art. 4.2, 25.

73   *Wyatt & Dashwood*, 14.

74   See, eg, Mark M. Nelson, "Protectionism Looms as Europeans Unify," *Wall Street Journal* (May 10 1988), 34.

75   Leslie Bennetts, "French Culture Minister Finds Empathy in US, "*New York Times* (Oct. 29 1986), C19.

76   Mervyn Rothstein, "Jack Lang, Creatively Engagé, Plots France's Cultural Future," *New York Times* (Jul. 26 1988), C17.

77 Clyde H. Farnsworth, "US Warns on Global Trade Talks," *New York Times* (Nov. 30 1988), D1.

78 "US Warns on Global Trade Talks," D1, D9.

79 "US Warns on Global Trade Talks," D1.

80 "US Warns on Global Trade Talks," D1.

81 Ann Devroy, "Hills to Be Trade Envoy," *Washington Post* (Dec. 7, 1988), A1.

82 "US Says GATT Aims Not Harmed By Talk Of Yeutter Replacement," Reuter (Dec. 6, 1988), available in LEXIS, News library, Reuter file.

83 Clyde H. Farnsworth, "Senate Panel Moves Swiftly To Approve Trade Nominee," *New York Times* (Jan. 28 1989), 7.

84 Irvin Molotsky, Bush's Selections for the United Nations, the CIA and Top Economic Posts; Carla Anderson Hills, Special Trade Representative, *New York Times* (Dec. 7, 1988), B14.

85 Elizabeth Chute, "Two Senators Express Reservations About Bush's Choice for USTR Post," *American Metal Market* (Dec. 16, 1988), available in LEXIS, News library, ASAP file.

86 Randall Mikkelsen, "Carla Hills: Washington Superlawyer to Become Top US Trader," Reuter (Dec. 6 1988), available in LEXIS, News library, Reuter file.

87 *Nomination of Carla Anderson Hills: Hearing S. Hrg. 101-52 Before the Committee on Finance United States Senate*, 101st Cong., 1st. Sess. 1 et. seq. (1989).

88 *Nomination of Carla Anderson Hills*, 16.

89 Louis Uchitelle, "A Crowbar For Carla Hills," *New York Times* (10 June, 1990), section 6, pt. 2, 20.

90 The United States Trade Representative has the diplomatic rank of ambassador, but in the Bush administration, as in others, was also a political appointee and member of the cabinet.

91 *Nomination of Carla Anderson Hills*, 1.

92 *Nomination of Carla Anderson Hills*, 18.

93 *Nomination of Carla Anderson Hills*, 9.

94 *Nomination of Carla Anderson Hills*, 5-7.

95 *Wyatt & Dashwood*, 45.

96 *Wyatt & Dashwood*, 44.

97 *Wyatt & Dashwood*, 44, n. 55.

98 Raymond Snoddy, "EC Proposals on Broadcasting Criticised," *Financial Times* (Feb. 18 1988), 10.

99 William Dawkins, "Television Proposals Rebuffed," *Financial Times* (Mar. 23 1988), 2.

100 "European Commission Stands Firm on Draft Directive," *New Media Markets* (Mar. 30, 1988), available in LEXIS, News library, Newmed file.

101 "European Commission Stands Firm on Draft Directive,"

102 Ministers' deputies to meet in attempt to reach agreement, *New Media Markets* (Oct. 12 1988), available in LEXIS, News library, Newmed file.

103 "European Convention on Transfrontier Television," May 5, 1989, art 10.1, *European Conventions and Agreements* (1990), 5:243 .

104 Raymond Snoddy, "Europe Compromises on TV Rules," *Financial Times* (Nov. 25, 1988), 16.

105 Raymond Snoddy, "Blow to EC Commission on TV Controls," *Financial Times* (Dec. 7, 1989), 2.

106 William Dawkins, "Ministers back EC Accord on TV Rules," *Financial Times* (Mar. 15, 1989), 2.

107 "William Dawkins, EC Agrees Rules for Cross-Border Television," *Financial Times* (Apr. 14 1989), 2.

108 Pierre Angel Gay, "Bruxelles demande la modification de la réglementation française," *Le Monde* (May 23, 1991), 34.

109 The draft of the common position of the council does not appear to have been published. However, the text of article 4(1) can be found in [European Parliament] Decision (Cooperation procedure: second reading)concerning the common position of the Council on the proposal from the Commission for a directive on the coordination of certain provisions laid down by law, regulation or administrative action in Member States concerning the pursuit of television broadcasting activities, 1989 O.J. (C 158) 138, 139.

110 William Dawkins, "European Broadcasting Becomes Battleground For A Pot Of Gold; The European Market," *Financial Times* (Sept. 11, 1989), 4.

111 Martin du Bois & Peter Truell, "EC Ministers Back Open TV Market, Local Programs," *Wall Street Journal*, Apr. 10, 1989), B7.

112 "EC Ministers Back Open TV Market, Local Programs."

113 "EC Ministers Back Open TV Market, Local Programs."

114 The European Parliament's amended article 4(1) read:

> The Member States, shall ensure, using appropriate and legally effective means and according to a progressive timetable commensurate with the prevailing situation, that within four years after the entry into force of this Directive all television broadcasters reserve the majority of this transmission time for European works ... [thereafter following the Council of Europe text].

115 *Europe 1992: Hearing before the Subcomm. on Trade of the House Comm. on Ways and Means*, 101st Cong., 1st Sess. 7 (1989).

116 *Europe 1992*, 7.

117 *Europe 1992*, 28.

118 *Europe 1992*, 7.

119 *Europe 1992*, 10.

120 Elizabeth Wehr, "Japan India, Brazil Cited for Import Barriers," *Congressional Quarterly* (1989) 1242-43.

121 *USTR Identification of Priority Practices and Countries Under Super 301 and Special 301 Provisions of the Omnibus Trade and Competitiveness Act of 1988: Hearing Before the Subcomm. on Trade of the House Comm. on Ways and Means*, 101st Cong., 1st Sess. 15 (1989).

122 Clyde H. Farnsworth, "US Fights Europe TV-Show Quota," *New York Times* (June 9, 1989), D1.

123 "US Fights Europe TV-Show Quota," D1.

124 Peter Riddell, "Delors Believes US Fears Over 1992 Allayed," *Financial Times* (June 16, 1989), 6.

125 Peter Montagnon, "US Concern Over EC Plans For Broadcasting," *Financial Times* (Jul. 25, 1989), 6.

126   David Shribman, "Working Profiles: Top-Notch Lobbyists on Tape Royalties," *New York Times* (Nov. 24, 1982), A20.

127   Richard W. Stevenson, "The Spirited and Erudite Oration That Could Fail," *New York Times* (Dec. 9, 1990) Sec. 3, 8.

128   "The Spirited and Erudite Oration That Could Fail," 8.

129   "EC Ministers Back Open TV Market, Local Programs," B7.

130   William Dawkins, "US Film Makers Step Up Attack On EC Television Proposals," *Financial Times*, (Aug. 1, 1989), 2.

131   "Can Madrid save the directive?" *New Media Markets* (June 21, 1989), available in LEXIS, News library, Newmed file.

132   "Can Madrid save the directive?"

133   "Can Madrid save the directive?"

134   Peter Montagnon, "Europe TV Rules On Hills Agenda," *Financial Times* (Sept. 8, 1989), 3.

135   "Europe TV Rules On Hills Agenda," 3.

136   William Dawkins, "European Broadcasting Becomes Battleground For A Pot Of Gold," *Financial Times* (Sept. 11, 1989), 4.

137   Paul Montgomery, "US Trade Official 'More Positive' on Europe," *New York Times* (Sept. 17, 1989), 27.

138   "US Trade Official 'More Positive' on Europe," 27.

139   "Unchaining Europe's TV," *Financial Times* (Sept. 14, 1989), 30.

140   "Last minute lobbying on trans-frontier rules," *New Media Markets* (Sept. 27, 1989), available in LEXIS, News library, Newmed file.

141   David Buchan, "EC may give green light to TV directive," *Financial Times* (Oct. 3, 1989), 3.

142   David Buchan, "EC ministers agree minimum TV standards," *Financial Times* (Oct. 4, 1989), 2.

143   *Council Directive 89/552/EEC on the coordination of certain provisions laid down by law, regulation or administrative action in Member States concerning the pursuit of television broadcasting activities,* 1989 O.J. (L 298), 23.

144   "EC ministers agree minimum TV standards," 2.

145   "EC ministers agree minimum TV standards," 2.

146   "Last minute lobbying on trans-frontier rules," *New Media Markets* (Sept. 27, 1989), available in LEXIS, News library, Newmed file.

147   See eg, E.S. Browning, "Hills Hopes Talks Will Prevent A Protectionist 'Fortress Europe'," *Wall Street Journal* (Sept. 12, 1989), A12.

148   William Dullforce, "US challenges EC television ruling," *Financial Times* (Oct. 12, 1989), 6.

149   Steven Greenhouse, "Europe Reaches TV Compromise; US Officials Fear Protectionism," *New York Times* (Oct. 4, 1989), A1, D20.

150   "Europe Reaches TV Compromise; US Officials Fear Protectionism," D20.

151   "Europe Reaches TV Compromise; US Officials Fear Protectionism," D20.

152   Peter Truell, "US Criticizes EC Over Issue of TV, Seeks Arbitration," *Wall Street Journal* (Oct. 11, 1989), A14. The placing of inverted commas around the word 'Europeans'

suggests the reporter worked from a printed transcript of Hills' remarks – and that the questions of the idea of European identity was a deliberate move on her part.

153   "US Criticizes EC Over Issue of TV, Seeks Arbitration," A14.

154   "A Crowbar For Carla Hills," 21.

155   Ron Scherer, "US Debates Policy on Europe in 1992," *Christian Science Monitor* (May 18, 1989), 1.

156   "US Debates Policy on Europe in 1992," 1.

157   Clyde H. Farnsworth, "US Cautions Europe on Protectionist Moves," *New York Times* (Oct. 6, 1989), D2.

158   "US Cautions Europe on Protectionist Moves," D2

159   Clyde H. Farnsworth, "Decisions By Gatt Accepted," *New York Times* (13 Nov. 1989), D1.

160   "Decisions By Gatt Accepted," D1.

161   "Decisions By Gatt Accepted," D1.

162   "Europe Seeks Film, TV Bar," *New York Times* (June 21, 1990), D17.

163   Decret No. 90-66 du 17 janvier 1990, *Journal Officiel* (Jan. 18, 1990); *Gazette du Palais* (Jan. 31-Feb. 1, 1990), 121.

164   Decret No. 90-66, Arts 3, 4.

165   Decret No. 90-66, Arts 7, 8.

166   Decret No. 90-66, Art. 9.

167   Pierre-Angel Gay, "Le gouvernement rend publiques les nouvelles obligations des télévisions," *Le Monde* (Jan. 19, 1990),16.

168   See *Desperately Seeking the Audience*, 118-120.

169   Jean-François Lacan, "Les frontières de la télévision," *Le Monde* (Aug. 28, 1990), 1, 23.

170   Pierre-Angel Gay, "La CLT remet en cause la réglementation française de l'audiovisuel," *Le Monde* (March 5, 1991), 26.

171   Pierre Angel-Gay, "Vers l'assouplissement des règles imposées aux télévisions," *Le Monde* (Apr. 16, 1991), 22.

172   "Vers l'assouplissement des règles imposées aux télévisions," 22.

173   Piere Angel-Gay, "Le CSA souhaite un reamenagement des obligations des chaînes," *Le Monde* (Apr. 5, 1991).

174   "Le CSA souhaite un reamenagement des obligations des chaînes."

175   "Bruxelles demande la modification de la réglementation française," 34.

176   Yves-Marie Labé, "Compromis entre Paris et Bruxelles sur les quotas audiovisuels," *Le Monde* (Aug. 2, 1991).

177   "Compromis entre Paris et Bruxelles sur les quotas audiovisuels."

178   "Compromis entre Paris et Bruxelles sur les quotas audiovisuels."

179   "Compromis entre Paris et Bruxelles sur les quotas audiovisuels."

180   Loi No. 92-61 du 18 janvier 1992, Modifiant les articles 27, 28, 31 et 70 de la loi no 86-1067 du 30 septembre 1986 relative à la liberté de communication, *Journal Officiel* (Jan. 21, 1992), 970.

181   "Le Conseil constitutionnel entérine le pouvoir du CSA à moduler les quotas selon les chaînes," *Le Monde* (18 Jan., 1992), 18.

182   Michel Colonna d'Istria & Yves-Marie Labé, "Un entretien avec M. Georges Kiejman," *Le Monde* (Oct. 23, 1991), 25.

183   Annick Cojean, "Mme. Tasca découvre la réussite des quotas canadiens," *Le Monde* (March 22, 1990), 22.

184   Marianne Ferguson, "Canadian Broadcasting," in Jay G. Blumer & T.J. Nossiter eds., *Broadcasting Finance in Transition: a Comparative handbook* (1991), 158-187. See also, Michael Braun & Leigh Parker, "Trade in Culture: Consumable Product or Cherished Articulation of a Nation's Soul?" Denver Journal of International Law & Policy 22 (1993) 157-67. New York, Oxford: Oxford University Press.

185   Clyde H. Farnsworth, "US Is Changing Its Tune On Liberalization of Trade," *New York Times* (Oct. 29, 1990), D1, D4.

186   Keith Bradsher, "Trade Plan Criticized, Stalling World Talks," *New York Times* (Dec. 24, 1991), D2.

187   Jean-Michel Frodon, "Un entretien avec M. Dominique Wallon," *Le Monde* (March 11, 1992), 14.

188   "Un entretien avec M. Dominique Wallon," 14.

189   Europeans, like others, had watched with interest the Japanese arrival in Hollywood, with the purchase of Columbia Pictures by the Sony Corporation, and that of MCA by Matsushita (since sold to the Canadian conglomerate Seagram).

190   "Un entretien avec M. Dominique Wallon," 14.

191   Alan Riding, "Only the French Elite Scorn Mickey's Debut," *New York Times* (Apr. 12, 1992), A1, A13.

192   "Only the French Elite Scorn Mickey's Debut."

193   "Only the French Elite Scorn Mickey's Debut."

194   Pierre Merlin, "La mariée n'est pas si belle ...," *Le Monde* (Apr. 15, 1992.

195   Emmanuel de Roux, "Pour seduire les Européens en France, les Américains ont gardé Mickey mais ont recruté Jules Verne," *Le Monde* (Apr. 13, 1992.

196   "Only the French Elite Scorn Mickey's Debut," A13.

197   "Only the French Elite Scorn Mickey's Debut," A13.

198   Bob Davis & Asra Q. Nomani, "Clinton Team Mulls Stance On Trade Talks," *Wall Street Journal*, Dec. 9, 1992), A2.

199   Alan Riding & Keith Bradsher, "Europeans Agree With US on Cutting Farm Subsidies; French Withhold Support," *New York Times* (Nov. 21, 1992), A1.

200   Alan Riding, "French Now Agree The Lack a Veto over Farming Pact," *New York Times* (Nov. 24, 1992), A1.

201   Bob Davis, "Tough Trade Issues Remain as E.C., US Agree on Agriculture," *Wall Street Journal*, Nov. 23, 1992), A1, A6.

202   "Clinton Team Mulls Stance On Trade Talks," A2.

203   "France's View Of Trade Talks," *New York Times* (Jan. 6, 1992), D2.

204   Philippe Lemaitre, "La France demande une renégociation de l'ensemble des sujets du GATT," *Le Monde* (Dec. 5, 1992), 21.

205 Bob Davis, "In Global Trade Drama, Movie Man Jack Valenti Stars as Chief defender of Hollywood's Honor," *Wall Street Journal*, Dec. 9 1993), A18.

206 Bernard Weinraub, "David Geffen, Still Hungry," *New York Times* (May 2, 1993, sec. 6, 28.

207 "David Geffen, Still Hungry," 28.

208 "Carla's boys," *Financial Times* (Mar. 25, 1993), 21.

209 See, eg, Stuart Auerbach, "Kantor a Newcomer to an Intricate Field," *Washington Post*, Dec. 25, 1992), A23.

210 See, eg, Roger Cohen, "Culture Dispute With Paris Now Snags World Accord," (Dec. 8, 1993), A1.

211 "Culture Dispute With Paris Now Snags World Accord,"

212 John M. Broder, "Comeback Kid Kantor Makes Clinton Team," *Los Angeles Times* (Dec. 25 1992), A40.

213 Bob Davis, "Clinton Isn't Expected to Urge a Delay In Current Discussions on World Trade," *Wall Street Journal*, Dec. 14, 1992 at A2, A4.

214 Bhushan Bahree & Bob Davis, "French Objection to Lower Farm Tariffs Will Likely Delay World Trade Talks," *Wall Street Journal* (Dec. 17, 1992), A4.

215 Claudine Mullard, "Les États-Unis ne signeront pas une revision du GATT qui fasse de la culture un secteur d'exception," *Le Monde* (Marc. 11, 1993), 17.

216 "Les États-Unis ne signeront pas ..." 17.

217 Jean Claude Carrière, "Nous sommes pour la co-existence," *Le Monde* (Mar. 24, 1993), 2.

218 Jack Lang, "L'identité européenne," *Le Monde* (Mar. 24, 1993), 2.

219 Alain Modot, "Lettre au lobbyiste," *Le Monde* (March 24, 1993), 2.

220 Dominique Wallon, "Préserver la liberté de choix," *Le Monde* (Mar. 24, 1993), 2.

221 Keith Bradsher, "GATT Chief Says US Delays Pact," *New York Times* (Apr. 5, 1993), D1.

222 Roger Cohen, "French Disavow Accord on Farm-Trade Subsidy," *New York Times* (May 14, 1993 at D2.

223 "French Disavow Accord on Farm-Trade Subsidy," D2.

224 The Balladur government broke up Lang's "super-ministry" which had included culture, communications and, latterly, national education. Carignon was thus the senior minister in the new administration concerned with television matters. "M. Carignon sera également chargé de l'action audiovisuelle extérieure," *Le Monde* (Apr. 22, 1993),15.

225 Yves Mamou, "Alain Carignon 's'interroge' sur les quotas de diffusion posés aux télévisions," *Le Monde* (June 9, 1993), 1, 16.

226 Danièle Heymann & Emmanuel de Roux, "Un entretien avec Jacques Toubon," *Le Monde* (June 9, 1993), 1, 16.

227 Roger Cohen, "New GATT Chief Turns Up Heat, *New York Times*, July 2, 1993 at D1.

228 Andrew Pollack, "Big Powers' Free-Trade Talks Stall," *New York Times* (June 25, 1993), D1.

229 David P. Hamilton, *et al.*, "Trade Ministers Remain Divided at Tokyo Talks," *Wall Street Journal*, June 25, 1993), A2.

230 Andrew Pollack, "Many Loose Ends Must Be Tied Up," *New York Times* (July 8, 1993), A8.

231 Roger Cohen, "Barbarians at the Box Offices," *New York Times* (July 11, 1993) sec. 9, 3.

232   UIP/Universal/Amblin, 1993.

233   Yves-Marie Labé, "M. Carignon propose plusieurs mesures pour favoriser 'le rayonnement de la culture française,'" *Le Monde* (Aug. 31, 1993), 11.

234   Alain Rollat, "Une pléiade de vedettes à la rescousse," *Le Monde* (Sept. 17, 1993), 18.

235   "Une pléiade de vedettes à la rescousse," 18.

236   See Yves Mamou, "Ted Turner à la conquête de l'Europe," *Le Monde* (Sept. 19-20 1993), section Radio-Télévision, 28.

237   "Le group Turner affirme que M. Carignon va 'perdre son combat' contre les chaînes américaines," *Le Monde* (Sep. 10, 1993), 8.

238   "La Lyonnaise communication critique le CSA," *Le Monde* (Sep. 10, 1993), 8.

239   Julie Wolf & Charles Goldsmith, "EC Ministers Meet to Placate Opposition By France to Blair House Agreement," *Wall Street Journal*, Sep. 20 1993), B48.

240   "Jack Lang soutient Alain Carignon contre 'l'agression américaine,'" *Le Monde* (Sept. 19-20 1993), 9.

241   Alain Rollat, "Le véto de Mitterrand 'l'Indien,'" *Le Monde* (Oct. 10-11 1993), section Radio Télévision, at 34.

242   Yves Mamou, "L' "exception culturelle" définie en six points," *Le Monde* (Oct. 7, 1993), 17.

243   "L' 'exception culturelle' définie en six points," 17.

244   "EC Movie Protection Sought," *Wall Street Journal* , Oct. 5, 1993), A13.

245   Yves Mamou, "Jacques Delors à la rescousse de l'"exception culturelle," *Le Monde* (Oct. 15, 1993 20.

246   "Jacques Delors à la rescousse de l'"exception culturelle," 20.

247   Columbia, 1993.

248   Kathleen O'Steen, "Helmer duo decries quotas," *Daily Variety* (Oct. 5, 1993), 1.

249   *La Battaglia di Algeri*, Casbah/Igor, 1965.

250   The final cut is the finished version of the work print to which the negative is conformed in order to strike the release prints that are to be exhibited in theatres. Who has the ultimate authority to approve this version of a film is a significant negotiating point between producers and directors and also between producers and distributors. John W. Cones, *Film Finance & Distribution* (1992), 188-189. Los Angeles: Silman-James Press.

251   Danièle Heymann, "Les dinosaures et le Lion," *Le Monde* (Sep. 10 1993).

252   Leonard Klady, "Spielberg, Scorsese in GATT spat," *Daily Variety*, (Oct. 29 1993) 1.

253   Renn Productions/Films A2/Rai2/DD Productions, 1986.

254   Renn Productions/Films A2/Rai2/DD Productions, 1986.

255   Henri Behar & Danièle Heymann, "Les profitosaures," *Le Monde* (Oct. 20 1993).

256   Jean-Luc Bardet, "'Jurassic Park' contre 'Germinal,'" Agence France Presse (Oct. 20 1993), available in LEXIS, Presse library, AFP file.

257   Frederic Castel, "Mickey Kantor a vu trois fois Jurassic Park, Leon Brittan en a 'entendu parler,'" Agence France Presse (Oct. 13, 1993), available in LEXIS, Presse library, AFP file.

258   Emmanuel Serot,"'M. Balladur n'a rencontré 'aucun dinosaure dans la faune politique,'" Agence France Presse (Oct. 21 1993), available in LEXIS, Presse library, AFP file.

259   The original uses "franchouillardise," an untranslatable slang word that gives an ironic and absurd twist to the idea of Frenchness.

260   "'*Jurassic Park*' contre '*Germinal*.'"

261   "Les entrées à Paris," *Le Monde* (Oct. 28, 1993).

262   Jennifer Clark et al., "Euros Bury Dinos, Fete 'List' Auteur," *Daily Variety* (Mar. 7 1994), 55.

263   "Bill Clinton rejette l'idée d'un traitement spécifique pour l'audiovisuel," *Le Monde* (Oct. 16, 1993), 20.

264   Peter Sutherland, "If GATT Fails, We All Lose," *Wall Street Journal* (Oct. 19 1993), A20.

265   Brooks Boliek, "Clinton backs H'wood in GATT audiovisual debate," *Hollywood Reporter* (Oct. 15, 1993), available in LEXIS, News library, THR file.

266   "Clinton backs H'wood in GATT audiovisual debate."

267   At that time, the MPAA members were Columbia Pictures, MGM/UA, Paramount, Twentieth Century-Fox, Universal Studios, Walt Disney and Warner Brothers.

268   "Mitterrand warns of US domination," Agence France Presse (Oct. 16 1993), available in LEXIS, News library, AFP file.

269   "Bill Clinton rejette l'idée d'un traitement spécifique pour l'audiovisuel," 20. Annex 2106 of the NAFTA provides for Canada's "cultural industries" generally to receive, notwithstanding provisions in the agreement to the contrary, the same protection as they would under the Canada-United States Free Trade Agreement. *North American Free Trade Agreement* (1993) 1:21-11. Ottawa: Canada Communication Group. Cultural industries include persons engaged in "the distribution, sale or exhibition of film or video recordings" and in all television broadcast, cable and satellite activities. NAFTA art 2107, 21-7. Article 2005 of the Canada-United States Free Trade Agreement exempts cultural industries from most provisions of the treaty. *International Law Materials* 27 (1988), 281, 396.

270   Yves Mamou, "M. Toubon accuse de 'dérapage' la Commission européenne," *Le Monde* (Nov. 2, 1993), 16.

271   On November 1, 1993, the Treaty on European Union (or Treaty of Maastricht) entered into force, and the EC became transformed into the European Union, or EU.

272   Yves Mamou, "Les juristes de Bruxelles en faveur de l'exception culturelle, '" *Le Monde* (Nov. 2, 1993),16.

273   Roger Cohen, "France Now Faces US on Trade Issue," *New York Times* (Nov. 19, 1993), A7.

274   Yves Mamou, "Audiovisuel: l'exception culturelle reste une pomme de discorde," *Le Monde* (Dec. 7 1993), 20.

275   "Audiovisuel: l'exception culturelle reste une pomme de discorde," 20.

276   Bob Davis & Bhushan Bahree, "Trade Accord By US And E.C. Runs Into Snags," *Wall Street Journal*, Dec. 6 1993), A3.

277   "Trade Accord By US And EC Runs Into Snags," A3.

278   Philippe Lemaitre, "Le Conseil des ministres des Douze a pris acte des progrès accomplis sur le GATT," *Le Monde* (Dec. 9 1993), 18.

279   Roger Cohen, "US Seeks to Bring France Into Trade Pact's Fold," *New York Times* (Dec. 4 1993), 37.

280   Bob Davis, "US and EC Reach Accord on Farm Trade," *Wall Street Journal* (Dec. 8 1993), A3. Both France and the US shifted position to allow the deal to go through.

281   Yves Mamou, "La volte-face de Leon Brittan," *Le Monde* (Dec. 11 1993), 1.

282   "La volte-face de Leon Brittan," 20.

283   "La volte-face de Leon Brittan," 20.

284   "La volte-face de Leon Brittan," 20.

285   "La volte-face de Leon Brittan," 20.

286   "La volte-face de Leon Brittan," 20.

287   Asra Q. Nomani & Bhushan Bahree, "Gatt Teams Push Final Efforts to Set Global Trade Pact as Deadline Looms," *Wall Street Journal*, (Dec. 9 1993), A3.

288   Bob Davis, "In Global Trade Drama, Movie Man Jack Valenti Stars as Chief Defender of Hollywood's Honor," A18.

289   "In Global Trade Drama, Movie Man Jack Valenti Stars as Chief Defender of Hollywood's Honor," A18.

290   "In Global Trade Drama, Movie Man Jack Valenti Stars as Chief Defender of Hollywood's Honor," A18.

291   "In Global Trade Drama, Movie Man Jack Valenti Stars as Chief Defender of Hollywood's Honor," A18.

292   Yves Mamou, "Audiovisuel: des positions claires mais bloquées," *Le Monde* (Dec. 15 1993), 21.

293   "In Global Trade Drama, Movie Man Jack Valenti Stars as Chief Defender of Hollywood's Honor," A18.

294   Roger Cohen, "Europeans Back French Curbs on US Movies," *New York Times* (Dec. 12 1993) , sec. 1, 24.

295   "Europeans Back French Curbs on US Movies," 24.

296   Asra Q. Nomani & Lawrence Ingrassia, "Breakthroughs In Trade Talks Are Announced," *Wall Street Journal* (Dec. 13 1993), A3.

297   Roger Cohen, "Film Issue Snags Trade Talks: Anti-Dumping Pact Reached," *New York Times* (Dec. 13 1993), A1, D5.

298   Roger Cohen, "With Time Waning, Europeans Reject US Movie Compromise," *New York Times* (Dec. 14 1993), A1.

299   Bob Davis & Asra Q. Nomani, "Officials Close To Completing A Trade Accord," *Wall Street Journal*, (Dec. 14. 1993), A3.

300   Craig R. Whitney, "Germans Whisper Softly in Trade Rivals' Ears," *New York Times* (Dec. 14 1993), D7.

301   Bob Davis & Lawrence Ingrassia, "After Years of Talks, GATT is at Last Ready To Sign Off on a Pact," *Wall Street Journal*, Dec., 15 1993), A1, A7.

302   "After Years of Talks, GATT is at Last Ready To Sign Off on a Pact," A1.

303   Alan Riding, "Months of Risk, Moments of Isolations, Now Boasts of Triumph," *New York Times* (Dec. 15 1993), D19.

304   Keith Bradsher, "US And Europe Clear The Way For A World Accord On Trade, Setting Aside Major Disputes," *New York Times* (Dec. 15 1993), A1, A18.

305 Advisory Committee for Trade Policy and Negotiations, *A Report to the President, the Congress, and the United States Trade Representative Concerning the Uruguay Round of Negotiations on the General Agreement on Tariffs and Trade* (1994), 59-60 .

306 "After Years of Talks, GATT is at Last Ready To Sign Off on a Pact," A1.

307 Bernard Weinraub, "Clinton Spared Blame By Hollywood Officials," *New York Times* (Dec. 15 1993), D1, D9.

4
After the GATT

The final quota battle

The GATT victory emboldened those who believed that the Directive itself was an unsatisfactory compromise. France, it will be recalled, had gone further in its implementation of the Directive and imposed a 60 per cent quota for European works, going beyond the "majority" language of the Directive. It had further decreed that 50 per cent of programs broadcast in television should be French works. It also defined European works more tightly than the Commission and removed such weasel words as "where practicable."

This implementation of the Directive in fact mirrored national quotas of similar force that had been applied earlier. At the same time, as has been seen, from 1985 France underwent both an expansion and a transformation of its television system. France also had a highly regulated advertising market, which limited the potential for growth in television ad revenues. In just a couple of years, France had two-thirds more broadcast hours to fill (probably more, because the networks generally expanded their broadcasting time), little more cash to fill them with and a brand new for-profit sector needing to amortize substantial investments and startup costs. This was the moment the government chose to make programs more expensive by implementing stringent quotas, and by policing them with fines.

There were two results: first, a crisis in the production industry as broadcasters squeezed costs. Unlike the US, French producers could not viably use deficit financing because they did not have a secondary market to resell their programs into. The second result was that one of the new private networks, La Cinq, went out of business at a time when audience demand was create new television services all over the world.[1] In April 1992, more than a year a half before the brinkmanship of the GATT row reached its climax, La Cinq went off the air, clear proof ignored by both France and Hollywood that the biggest victims of program quotas were likely to be European broadcasters themselves.

Despite this debacle, the French reaction to its GATT victory was to attempt to tighten the screw. With the audiovisual sector expressly exempted from the Uruguay Round, the EU could toughen its quotas without infringing the new agreement. Europe's – and France's – sense of having won a victory was comforted by the United States continuing to threaten trade sanctions, Mickey Kantor declaring himself to be "profoundly disturbed" and "very pessimistic" about the application of the Directive.[2]

The challenge for France was that the European Commission was preparing a second Green Paper consultative document on audiovisual policy, which would review the operation of the Directive. Communications minister Alain Carignon signaled in advance of the commission publishing its findings, that he wished the quotas to be strengthened.[3] At the same time, he sought to out-Lang Jack Lang by evoking "battles" and "war" and expressing the fear that Europe's GATT victory might be equivalent to the heroic – but ultimately fruitless – charge of the French cavalry upon the Prussians at Reichshoffen in August, 1870.[4]

Carignon's highly-public efforts were blunted in two ways. He found himself in conflict with the culture minister, Jacques Toubon, who retained responsibility for the cinema and resented Carignon's encroachment onto his turf.[5] This difference slowed the development of a clear government policy on the next step in the quota debate. Carignon's other problem was that everyone else seemed to believe that the war was over. Jack Valenti, emollient, distanced himself from the positions the US administration had taken (at his insistent prompting) over GATT and declared that his work was to "find an area of agreement among film producers."[6] On the European side, the new culture commissioner, João de Deus Pinheiro, hastened to tell an American film industry audience that the "rhetoric" and "hyperbole" of the GATT negotiations were past and that his role was not "to launch any kind of war."[7] Even when Mickey Kantor railed in public against Europe's "profoundly protectionist" audiovisual policy and swore to open up the European television market, French analysts saw only pandering to internal US politics as the Clinton administration attempted to steer the GATT accord towards Congressional ratification. And Sumner Redstone, new owner of Paramount Pictures, told the French press that the GATT audiovisual question was "more philosophic than commercial" and that national channels in Europe still had "a large margin for using American products" under the existing quota system.[8] The air seemed thick with amity.

When the Commission's Green Paper was published, the question of quotas, present and future, was generally skirted around. It ducked the question of the effectiveness of the current quotas, noting simply that the highest-rated programs tended to be nationally-produced (with the unstated implication that these shows would have been made in any case without the aid of quotas).[9] Although the Commission concluded that no member-state had properly transposed the Directive into national law, it took no action against any state for non-compliance with the quotas provisions – presumably because of their ambiguous language and non-binding status.[10] The Commission did, however, begin proceedings against three countries – Belgium, Italy and the UK – for incorrectly incorporating other parts of the Directive into national laws. While arguing that existing quota standards would have to be applied, policed and enforced more consistently by member states (possibly under the control of the

ECJ), the Green Paper also avoided suggesting any changes to the existing regime.[11] The Commission's own think-tank on audiovisual policy went much further, proposing a tightening of the quota by particular timeslots, and a redefinition of the term "European work" to force broadcasters to air non-national but European programs. The think tank's report was quietly shelved: although published, it prominently bore the disclaimer that it did not reflect the position of the European Commission.[12]

This was caution taken to the point of inaction, and was not what France had sought. The French proposal to the Commission prior to the publication of the Green Paper called for striking the "where practicable" language of the Directive and for a 50 per cent quota on new technologies. (A "fallback position" proposed forcing broadcasters airing non-European works to spend 10 per cent of revenues on European production or 30 per cent of budget on acquiring European programs.)[13] France hoped to push this agenda as the EU moved forward to a new audiovisual directive. Nevertheless, as EU culture ministers met in Athens in April 1994 to launch the revision process, France had still made no headway with the German, British or Dutch governments over either a new quota regime or the granting of rights to governments to block non-complying services from other member-states. Further, with the arrival on the political scene of Silvio Berlusconi, who eventually became his country's prime minister, France was anxious that Italy's traditional support for its position might evaporate.[14]

The United States, doubtless sensing the lack of general support for the French posture, began to adopt a policy that was both moderate and sustainable: opposition to the extension of the quota regime, while toning down calls for its outright abolition. At the same time, the US administration attempted to cool the conflict by downplaying the possibility of sanctions against Europe over telecommunications and audiovisual policy.[15] Jack Valenti, too, spoke of being encouraged by signs of European "compromise" on the quota question. For his part, the culture commissioner Pinheiro spoke of the "common values" of Europe and the US and the prospects for the two to engage together in "a vaster economic prosperity and cultural richness."[16]

In the face of this closing of ranks, France's main hope was to use its forthcoming six-monthly presidency of the EU Council, beginning in January 1995, as a springboard for pushing the audiovisual agenda.[17] The new communications minister, Nicolas Sarkozy, announced that the audiovisual question would be a "priority" of France's presidency.[18] However, before this could happen, a new directive was drafted by Pinheiro's cultural affairs directorate at the Commission. As concerned quotas, the text represented a substantial move towards the French position, as expressed in its pre-Green Paper submission: the "where practicable" language to be eliminated, the definition of European works to be tightened, and any non-European channels specialized in showing films (such as Ted Turner's TNT) to be required to invest in European production at a level "equivalent" to that of the quotas.[19] On the other hand, the draft proposed giving new market entrants five years in which to meet quota requirements and did not seek to expand the quotas to "video-on-demand" services being developed by the telecommunications industry.[20]

Pinheiro's draft caused a huge row within the Commission. He had originally hoped that the text would be adopted in late November;[21] instead its consideration began to be bounced from week to week as internal wrangling continued over the text. The powerful industry commissioner, Martin Bangemann, who helped engineer the 1989 compromise over the Directive, signaled his continued opposition to mandatory quotas. The directorate responsible for the single market said the proposal would deter new entrants, while the consumer policy service of the Commission argued that the measure would eliminate customer choice.[22] With the commissioners deadlocked, the postponements continued.[23]

At the same time, the US continued to emphasize a "new spirit of cooperation." As Pinheiro launched his draft, Jack Valenti of the newly-renamed MPA (the words "of America" having been diplomatically expunged) came to Brussels to announce a \$40,000 grant for training European filmmakers with more such ventures to come. Although worried by Pinheiro's draft, he believed the EU would ultimately take a different approach.[24] The MPA also appeared to have refined its lobbying efforts in Brussels. An internal MPA memorandum leaked to the press by the French producers' association in December revealed, despite hyperbolic editorializing,[25] that Hollywood knew about as much concerning the progress of Pinheiro's draft as had been already revealed in the press. On the other hand, the memo showed that the MPA, both directly and through its member companies, had made worthwhile contacts with several of the Commission directorates implicated in the new Directive.[26]

But even with the American behind-the-scenes pressure, the French side recognized that the biggest obstacle to tougher quotas was institutional pressure within the Commission and political opposition in the EU. These counter-currents appeared to be pushing for the idea of replacing the quotas altogether with a levy on production budgets. In the arcane world of inter-directorate Commission rivalries, the following rationale was advanced for this clearly impossible solution: the proponents of this idea knew it would be so unacceptable to the French that they would block the revised Directive altogether, thereby leaving the status quo intact.[27] However, there was a simpler explanation for the entropy that had overtaken the audiovisual directive. The European Commission was in the throes of changing president: the incomer, Jacques Santer from Luxembourg, had the power to reallocate the commissioners' portfolios. (The outgoing president, Jacques Delors, a Frenchman, was viewed as essentially sympathetic to the French position. It was feared by France that Santer would take a more free-market approach to the audiovisual question, from his closeness to Luxembourg's extensive commercial television interests.) Despite France's efforts, and at the behest of its *bête noire*, Leon Brittan, consideration of the draft directive was postponed until the new Commission was installed, on January 23, 1995.[28] (The reasons for the postponement were almost certainly entirely internal to the

Commission, why is why commissioners reacted with embarrassment to the activities of the US ambassador to the EU, Stuart Eizenstat, who had telephoned several of them on the eve of the meeting to urge the delay. "There are limits," an embarrassed commission official declared.[29]

The tactic of suggesting the suppression of quotas altogether had the effect of undermining France's position. President Mitterrand announced that he was against "going back" on the Directive or the GATT agreement, but not that he supported the tougher new proposals of his country.[30] There was further anxiety when the incoming Commission president described quotas as "artificial" and said he preferred incentives to local production rather than quotas (which he acknowledged nonetheless were likely to be maintained).[31] Even after an avalanche of French fury – not least because Santer had chosen to reveal his innermost thoughts to an American newspaper – Santer stuck to his position, favoring only short term quotas and insisting that they "should not last an eternity."[32]

The quota wrangle was the focus of a two day informal meeting of EU culture ministers in Bordeaux on 13-14 February.[33] But there was no agreement at the meeting and the new EU culture commissioner, Marcelino Oreja, was reduced to telling the European Parliament shortly afterwards that the quota system was "all we've got," although maybe it should be "time-limited."[34] Worse still, France found itself isolated at the Bordeaux meeting, with such traditional supporters as Spain slipping away from the hardline position, and only Greece remaining firm.[35]

France's sense of beleaguerment could only have increased at the conjuncture of two events. First, the bizarre story emerged that the CIA had attempted to bribe French public servants, including a senior official involved in audiovisual policy during the GATT negotiations, by means of wads of FFr 500 notes.[36] It was alleged that the CIA sought details of France's negotiating position on films and entertainment – a position, as had been seen, that was always unbending and at no time unclear to the naked eye. Yet at the same time as this proof of American perfidiousness was being revealed, a second event of equal surprise to the French unfolded in Brussels. Vice President Al Gore met Jacques Santer and declared that "for the moment, we are not against quotas, if they are a means of reinforcing the European audiovisual [sector]."[37]

This declaration returned the US administration to the classic position it had held for almost seventy years: to oppose quotas in principle, but to accept the best deal available. It told the EU that there would be no more GATT-like pitched battles as long as the 1989 Directive was not made tougher: indeed, with the acceptance of quotas, even the threat of other, non-GATT sanctions, muted for more than a year, disappeared. Gore's statement also isolated France even further from its European partners: only French intransigence stood between them and an end to the corroded and poisoned relations with Washington occasioned by the bitter GATT negotiations.

The new EU culture commissioner, Marcelino Oreja, nevertheless hoped to engineer a compromise position. In a new draft Directive, he proposed deletion of the "where practicable" language but a 10-year limit on the lifetime of the quotas.[38] Despite widely-voiced misgivings, the Commission approved this plan, certain in the knowledge that it would face entrenched opposition from the forthcoming Council meeting of culture ministers scheduled for 3-4 June.[39] The new plan meant a short-term tightening of quotas – and stepping over the line drawn by Al Gore after his meeting with Jacques Santer in February. Nonetheless, and despite a little grandstanding from the Speaker of the House of Representatives, Newt Gingrich, the official administration line, according to ambassador Eizenstat, remained that of quiet diplomacy and attempting to influence the direction of the EU's debate.

Further, the problem with the Oreja plan was that it ran directly counter to the majority position of the EU culture ministers at their Bordeaux meeting in February. With support for Oreja's proposal only sure from Greece and Belgium and with a French presidential election looming, France availed of its advantages as EU president, and postponed discussion of the issue.[40] A new meeting was ultimately scheduled for Luxembourg on 21 June but, in the end, France did not attempt to push the measure through.[41] Wishing to avoid an embarrassing defeat, France then pulled the issue off the agenda for the European summit in Cannes at the end of June, the culmination of the country's six-month EU presidency.[42]

In the wake of the Cannes postponement, the next target date for the Council of culture ministers was set for 20 November in Brussels. Spain, as the new EU president, attempted to broker a compromise involving a commission to supervise the implementation of quotas, but this failed to gain support.[43] A follow-up plan produced the inevitable compromise: change nothing, and review the situation again in five years.[44] As in 1989, the prospect of deadlock brought the recognition that a "political agreement" had to be secured.[45]

On 20 November, the Council, meeting in its formation of culture ministers, unanimously agreed the revision of the Directive. The 1989 quota regime was left intact, a "contact committee" was established to monitor the operation of the quotas, and provision was made for the directive to be reviewed after five years by an independent body. Moreover, the quota regime would not be extended to new technology-driven services, such as the Internet or the pay-per-view "video on demand" outlets that were being developed in Europe.[46] The latest French culture minister, Philippe Douste-Blazy, congratulated himself on maintaining the quotas.[47] And Jack Valenti said nothing. He had already declared that the quota and subsidy issues were "for the European Union alone to decide": the MPA would live with them.[48] In a gesture of peace, Valenti had offered training scholarships to young European filmmakers and cash to dub European films for the American market.[49] After eleven-and-a-half-years of bitterness, Europe and Hollywood appeared, finally, to have found, however, wearily, a *modus vivendi*.

However, there were further obstacles to overcome, which lay in new forms of decision making that the EU had recently adopted. The constitutional arrangements for the implementation of a legislative act by the EU changed between 1989 and 1995. Where once the views of the European Parliament could simply be heard and then ignored by the Commission and Council, the Treaty on European Union had shifted the balance of power between the different organs of the EU in the Parliament's direction. Article 128 of the EC treaty, as amended by Maastricht, provided for EU action, *inter alia*, in the audiovisual sector.[50] Article 128 further prescribed the provisions of a procedural clause of the treaty, article 189b, as those to be followed in order to adopt new measures pursuant to the article.

In its turn, article 189b provides that a common position of the Council – such as that adopted on 20 November on the audiovisual directive – must be ratified by Parliament. If Parliament amends the common position, it must be returned to the Council. After the Commission delivers an opinion on the amendments, the Council votes on the amended position: if this is rejected, then the Council and Parliament must convene a Conciliation committee to reconcile the divergent positions. If the Conciliation committee fails to produce an agreed version, the Council may vote on the original text in order to adopt it. In most cases, this is by the qualified majority form of weighted voting used for most EU acts, However, in the case of cultural matters, the Council vote must be unanimous.[51]

It will be recalled that the original Directive avoided framing its goals in cultural terms because these lay outside the enumerated powers of the EC at that time. By 1995, culture was not only within the powers of the post-Maastricht EU, but the audiovisual sector was expressly a cultural domain. If the European Parliament were to amend the common council position on quotas, and a Conciliation committee failed to reconcile the two bodies' different versions, then there would have to be a unanimous vote in Council to bring the Directive into effect. In other words, France would have to support it.

On St. Valentine's Day, 1996, following an "orgy" of lobbying by film stars, companies and trade associations, the European Parliament voted, by 292 votes to 195, to amend the common position agreed on 20 November. One amendment expunged the "where practicable" language, and enjoined member-states, just as the Parliament's thwarted efforts of 1989 had attempted, to enforce the quotas by "legally effective means."[52] The amendment comprehended the new technology-driven services excluded from the common position, and also adopted a narrower definition of "works," thereby tightening the practical effect of the quotas.[53] Jack Lang, now sitting in the Parliament, hailed the vote as "a decisive step in the construction of a true Europe of culture."[54]

However, American reaction to the Parliament's moves remained muted. One week after the vote, Jack Valenti addressed a London meeting on "key issues facing European cinema." He did not mention quotas at all.[55] On 19 March, ambassador Eizenstat appeared before the United States Senate Banking, Housing and Urban Affairs Committee at a hearing on his confirmation as under-secretary of commerce for international trade. Eizenstat's prepared statement of nearly 5,000 words both reviewed his activities as US ambassador to the EU and outlined the program he would pursue if confirmed. Just 28 words were devoted to the quota issue. US policy, Eisenstat said, was aimed at "preventing any further tightening of the EU Broadcasting Directive" and "indeed, working to eliminate [the quotas] over time."[56]

Coincidentally, the French authorities were discovering the difficulties of policing the stricter form of quotas they had themselves adopted. On 13 February, one day before the parliamentary vote, the French television regulator, the CSA, ordered France's leading television network, TF1, to invest FFr 45 million (around $9 million) in European production for persistent breach of the quotas.[57] It was the third successive year in which TF1 had failed to meet its quota of European works broadcast by the network. In 1993, TF1 fell short of its target by 238 hours; the CSA required it to pay FFr 18 million. In 1994, the deficit had fallen to 87 hours; the compensatory payment was cut, slightly, to FFr 15.5 million. The 1995 shortfall was lower still, at 65 hours, or one-and-a-quarter hours of prime time programming per week.[58] Although the sanction was substantial, it reflected the realities of the situation. Four of the nine members of the CSA had called for TF1 to be fined directly, rather than merely be required to invest in programming. But a slim majority, including the CSA's chairman, Hervé Bourges, preferred a negotiated agreement with the miscreant network. The problem, according to TF1's vice-chairman, Etienne Mougeotte, was not that the company could not meet its quota for *French* works, but that it could not find enough good quality non-French *European* programs to fill its schedules. "Between a German series and an American series, it's always the latter that will be chosen," Mougeotte admitted.[59] (Five months later, the CSA would renew TF1's broadcasting license for a further five years.)[60]

In the international field, however, France continued to push for stricter quotas. At a meeting of European culture ministers in Bologna on 23-24 April, France, supported by Belgium, made an additional demand that the revised directive should include language preventing television services from relocating to other countries to avoid stricter quota regimes in their home state. Its efforts to tighten quotas beyond the 20 November common position were unavailing, however. Recognizing the danger of unraveling the common position, the culture commissioner, Marcelino Oreja, described the November compromise as one that had so weakened the directive that "a puff of wind could bring it down."[61]

As required by article 189b, the Commission produced its final position on the revised Directive, agreeing to just one of the Parliament's technical amendments, on the definition of a television program as "an animated sequence of images with or without sound."[62] On 7 May, claiming a "serious constitutional breach," Luciana Castellina, chairwoman of the European Parliament's Culture Committee, complained to Oreja that the Commission had openly encouraged the Council to ignore the Parliament's opinion which had been treated as "a mere formality," and not as "an integral part of the decision-making procedure."

The reality was that the split among the member states was such as to make any departure from the November compromise impossible. At the same time as France tried to tighten the quotas, countries such as Germany and the United Kingdom reiterated their desire to abandon them altogether. Initially, the Italy, as president of the EU, sought to delay a Council vote at the scheduled June meeting in Luxembourg.[63] The new Italian government of Romano Prodi was less sympathetic than its predecessors to arguments against the quotas and was anxious to avoid a row with the Parliament, and, with Luciana Castellina, an Italian.[64] However, Italy also shared the exhaustion of its European colleagues. "We want to move on," its minister for posts and telecommunications, Antonio Maccanico, told the Council. "I say take it or leave it."[65] In the end, Italy decided to put the Directive on the agenda, and on 11 June the Council voted unanimously to adopt the November text of the new Directive and thereby override the Parliament's objectives.[66] The unanimous vote of the Council meant that, in order to create a Conciliation committee composed of Parliament and Council representatives that would work on a new joint draft of the Directive,[67] an absolute majority of the Parliament's members — 314 — would have to vote in favor. In the end, the vote in Parliament produced a healthy tally of 291 to 170 in favor of making the quotas tougher, but an insufficient majority to force the creation of the Conciliation committee.

The new Directive was not finally adopted by the Parliament and Council until 30 June, 1997, as the two bodies hammered out differences over sporting events and the protection of minors.[68] But the quota issue was finally over. Only Jack Lang, whose Mexico City speech nearly 15 years earlier had lit the fuse of the entire debate, kept blasting to the very end, irresistibly reminiscent of Monty Python's Black Knight. "Washington can be reassured," he declared after the Parliament's vote, "[that] the majority of Europeans lie down when America tells them to."[69]

The impact of the Directive

But did the Directive work? That is, did it succeed in its aim of stemming the tide of American programs flowing into Europe? After all, the revised Directive merely retained the status quo; the quotas, over which so much time has been spent, are sill there. The question is hard to answer, since it requires proving a negative. One approach would be to assess the extent to which the quotas were breached, and, perhaps more significantly, where the outer limits of the quotas were skirted by those who stayed within the law. The closer broadcasters got to the 50 per cent threshold, the more likely it was that they would have desired to cross it had not the Directive, as implemented by their local laws, prevented them. Fortunately, the Directive provided for EU members-states to report every two years on the achievement of the television quotas in their countries.[70]

We have already seen that European broadcasters programmed a majority of European works before the quotas were implemented. According to the data gathered by the European Commission from member-states, this is what the European television landscape looked like after three years of compliance with the Directive:

Table 10: National Compliance with Article 4 of the EC's *Television Without Frontiers* Directive, 1992[71]

Country	Station	Owner	% European works
Belgium			
	BRTN(TV1)	Public	64.1
	BRTN(TV2)	Public	92.3
	Canal + TVCF	**Private**	**41.6**
	Filmnet Plus	**Private**	**24.3**
	RTBF1	Public	68.0
	RTL-TVi	Private	52.4
	Tele 21	Public	95.0
	VTM	**Private**	**38.1**
Denmark			
	Danmark Radio	Public	79.0
	TV2/Danmark	Private	53.0
Germany			
	3-SAT	Public	92.0
	ARD	Public	90.1
	Eins Plus	Public	91.5
	Premiere	Private	50.0
	PRO-7	**Private**	**34.1**
	RTL	**Private**	**49.0**
	SAT-1	Private	53.4
	ZDF	Public	80.9
Greece			
	Antena	Private	61.9
	ET1	Public	76.7
	ET2	Public	65.7
	ET3	Public	82.3
	Mega	Private	52.5
	New Channel	**Private**	**40.3**
Spain			
	Antena-3	Private	52.0
	Canal Plus	**Private**	**44.0**
	Canal Sur Andalucia	Public	68.0
	Canal-33	Public	89.0
	Canal-9	**Private**	**48.0**
	EITB-1	Public	73.0
	EITB-2	Public	69.0
	Tele-5	**Private**	**47.0**
	TeleMadrid	**Private**	**49.8**
	TV-3	**Private**	**49.0**
	TVE-1	Public	59.0
	TVE-2	Public	67.0
	TVGalicia	Public	57.0
France			
	Canal +	Private	57.9
	Canal J	Private	53.0
	Canal Jimmy	**Private**	**46.0**
	Ciné-Cinéfil	Private	53.0

	Ciné-Cinémas	Private	53.0
	FR2	Public	74.8
	FR3	Public	76.9
	M6	Private	63.2
	MCM/Euromusique	Private	58.0
	Planète	Private	77.0
	TF1	Private	66.0
Ireland			
	RTE-1 & Network 2	Public	75.0
Italy			
	Beta-TV	Private	60.0
	Canale 5	Private	72.0
	Italia-1	**Private**	**39.8**
	RAI-1	Public	73.0
	RAI-2	Public	61.0
	RAI-3	Public	67.0
	Rete-4	**Private**	**39.5**
	Tele+1	**Private**	**31.7**
	Tele+2	Private	98.2
	Tele+3	Private	73.0
	TeleMontecarlo	**Private**	**40.3**
Luxembourg			
	RTL 4	**Private**	**39.7**
	RTL HeiElei	Private	98.0
	RTL Télé	**Private**	**48.0**
	RTL TV	**Private**	**46.2**
	RTL TVi	**Private**	**41.3**
Netherlands			
	NED.1	Public	74.0
	NED.2	Public	65.0
	NED.3	Public	89.0
Portugal			
	Canal 1	Public	52.0
	Canal 2	Public	62.0
United Kingdom			
	Adult Channel	**Private**	**49.7**
	Arts Channel	Private	67.0
	Asia Vision	**Private**	**4.3**
	BBC World Service TV	Public	99.8
	BBC-1	Public	71.5
	BBC-2	Public	70.0
	Bravo	**Private**	**29.2**
	Channel 4	Private	67.3
	Channel Guide	Private	100.0
	Children's Channel	Private	52.8
	China News Europe	**Private**	**0.0**
	Discovery Channel	Private	51.3
	HVC	**Private**	**24.9**
	ITV	Private	65.4
	Japan Satellite TV	**Private**	**0.0**
	Kindernet	Private	60.3

Landscape Channel	Private	100.0
Learning Channel	Private	98.3
Mid. E. B'dcasting Ctr.	**Private**	**25.9**
Movie Channel	**Private**	**16.4**
MTV Europe	Private	84.3
Muslim TV Ahmadiyya	**Private**	**0.0**
Parliamentary Channel	Private	100.0
Quantum TV	**Private**	**0.0**
Regal Shop	**Private**	**13.3**
Sky Movies +	**Private**	**13.7**
Sky Movies Gold	**Private**	**19.1**
Sky News	Private	64.3
Sky One	**Private**	**8.5**
Sky Sports	Private	65.2
Super Channel	Private	70.9
Supershop Limited	**Private**	**0.0**
The Box	Private	62.0
TV 1000	**Private**	**22.9**
TV Asia	**Private**	**19.4**
TV3 B'dcasting Denmark	**Private**	**15.6**
TV3 B'dcasting Norway	**Private**	**23.4**
TV3 B'dcasting Sweden	**Private**	**24.8**
UK Gold	Private	63.3
Vision	**Private**	**27.8**

There were some minor methodological problems in the survey. For instance, Belgium and Luxembourg both reported on the same service, RTL-TVi, which is Luxembourg-owned but established in Belgium. According to one survey, the station complied with the directive; the other said it did not.

Nevertheless, some conclusions can be drawn from the Commission's data. Compliance, of course, is a slippery word, given that an apparently non-complying country might plead the "wherever practicable" language of the Directive to explain an apparent failure to meet its terms. However, of 110 services surveyed, 70 (63.6 per cent) were in compliance with the Directive. All 33 public broadcasters complied, as well as 37 private broadcasters. Virtually all the major private networks in Europe met their quota obligations.

Of the 40 stations that did not comply, eight were pay-television companies broadcasting new feature films, European origin versions of which are in short supply. A further seven were services broadcasting in non-European languages such as Japanese and Arabic. The remainder were generally new services that had yet to reach the point where they could afford to invest in production.

While these statistics show general compliance, they also point to wide differences in the way different states implemented the Directive. In Luxembourg, for instance, where most of the listed stations are cross-border broadcasters, relying for income on audiences in neighboring countries, compliance was in the range of 40 per cent European works rather than the mandated 50 per cent. In the UK, used as base for a large number of satellite channels beamed to other parts of Europe, compliance was very low – except for the national broadcasters who reach the preponderance of the population.

By contrast, where the local quota regime was strict, as in France, compliance was very high, with the national broadcasters all showing substantial amounts of European programming, and nearly all the cable services also providing a majority of European works.

A second report, covering the years 1993 and 1994,[72] painted the same picture, demonstrating that some 91 out of 148 broadcasters (61.5 per cent) complied with the quotas, including "the bulk of mainstream terrestrial broadcasters with high audience ratings."[73] Moreover, as before, "the channels which did not manage to achieve the majority requirement were for the most part recently launched and/or satellite channels with limited audience share."[74]

A third report, published in 1998, covered the years 1995 and 1996 and provided an assessment of the six years of operation of the Directive from 1991-1996.[75] The results were as follows:

Table 11: National Compliance with Article 4 of the EC's *Television Without Frontiers* Directive, 1995-96[76]

Country	Station	Owner	% European works 1995	1996
Belgium				
	BRTN(TV1)	Public	64.3	64.1
	BRTN(TV2)	Public	69.7	65.5
	Canal + TVCF	**Private**	**42.5**	**52.4**
	Club RTL	**Private**	**29.1**	**30.7**
	Filmnet 1	**Private**	**34.0**	**25.0**
	Filmnet 2	**Private**	**34.0**	**25.0**
	Kanaal 2	**Private**	**n/a**	**23**
	RTBF1	Public	74.0	80.0
	RTL-TVi	**Private**	**45.6**	**43.7**
	Supersport	Private	74.0	75.0
	Tele 21	Public	91.0	71.0
	VTM	**Private**	**48.0**	**62.0**
Denmark				
	DK4	Private	100.0	100.0
	DR1	Public	77.0	79.0
	DR2	Public	n/a	76.0
	Erotica	**Private**	**n/a**	**11.0**
	TV Bio	**Private**	**n/a**	**32.0**
	TV2	Private	61.0	65.0
Germany				
	3-SAT	Public	90.3	90.3
	ARD	Public	90.3	90.3

	Deutsche Welle TV	Public	95.0	96.0
	DSF	Private	86.0	87.0
	Kabel 1	**Private**	**24.6**	**31.3**
	Onyx Music Television	Private	n/a	n/a
	Premiere	**Private**	**35.1**	**31.2**
	PRO-7	Private	45.8	47.0
	RTL	Private	54.0	59.0
	RTL-2	**Private**	**31.0**	**32.0**
	SAT-1	Private	65.0	63.0
	Super RTL	**Private**	**26.5**	**29.8**
	TM3	Private	64.0	63.0
	VH-1	Private	n/a	n/a
	VIVA	Private	70.0	70.0
	VIVA-2	**Private**	**40.0**	**40.0**
	VOX	**Private**	**15.9**	**31.5**
	WRTV	Private	n/a	99.0
	ZDF	Public	85.1	79.3
Greece				
	Antena 1	Private	70.3	76.0
	ET1	Public	86.0	85.0
	ET2	Public	57.2	56.9
	ET3	Public	60.8	61.7
	Mega	Private	56.0	61.0
	New Channel	Private	53.3	53.5
	Seven X	Private	71.0	65.0
	Skai 100.4	Private	53.0	52.5
	TV Makedonia	Private	93.0	95.0
	Aristera Sta FM 902 TV	Private	n/a	53.0
	Kanali 5	Private	n/a	n/a
Spain				
	Antena-3	**Private**	**43.0**	**42.0**
	Canal Plus	**Private**	**39.0**	**40.0**
	CST	Public	61.0	62.0
	ETB-1	Public	81.0	78.0
	ETB-2	Public	55.0	51.0
	Tele-5	**Private**	**33.0**	**38.0**
	TV-3	Private	66.0	65.0
	TV-33	Public	79.0	79.0
	TVAM	Private	52.0	53.0
	TVE-1	Public	58.0	50.0
	TVE-2	Public	77.0	76.0
	TVG	Public	72.0	75.0
	TVV	Public	58.0	53.0
	France Arte	Public	85.6	84.1
	Canal +	Private	58.2	65.0
	Canal J	Private	63.7	72.0
	Canal Jimmy	Private	53.6	52.0
	Ciné-Cinéfil	Private	60.0	61.5
	Ciné-Cinémas	Private	52.6	54.3
	France 2	Public	77.9	79.6
	France 3	Public	69.8	67.9

	La Cinquième	Public	88.2	83.9
	M6	Private	66.1	63.5
	MCM/Euromusique	Private	85.3	86.7
	Muzzik	Private	n/a	95.7
	Paris Première	Private	91.0	95.0
	Planète	Private	80.0	80.0
	Série Club	Private	55.0	55.5
	TF1	Private	64.2	66.8
	TMC	Private	56.6	61.6
	Voyage	Private	n/a	70.6
Ireland				
	RTE-1 & Network 2	Public	76.0	88.0
Italy				
	Canale 5	Private	76.2	75.5
	Italia-1	**Private**	**43.2**	**38.8**
	RAI-1	Public	75.1	70.0
	RAI-2	Public	63.1	61.9
	RAI-3	Public	79.7	75.6
	Rete Mia	Private	n/a	n/a
	Rete-4	**Private**	**37.3**	**40.9**
	TBS Rete	Private	n/a	n/a
	Telepiù 1	**Private**	**34.8**	**35.0**
	Telepiù 2	Private	100.0	100.0
	Telepiù 3	Private	83.3	96.2
	TMC	Private	n/a	n/a
	TMC 2	Private	n/a	n/a
Luxembourg				
	Club RTL	Private	29.05	30.7
	RTL 4	Private	48.1	52.5
	RTL 5	**Private**	**33.6**	**29.3**
	RTL 7	**Private**	**n/a**	**39.2**
	RTL 9	Private	52.5	58.9
	RTL Télé Lëtzebuerg (HeiElei)	Private	100.0	100.0
	RTL Television	Private	54.1	59.51
	RTL TVI	**Private**	**45.6**	**43.7**
Netherlands				
	NED.1	Public	67.0	73.0
	NED.2	Public	77.0	85.7
	NED.3	Public	78.0	82.5
	TV 10	Private	45.0	48.0
	Veronica	Private	37.6	70.9
	SBS 6	**Private**	**30.9**	**0.7**
	Canal +	**Private**	**15.0**	**18.0**
	Music Factory	Private	> 50.0	> 50.0
	The Box	Private	± 70.0	± 70.0
Austria				
	ORF 1	**Public**	**48.4**	**40.8**
	ORF 2	Public	85.1	79.6
Portugal				
	Canal 1	Public	45.7	55.1
	TV 2	Public	70.9	62.4

	RTP I	Public	99.4	99.9
	SIC	**Private**	**30.7**	**37.9**
	TVI	**Private**	**21.6**	**23.8**
Sweden				
	[Sveriges Utbildnings-radio AB][77]	n/a	96.0	99.0
	FilmNet Plus	**Private**	**10.0**	**11.0**
	FilmNet the Complete			
	Movie Channel	**Private**	**10.0**	**11.0**
	SVT 1	Public	80.0	82.0
	SVT 2	Public	90.0	86.0
	The Adult Channel	Private	n/a	n/a
	TV 1000	**Private**	**35.0**	**32.5**
	TV 1000 Cinema	**Private**	**35.0**	**20.5**
	TV 4	**Private**	**43.0**	**50.0**
	TV 6	**Private**	**47.0**	**50.0**
	Z TV	Private	79.0	80.0
Finland				
	MTV 3	Private	57.0	57.0
	TV 1	Public	84.0	81.0
	TV 2	Public	85.0	76.0
United Kingdom				
	3+	**Private**	**n/a**	**24.0**
	Adult Channel	**Private**	**38.0**	**38.0**
	Ag Vision	Private	100.0	100.0
	Asianet	**Private**	**10.0**	**7.0**
	BBC Prime	Public	100.0	100.0
	BBC World	Public	97.0	98.0
	BBC-1	Public	68.0	67.0
	BBC-2	Public	72.0	73.0
	Box Music TV	Private	66.0	67.0
	Bravo	**Private**	**54.0**	**47.0**
	Carlton Food Network	Private	n/a	83.0
	Carlton Select	**Private**	**15.0**	**20.0**
	Cartoon Network	**Private**	**15.0**	**20.0**
	Challenge TV	**Private**	**25.0**	**36.0**
	Channel 4	Private	57.0	57.0
	Chinese Channel	**Private**	**4.0**	**5.0**
	Chinese News & Entertainment	**Private**	**1.0**	**2.0**
	Christian Channel	**Private**	**n/a**	**24.0**
	CNBC	Private	n/a	54.0
	Cultural Television	Private	100.0	100.0
	Discovery Channel	Private	55.0	55.0
	Disney Channel UK	**Private**	**19.0**	**19.0**
	EBN	Private	90.0	80.0
	Fox Kids	**Private**	**n/a**	**19.0**
	GSB Goodlife TV	Private	n/a	85.0
	GSB Men + Motors	Private	n/a	85.0
	GSB Plus	Private	n/a	100.0
	GSB Talk TV	Private	n/a	59.0
	Het Weer Channel	Private	n/a	100.0
	History Channel	**Private**	**14.0**	**21.0**

Home Video Channel	Private	**14.0**	**21.0**
ITV	Private	71.0	70.0
JSTV	Private	**0.0**	**0.0**
Kanal 5	Private	**n/a**	**15.0**
Kindernet CV	Private	90.0	77.0
Landmark Travel Channel	Private	**39.0**	**47.0**
Landscape Channel	Private	100.0	100.0
Live TV	Private	86.0	86.0
MBC Ltd	Private	**14.0**	**23.0**
MED TV	Private	99.0	78.0
Movie Channel	Private	**18.0**	**17.0**
MTV Central	Private	80.0	83.0
MTV North	Private	80.0	83.0
MTV South	Private	80.0	83.0
Muslim TV Ahmadiyyah	Private	94.0	81.0
Namaste TV	Private	**8.0**	**13.0**
NBC	Private	46.0	58.0
Nickelodeon	Private	**27.0**	**25.0**
Paramount Comedy Channel	Private	**1.0**	**7.0**
Parliamentary Channel	Private	100.0	95.0
Performance – The Arts Channel	Private	70.0	73.0
Playboy TV	Private	**n/a**	**6.0**
S4C	Private	100.0	100.0
Sat-7	Private	**25.0**	**25.0**
Sci-Fi Europe	Private	**2.0**	**8.0**
Sky 2	Private	**0.0**	**27.0**
Sky Movies	Private	**25.0**	**13.0**
Sky Movies Gold	Private	**27.0**	**20.0**
Sky One	Private	33.0	38.0
Sky Scottish	Private	**n/a**	**25.0**
Sky Soap	Private	**4.0**	**7.0**
Sky Travel Channel	Private	**23.0**	**32.0**
Step-Up	Private	100.0	100.0
TCC	Private	**21.0**	**22.0**
TCC Nordic	Private	**n/a**	**21.0**
Television X	Private	**47.0**	**47.0**
TLC	Private	67.0	50.0
TNT	Private	**22.0**	**33.0**
TV 1000 Sverige	Private	**36.0**	**32.0**
TV3 Denmark	Private	**36.0**	**54.0**
TV3 Norway	Private	**34.0**	**47.0**
TV3 Sweden	Private	**41.0**	**55.0**
UK Gold	Private	54.0	51.0
Vision Channel	Private	**39.0**	**49.0**

This third report permits some broad conclusions to be drawn about the effect of the quota laws. By 1996, of 214 channels surveyed. some 72, or 66.4 per cent, were in compliance with the Directive. While the compliant proportion is not very different from the nearly 64 per cent complying in 1992, the overall survey strongly suggests that the quotas did not contribute greatly to the portion of

European works broadcast. By and large, the non-complying broadcasters fell into three categories: pay-television services; new channels and specialist broadcasters. In Germany, France, Spain, Italy and the United Kingdom – the principal European markets – the major public and private terrestrial broadcasters reaching the highest audiences all complied. There was scant evidence of "skirting" the 50 per cent mark to obtain minimal compliance: just 21 stations, or less than one-tenth, were clustered in the 47-53 per cent range and of these just one was a significant terrestrial broadcaster, RTE-1 of Spain. Of the big for-profit broadcasters, RTL of Germany showed 59 per cent European works in 1996, TF1 of France had 66.8 per cent, ITV of Britain 70 per cent and Canale 5 of Italy 75.5 per cent. This is much more than token compliance, and suggests that these networks in highly competitive markets carried substantial amounts of European programming because they wanted to, not because they had to.

The compliance level is also notable because of the growth in the number of channels surveyed, up from 110 in 1992 to 214 in 1996. Of this additional 104 channels, 16 were added as a result of the accession of Austria, Finland and Sweden to the EU; the remaining 88 were from the 12 EU nations surveyed in 1992, representing a rise of 80 per cent in the number of channels. As discussed previously, one would expect a proliferation of channels to create greater demand for cheaper foreign programs. Certainly, judging from the non-complying broadcasters, it appears that the new entrants, as would be expected, looked outside Europe for a substantial part of their schedules. However, as noted above, the percentage of complying channels rose slightly, even in this period of considerable expansion. This means that the existing channels, also as could be predicted, increased their use of European programming as a function of market demand and competition. The viewers voted. They turned out to be good Europeans, after all.

1   This is a thumbnail account of a lengthy and complicated story. For greater detail, see generally Chamard & Kieffer, *La Télé: Dix ans d'histoires sécrètes* (1992). Paris, Flammarion.

2   "Les États-Unis menacent l'Europe de sanctions," *Le Monde* (Jan. 14, 1994), 14.

3   "Les États-Unis menacent l'Europe," 14.

4   Alain Carignon, "L'Europe n'a pas de temps à perdre," *Le Monde* (Jan. 18, 1994) 20.

5   Yves Mamou, "M. Carignon mobilise les professions de l'audiovisuel pour les prochaines échéances européennes," *Le Monde* (Jan. 21, 1994), 11.

6   Alain Woodrow, "Jack Valenti: 'La concurrence stimule la qualité,'" *Le Monde* (Feb. 15, 1994), 9.

7   Claudine Mulard, "La Commission européenne veut rassurer les producteurs indépendants de Hollywood," *Le Monde* (Mar. 8, 1994), 21.

8   Michel Colonna d'Istria & Yves Mamou, "Paramount Viacom International veut développer une 'stratégie de contenu,'" *Le Monde* (Mar. 17, 1994), 15.

9   *Strategy options to strengthen the European programme industry in the context of the audiovisual policy of the European Union*, COM(94) 96 final, § 4.3.1.

10 Yves Mamou, "Trois pays ne respectent pas la directive 'Télévision sans frontières,'" *Le Monde* (Jul. 9, 1994), 17.

11 *Strategy options*, § 5.1.2.

12 *Report by the Think-Tank on the Audiovisual Policy in the European Union* (1994) 37-39.

13 Yves Mamou, "La France propose des solutions alternatives aux quotas de diffusion," *Le Monde* (Mar. 19, 1994), 17.

14 Yves Mamou, "La réforme du cadre réglémentaire de l'audiovisuel en Europe est lancée," *Le Monde* (Apr. 23, 1994), 26.

15 Guy de Jonquières & Lionel Barber, "Super 301 is not for you, EU told," *Fin. Times* (Mar. 22, 1994), 4.

16 "Jack Valenti encouragé par les signes de compromis de l'Europe," *Le Monde* (Jun. 20, 1994).

17 The presidency of the Council is taken for six months by each member-state in rotation. The president takes the initiative to call meetings and set their provisional agendas. Boulouis, *Droit Institutionnel*, 87.

18 Yves Mamou, "Nicolas Sarkozy se dit determiné à règler tous les dossiers en suspens," *Le Monde* (Oct. 7, 1994), 14. France's efforts may have been blunted somewhat by the resignation of Alain Carignon on July 17. "Alain Carignon demissionne du gouvernement," *Le Monde* (Jul. 19, 1994). Carignon was convicted of corruption in November 1995. Maurice Peyrot, "Alain Carignon a été reconnu coupable de corruption." *Le Monde* (Nov. 18, 1995).

19 Yves Mamou, "'Télévision sans frontières' va être soumise à la Commission européenne" *Le Monde* (Nov. 17, 1994).

20 Suzanne Perry, "Draft legislation would tighten EU television quotas," Reuter (Oct. 26, 1994), available in LEXIS, News library, Reuec file.

21 Suzanne Perry, "DGX close to proposing 'Television Without Frontiers' changes," Reuter (Oct. 24, 1994), available in LEXIS, News library, Reuec file.

22 Suzanne Perry, "'TV Without Frontiers' proposals facing rocky road," Reuter (Nov. 28, 1994), available in LEXIS, News library, Reuec file.

23 Suzanne Perry, "Debate over European TV quotas delayed," Reuter (Dec. 12, 1994), available in LEXIS, News library, Reuec file.

24 Suzanne Perry, "Hollywood to help European filmmakers," Reuter (Nov. 3, 1994), available in LEXIS, News library, Reuec file.

25 "[T]hat confidential documents should leave the Commission and benefit American industry to the detriment of European industry calls into question the patriotism of certain European officials." "Nous contrôlons la situation de près," *Le Monde* (Dec. 29, 1994).

26 "Nous contrôlons la situation de près."

27 Yves Mamou, "MM. Sarkozy et Toubon demandent à Bruxelles le maintien des quotas de diffusion," *Le Monde* (Jan. 2, 1995).

28 Philippe Lemaitre, "L'examen de la directive 'Télévision sans frontières' par la Commission de Bruxelles est reporté au 23 janvier," *Le Monde* (Jan. 11, 1995).

29 Tom Buerkle, "UK Blocks Paris-Led Bid To Tighten TV Quotas," *Int'l Herald Tribune* (Jan. 5, 1995), available in LEXIS, News library, IHT file.

30 "M. Mitterrand affirme son opposition à un abandon des quotas de diffusion," Agence France Presse (Jan. 17, 1995) available in LEXIS, Presse library, AFP file.

31 Tom Buerkle, "EU's Leader Argues for Innovation, Not Quotas," *Int'l Herald Tribune* (Jan. 27, 1995), available in LEXIS, News library, IHT file.

32 "Nouvelles explications de M. Santer sur les quotas de diffusion," *Le Monde* (Feb. 6, 1995).

33 Pascal Bourdon, "Les quotas audiovisuels au centre d'une réunion des ministres de la Culture," Agence France Presse, Feb. 11, 1995, available in LEXIS, News library, AFP file.

34 "EU Eyes Quota Revision," *Daily Variety* (Feb. 17, 1995) available in LEXIS, News library, Dlyvrty file.

35 "La France de plus en plus isolée sur les quotas audiovisuels," *Le Monde*, (Feb. 16, 1995) 1.

36 Craig R. Whitney, "5 Americans Are Called Spies By France and Told to Leave," *N.Y. Times* (Feb. 23, 1995), A1.

37 Christian Spillmann, "Européens et Américains évitent toute polemique à Bruxelles," Agence France Presse (Feb. 25, 1995) available in LEXIS, Presse library, AFP file.

38 Janet McEvoy, "EU heads for tougher limits on Hollywood," Reuter (Mar. 21, 1995), available in LEXIS, News library, Reuec file.

39 Janet McEvoy, "Television plan already in trouble," Reuter (Mar. 22, 1995), available in LEXIS, News library, Reuec file.

40 Janet McEvoy, "Council postpones debate on TV directive," Reuter (Apr. 3, 1995), available in LEXIS, News library, Reuec file.

41 Janet McEvoy, "France still wants tougher TV import quotas," Reuter (Jun. 21, 1995), available in LEXIS, News library, Reuec file.

42 "France drops TV quotas drive from Cannes summit," Reuter (Jun. 23, 1995), available in LEXIS, News library, Reuec file.

43 "Spanish TV plan fails to fly," Reuter (Oct. 31, 1995), available in LEXIS, News library, Reuec file.

44 "EU members states cautious, not negative, on TV plan," Reuter (Nov. 9, 1995), available in LEXIS, News library, Reuec file.

45 "COPREPER clears TV Without Frontiers changes," Reuter (Nov. 15, 1995), available in LEXIS, News library, Reuec file.

46 Janet McEvoy, "Council agrees on television directive," Reuter, Nov. 20, 1995, available in LEXIS, News library, Reuec file.

47 "Maintien de la directive européenne 'Télévision sans frontières,'" *Le Monde* (Nov. 22, 1995).

48 "Une lettre de Jack Valenti," *Le Monde* (Nov. 10, 1995).

49 Janet McEvoy, "EU enters exciting week for Hollywood, EU film sector," Reuter (Nov. 10, 1995), available *in* LEXIS, News library, Reuec file.

50 *Basic Community Laws*, 93.

51 EC Treaty Art. 128.5.

52 Janet McEvoy, "Parliament calls for more television restrictions," Reuter (Feb. 14, 1996), available in LEXIS, News library, Reuec file.

53 "Broadcasting: Overwhelming Backing from Euro-MPS for TV Quotas," European Information Service, *Monthly Report on Europe* No. 137 (March 1, 1996), available in LEXIS.

54 Marcel Scotto, "L'UE renforce la directive 'Télévision sans frontières,'" *Le Monde* (Feb. 16, 1996).

55 In fact, in his absence owing to illness, Valenti's speech was read by another MPA official. "Remarks by MPA's Valenti on issues facing European cinema," Reuter (Feb. 22, 1996), available in LEXIS, News library, Reuec file.

56 Federal News Service (March 19, 1996), available in LEXIS-NEXIS.

57 Guy Dutheil & Yves Mamou, "Le CSA impose à TF1 une non-amende de 45 millions de francs," *Le Monde* (Feb. 21, 1996).

58 "Trois manquements successifs," *Le Monde* (Feb. 21, 1996).

59 "Le CSA impose à TF1 ..."

60 Yves Mamou, "Le CSA renouvelle les conventions de TF 1 et M 6," *Le Monde* (Aug. 1, 1996).

61 "Culture/Audiovisual Council: EU Ministers Dig In On TV Quotas Directive," *European Report* No. 2127 (April 27, 1996), available in LEXIS.

62 COM (96) 200. See also Janet McEvoy, "Council Seeking Television Accord on June 11," Reuter European Community Report (May 14, 1996).

63 Janet McEvoy, "TV Without Frontiers – a Battle for Influence," Reuter (June 3, 1996), available in LEXIS.

64 "Broadcasting: Council Embraces Commission Plan for Television Quotas," *European Report* (June 15, 1996), available in LEXIS.

65 Tom Buerkle, "EU Ministers Extend Accord On Nonbinding TV Quotas," *Int'l Herald Tribune* (June 12, 1996), available in LEXIS.

66 "Les ministres européens de la culture s'accordent sur les quotas à la télévision," *Le Monde* (June 13, 1996).

67 As provided by Article 189b of the EC treaty.

68 *Directive 97/36/EC of the European Parliament and of the Council of 30 June 1997, amending Council Directive 89/552/EEC on the coordination of certain provisions laid down by law, regulation or administrative action in Member States concerning the pursuit of television broadcasting activities.* O.J. No. L. 202 (Jul. 30, 1997). The remaining issues were resolved through the conciliation procedure by the end of April, 1997. "EP Background Note on Television Without Frontiers Directive," Reuters (May 5, 1997), available in LEXIS.

69 Tom Buerkle, "One EU Storm Calms, a 2d brews; Parliament Calls Truce In Fight With Hollywood," *Int'l Herald Tribune* (Nov. 13, 1996), available in LEXIS.

70 *Council Directive 89/552/EEC,* art. 4.3.

71 Adapted from *Communication from the Commission to the Council and the European Parliament on the application of Articles 4 and 5 of Directive 89/552/EEC Television without frontiers,* COM(94)57 final at 29-46. Entries in bold type indicate services that failed to broadcast a majority of European works, as required by Article 4, in 1992. I have supplied the ownership designation "public" or "private," as appropriate. Names of channels are given as they figure in the report, and may not correspond to actual usage by the channels themselves.

72 *Second Commission Report to the Council and Parliament on the implementation of Articles 4 and 5 of Directive 89/552/EEC "Television without frontiers",* COM(96)302 final.

73 Bull. EU 7/8 1996, point 1.3.246.

74 Bull. EU 7/8 1996, point 1.3.246.

75   *Third Communication from the Commission to the Council and the European Parliament on the application of Articles 4 and 5 of Directive 89/552/EEC "Television without frontiers"*, COM(98)199 final.

76   Adapted from *Third Communication from the Commission to the Council and the European Parliament on the application of Articles 4 and 5 of Directive 89/552/EEC "Television without frontiers"*, COM(98)199 final. Entries in bold type indicate services that failed to broadcast a majority of European works, in 1995 or 1996 or both.

77   The report entry does not name the channel, but identifies its owner.

5

Conclusions:
culture as a policy issue

The information that quotas were both ineffective per se and produced a result that would arrive without any regulation at all, though available long before the EU's three surveys, was almost entirely ignored during the EC's quota debate. The reasons are several. To begin with, it suited neither side's case. While Europe was not actually being threatened by an avalanche of American programming, Hollywood could no longer recite its traditional claim that it was being shut out of European markets. In fact, following the explosion of European television channels in the 1980s, Hollywood was almost drowning in the new cash flowing westward. Further, the European reaction to sudden and barely-controllable change in the audiovisual landscape had traditionally been to blame Hollywood and then seek to punish it. As with Galileo's telescope, it was easier to reiterate received wisdom than actually to look at the facts.

Another factor was Hollywood's influence on American foreign policy. Between the 1920s and 1940s, the MPPDA and its successors worked closely with successive US administrations in forming trade policy with respect to Hollywood's access to foreign markets. From the late 1940s onwards, it was the MPEA that occupied the front seat. Indeed, as the quota issue appeared to recede in the 1960s, the MPEA's role in dealing with foreign government policies – as opposed to the general questions of its members' commercial interests overseas – became much less pronounced. Although the MPAA continued to be a strong force in Washington on issues of domestic policy concerning the film industry, its foreign cutting edge appears to have been blunted by the years of relative peace internationally. Further, the one other big international policy issue that concerned the MPAA in the 1980s – intellectual property protection and the war against piracy – was shared by other powerful sectors, including the defense, high-technology and music industries. Whether or not the MPAA's lobbying efforts were well-targeted in this sphere, it could benefit from the umbrella provided by this much larger effort involving a far more significant potential economic benefit.

At the same time, as has been seen, US. administrations were having difficulty in keeping track of the entire European market integration project, much less the technical question of market access for television programs. When the US did, belatedly, become alarmed by the Directive, it fell into the trap of allowing its policy to be more or less directed by a trade association whose own grasp on the fundamental issues was less than total.

On the European side, the crucial player was France because, for good reason or bad, it thought the quota issue was more important than virtually anything else. A weakness of EC politics, as with any other political system, is that at times, some countries will concede issues where they disagree with the line being taken but prefer to gain advantages in other areas. Or, simply, they will decide that the matter in question is not sufficiently important to block. Once France, following the Mons Declaration, had formed its coalition of small countries, it was up to the UK and Germany to force an open rupture by using their blocking powers to impede the quotas. Having chosen not to do so, the television program policy of the entire EU was essentially hijacked by an administration whose position was driven almost totally by rhetoric and not by the facts of the matter.

The reasons for these violent differences run deep in relations between the United States and Europe in general, but particularly between America and France. Because, in the end, this economic argument is a question of culture; however, it is not the sort of culture Jack Lang had in mind. Instead, it is a culture of attitudes, connections and dealings that poisoned this affair. The enumerated goals that went into shaping the policies at stake – free trade, supporting European cinema and so on – may well be worthwhile values. But if they are, the arguments and strategies adopted by the various players in the incessant wrangling that has been described in this book had little, if anything, to do with the realization of these values.

Instead, what has been depicted here has been a series of repeated fears, about culture, economics, change, loss. These constantly reiterated anxieties are, however, punctuated by times of relative clarity and calm, where the fighting stops, for a while, or where the issue that has caused such fierce heat between different sides simply becomes moot. But these moments of calm are not periods of reflection for, when the old anxieties become tweaked once more by some new circumstance, the confrontations resume with the same fervor as before.

The sense of continuousness, the feeling that, even as this story comes to an end in the summer of 1997, the underlying issues will not go away, is due to a number of failures that act together.

Failure of consciousness

Virtually every statement quoted or position cited in this book is highly determined by ideology. America's position on free trade has always been equivocal and remains so. Yet, ideologically, its advocates appear always to regard it as an absolute, immutable value. This does not appear merely to be propaganda to intimidate the opponents of free trade, but an deeply-held belief. On the other side, the European view of America depends on so many layers of culture, image, history, practice, that it becomes hard to find a concrete or material basis for the holding of any particular position. These are, in a sense, imaginary worlds, that of free trade, and that of the European America. But there is also a pragmatic space where what might be termed ordinary contact occurs, the simple traffic of people and things, where it makes a difference if you are allowed to buy or sell a good unhindered, or if you can be regarded by the person with whom you are dealing as something less interesting than a devil. For this space to exist at all requires a certain effort of consciousness, a reluctance to caricature the world and a degree of comfort with complexity. The failure of consciousness reduces this complexity to something of the character of a comic-book.

Failure of systems

Throughout this book, we have seen people making mistakes. Often, this is particularly surprising given the resources to which these people have access, in terms of personnel, information and money. Yet at times, we see the US Department of Commerce incapable of producing an informed opinion on the integration of the European market, or the European Commission generating a policy document without even apparently reflecting that it has no chance of gaining the political support it needs to advance. Lobbyists have difficulty in identifying their own interests, while apparent victims of economic imbalances fail to recognize the true causes of their ills, preferring instead to attack obvious – but incorrect – targets.

Failures of policies

Perhaps the most impressive success in this whole story is also the most useless: France's ability, through complete determination, to shape the agenda and often to get its own way. Such an outcome is useless, as we have seen, because the underlying policy makes no sense. But pursuing a bad policy has a second adverse consequence: one is unlikely simultaneously to pursue a good one. Take the issue of European audiovisual production for television, for instance. There is a simple solution to much of the problem: harness Europe's public broadcasters so that, in the tradition of European broadcasting, they fulfill certain ideological and cultural desires of the state, by producing European works. This has generally not happened for two reasons: first, public broadcasting itself became somehow "unsound" in some European countries in the 1980s; secondly, governments have tried to curb the amount of taxes spent to keep large public broadcasting establishments going. Yet by focusing on what was clearly and permanently a sphere of state intervention, and leaving the commercial world of private television to private efforts, the cultural goal of providing a European bulwark to American images would have been accomplished, and the jeopardy in which essential trade relationships were placed could have been avoided.

Failures of restraint

There has not been very much war in this book: indeed, the periods when people actually were at war have largely been glossed over. Yet, for so much of the time, the rhetoric and attitudinizing of the two sides has been very reminiscent of war-mongering. (Of course, it's an oft-cited axiom that France and the United States are the only two major powers of the past 200 years that have not gone to war with each other.) The problem being, these various negotiations over film and television quotas over the past seventy-five years have often sounded less than the pursuit of war by other means than like the preparation for war itself. It is unlikely that a war will every break out over sales of television programs. But the degree of demonization, distortion and misrepresentation that each side engages in with relation to each other has a destabilizing effect that, in other circumstances, has lead to nastier escalations. Because the basis of so many of the acts here has been irrational, the fear that other, deeper forms of irrationality might break out can never completely be dispelled. After all, real wars do follow trade wars, and a trade war was something that was only barely averted here. Even if this is only a cold war, it's an unsettling one, all the same.

Failure of perspective

All these different failures add up to a simple one: the refusal to see issues clearly. There will be many occasions in policy conflicts where different interests are genuinely opposed, and will have to be resolved by one means or another. But this issue was not one of those occasions. One cannot help feeling that at no point in these long and bitter exchanges did anyone stop and ask themselves the question, "What's the truth here?" Instead, the parties start from predetermined positions and proceed accordingly. In some ways, what this book has attempted to do, in covering so much different type of ground, often rather thinly, has been to find out what the parties should have known about their own dispute. What was there in their cultural history, intellectual dealings, mutual suspicions and fears, industrial contacts, legal conflicts and so on, that made their confrontation so severe, so bitter. There is probably no such thing as perfect knowledge, certainly not in a situation with so many elements and as many deep roots as this. Nevertheless, there is such a thing as improved knowledge and also, when the stakes are so high, some responsibility to attempt to seek it out.

Bibliography and Filmography

Government and international agency documents

Council of Europe

European Convention on Transfrontier Television (May 10, 1989) in *European Conventions and Agreements* (1990).

European Commission

Amended Proposal for a Council Directive on the coordination of certain provisions laid down by law, regulation or administrative action in Member States concerning the pursuit of broadcasting activities: submitted by the Commission to the Council pursuant to article 149(3) of the EEC Treaty, COM(88) 154 final – SYN 52 1987 O.J.

Commission Proposal for a Council Directive on the coordination of certain provisions laid down by law, regulation or administrative action in Member States concerning the pursuit of broadcasting activities, 1986 O.J. (C. 179/05).

Communication from the Commission to the Council and the European Parliament on the application of Articles 4 and 5 of Directive 89/552/EEC Television without frontiers, COM(94)57 final.

Council Directive of 3 October 1989 on the coordination of certain provisions laid down by law, regulation or administrative action in Member States concerning the pursuit of television activities, 89/552/EEC, 1989 O.J. (L 298).

Directive 97/36/EC of the European Parliament and of the Council of 30 June 1997, amending Council Directive 89/552/EEC on the coordination of certain provisions laid down by law, regulation or administrative action in Member States concerning the pursuit of television broadcasting activities, 1997 O.J. (L. 202).

Opinion of the Economic and Social Committee on the proposal for a Council Directive on the coordination of certain provisions laid down by law, regulation or administrative action in Member States concerning the pursuit of broadcasting activities, 1987 O.J. (C. 232/16).

Proposal for a Council Directive on the coordination of certain provisions laid down by law, regulation or administrative action in Member States concerning the pursuit of broadcasting activities: submitted by the Commission to the Council, 1986 O.J. (C 179/05).

Proposal for a directive, COM (86) 146 final, 1988 O.J. (C. 49).

Report by the Think-Tank on the Audiovisual Policy in the European Union (1994).

Resolution of the Representatives of the Governments of the Member-States, 1984 O.J. (C. 204).

Second Commission Report to the Council and Parliament on the implementation of Articles 4 and 5 of Directive 89/552/EEC Television without frontiers, COM(96)302 final.

Strategy options to strengthen the European programme industry in the context of the audiovisual policy of the European Union, COM(94) 96 final.

Television Without Frontiers: Green Paper on the Establishment of the Common Market for Broadcasting, Especially by Satellite and Cable, Communication from the Commission to the Council, COM(84) 300 final, 14 June 1984.

Third Communication from the Commission to the Council and the European Parliament on the application of Articles 4 and 5 of Directive 89/552/EEC "Television without frontiers," COM(98)199 final.

European Parliament

Decision (Cooperation procedure: second reading) concerning the common position of the Council on the proposal from the Commission for a directive on the coordination of certain provisions laid down by law, regulation or administrative action in Member States concerning the pursuit of television broadcasting activities, 1989 O.J. (C. 158).

General Agreement on Tariffs and Trade

GATT Secretariat, *The General Agreement on Tariffs and Trade (GATT): What It Is and What It Has Done*, Document MGT/3/54 (2nd ed., Feb. 1954).

GATT Press Release, *Background Note on the Audiovisual Sector*, NUR 069, Oct. 14, 1993.

United States

Advisory Committee for Trade Policy and Negotiations, *A Report to the President, the Congress, and the United States Trade Representative concerning the Uruguay Round of Negotiations on the General Agreement on Tariffs and Trade* (1994).

Europe 1992: Hearing before the Subcommittee on Trade of the House Committee on Ways and Means, 101st Cong., 1st Sess. (1989).

Nomination of Carla Anderson Hills: Hearing S. Hrg. 101-52 Before the Committee on Finance, United States Senate, 101st Cong., 1st Sess. (1989).

USTR Identification of Priority Practices and Countries Under Super 301 and Special 301 Provisions of the Omnibus Trade and Competitiveness Act of 1988: Hearing Before the Subcommittee on Trade of the House Committee on Ways and Means, 101st Cong., 1st Sess. (1989).

Press articles

Articles from newspapers and magazines including *Congressional Quarterly*, *Daily Variety*, *The Economist*, *The Financial Times*, *The Hollywood Reporter*, *Le Monde*, *New Media Markets*, *The New York Times*, *Saturday Evening Post*, *Scientific American*, *Television Business International*, *The Wall Street Journal*, and the Agence France-Presse, Reuters and United Press International wire services are too numerous to cite here but are referenced individually in the footnotes.

Journal articles and book essays

"Final Report of the Ad Hoc Working Group on US Adherence to the Berne Convention," *Columbia-VLA Journal of Law & the Arts* 10 (1986), 547.

Audit, Bernard, "Note [on the Huston affair]," *Dalloz Sirey* (1990), J. 158.

Braun, Michael & Parker, Leigh, "Trade in Culture: Consumable Product or Cherished Articulation of a Nation's Soul?" *Denver Journal of International Law and Policy* 22 (1993),155.

Conley, Janet L., "Hollywood's Last Hurrah? 'Television Without Frontiers' Directive May Close Borders to the European Community's Broadcast Market," *University of Pennsylvania Journal of International Business Law* (1993), 87.

De Grazia, Victoria, "Mass Culture and Sovereignty: The American Challenge to European Cinemas, 1920-1960, *Journal of Modern History* 61 (1989), 53.

Filipek, Jon, "'Culture Quotas': The Trade Controversy over the European Community's Broadcasting Directive," *Stanford Journal of International Law* 28 (1992), 323.

Garrett, Lisa L., "Commerce versus Culture: The Battle Between the United States and the European Union Over Audiovisual Trade Policies," *North Carolina Journal of International Law and Commercial Regulation* 19 (1994), 553.

Ginsburg, Jane C., "A Tale of Two Copyrights: Literary Property in revolutionary France and America," *Tulane Law Review* 64 (1990), 991.

– & Sirinelli, Pierre, "Auteur, création et adaptation en droit international privé et en droit interne français. Réflexions à partir de l'affaire Huston," *Revue internationale du droit d'auteur* (Oct. 1991), 5.

Gunter, Barry "On The Future of Television Ratings," *Journal of Broadcasting & Electronic Media* 37 (1993), 359.

Hesse, Carla, "Enlightenment Epistemology and the Laws of Authorship in Revolutionary France, 1777-1793, in *Law and the Order of Culture* (Robert Post ed., 1991)

Hoskins, C. *et. al.*, "Television Programs in the International Market: Unfair Pricing?" *Journal of Communications* 39 (Spring 1989), 55.

Hubert-Lacombe, Patricia, "L'acceuil des films américains en France pendant la guerre froide (1946-1953)," *Revue d'histoire moderne et contemporaine* 33 (1986), 301.

Jarvie, Ian, "Dollars and Ideology: Will. H. Hays' Economic Foreign Policy 1922-1945," *Film History* 2 (1988), 207.

Jeancolas, Jean-Pierre, "L'arrangement Blum-Byrnes à l'épreuve des faits: les relations (cinématographiques) franco-américaines de 1944 à 1948," *1895* (Dec. 1993), 3.

Jeanne, René, "L'invasion cinématographique américaine," *Revue des Deux Mondes*, Feb. 15, 1930.

Jolas, Eugène, "Inquiry Among European Writers Into the Spirit of America," *transition* 13 (Summer 1928), 248.

Kael, Pauline, "Circles and Squares," *Film Quarterly* 12 (Spring, 1963).

Kaplan, Laurence G.C., "The European Community's 'Television Without Frontiers' Directive: Stimulating Europe to Regulate Culture," *Emory International Law Review* 8 (1994), 225.

Lichty, Lawrence W. "Ratings in the Real World: A Reply to Gunter," *Journal of Broadcasting & Electronic Media* 37 (1993), 483.

Lupinacci, Timothy M., "The Pursuit of Television Broadcasting Activities in the European Community: Cultural Preservation of Economic Protectionism?" *Vanderbilt Journal of Transnational Law* (1991), 112.

Margairaz, Michel, "Autour des accords Blum-Byrnes: Jean Monnet entre le consensus national et le consensus atlantique," *Histoire, Économie, Société* (1982), 439.

Murphy, Robert, "Under the Shadow of Hollywood" in *All Our Yesterdays: 90 Years of British Cinema* (Charles Barr ed., 1986). London: British Film Institute.

Peck, N.C.M., "Transfrontier Television and Europe 1992: A Common Position," *Temple International and Comparative Law Journal* (1990), 307.

Portes, Jacques, "Les origines de la légende noire des accords Blum-Byrnes sur le cinéma," *Revue d'histoire moderne et contemporaine* 33 (1986), 314.

Price, Monroe E., "The Market for Loyalties: Electronic Media and the Global Competition for Allegiances," *Yale Law Journal* 104 (1994), 667.

Ross, Brian L., "'I Love Lucy,' But the European Community Doesn't: Apparent Protectionism in the European Community's Broadcast Market," *Brook Journal of International Law* (1990), 529.

Sarris, Andrew, "Notes on the Auteur Theory in 1962," *Film Culture* (Winter, 1962-63).

– "The Auteur Theory And The Perils Of Pauline," *Film Culture* 26 (Summer, 1963).

Schwartz, Ivo, "La politique de la commission en matière de télévision," *Revue du marché commun* (1985), 494.

Sears, John F. "Bierstadt, Buffalo Bill and the Wild West in Europe," in *Cultural Transmissions and Receptions: American Mass Culture in Europe* (R. Kroes *et al.*, eds., 1993). Amsterdam VU University Press.

Smith, Clint, "International Trade in Television Programming and GATT: An Analysis of Why the European Community's Local Program Requirement Violates the General Agreement on Tariffs and Trade," *International Trade & Business Lawyer* 10 (1993), 97.

Tunstall, Jeremy, "Media Imperialism?" in *American Media and Mass Culture* (Donald Lazere, ed., 1987). Berkeley, London: University of California Press.

Wallace, Rebecca & Goldberg, David, "The EEC Directive on Television Broadcasting," *Yearbook of European Law* 9 (1989), 175.

Wilkins, Kelly L., "Television Without Frontiers: An EEC Broadcasting Premiere," *Boston College International and Comparative Law Review* 14 (1991), 195.

Books

Agulhon, Maurice, *The Republican Experiment, 1848-1852* (1983). Cambridge, Cambridge University Press.

Allen, Donald Roy, *French Views of America in the 1930s* (1979). New York, Garland.

Anderson, Benedict, *Imagined Communities* (rev. ed. 1991). London: Verso.

Ang, Ien, *Desperately Seeking the Audience*, (1991). London: Routledge.

Ang, Ien, *Living Room Wars: Rethinking Media Audience for a Postmodern World* (1996). London: Routledge.

Armes, Roy, *French Cinema* (1985). London: Secker & Warburg.

Azema, Jean-Pierre, *From Munich to the Liberation, 1938-1944* (1984). Cambridge, Cambridge University Press.

Bach, Steven, *Final Cut* (1985). London, Cape.

Barnum, P.T., *Struggles and Triumphs* (1869) (Carl Bode, ed. 1981). Harmondsworth, Penguin.

Baudelaire, Charles, *Oeuvres Complètes* (Claude Pichois, ed. 1975). Paris, Bibliothèque de la Pleíade.

Baudrillard, Jean, *Amérique* (1986). Paris, Editions Bernard Brasset.

Bazin, André. *French Cinema of the Occupation and Resistance* (1975) (François Truffaut ed., Stanley Hochman trans., 1981). New York, F. Ungar Publishing Company.

Berg, A. Scott, *Goldwyn* (1989). London, Hamish Hamilton.

Bernard, Philippe & Dubief, Henri, *The Decline of the Third Republic, 1914-1938* (1985). Cambridge, Cambridge University Press.

Berstein, Serge, *The Republic of De Gaulle, 1958-1969* (1993). Cambridge, Cambridge University Press.

Bigsby, C.W.E. (ed), *Super Culture: America Popular Culture and Europe* (1975). Bowling Green, Ohio: Bowling Green University Press and London: Elek.

Blumer, Jay G. & Nossiter, T.J. (eds), *Broadcasting Finance in Transition: a Comparative Handbook* (1991). New York, Oxford: Oxford University Press.

Boujut, Michel & Chancel, Jules (eds), *Europe-Hollywood et retour* (1992). Paris: "Autrement".

Boulouis, Jean, *Droit Institutionnel de l'Union Européenne* (5th ed. 1995). Paris: Editions Montchrestien.

Bourget, Paul, *Outre Mer: Impressions of America* (1896). London: T Fisher Unwin.

Brooks, Charles, *America in France's Hopes and Fears, 1890-1920* (1987). New York, London: Garland.

Brownstein, Ronald, *The Power and the Glitter: The Hollywood-Washington Connection* (1990). New York: Pantheon.

Carrière, Jean Claude, *The Secret Language of Film* (1994). New York: Radom House.

Caute, David, *The Great Fear: The Anti-Communist Purge Under Truman and Eisenhower* (1978). London: Secker & Warburg.

Cendrars, Blaise, *Hollywood, La Mecque du cinéma* (1936; reissued ed. 1987). Paris: Éditions Bernard Grasset.

Cleaver, Eldridge, *Soul On Ice* (1968). New York: McGraw Hill.

Colombet, Claude, *Propriété littéraire et artistique et droits voisins* (7th ed., 1994). Paris: Dalloz.

– *Grands principes du droit d'auteur et des droits voisins dans le monde* (2nd ed. 1992). Paris: Litec. UNSECO.

Cones, John W., *Film Finance and Distribution: A Dictionary Of Terms* (1992). Los Angeles: Silman-James Press.

Dadomo, Christian & Farran, Susan, *The French Legal System* (1993). London: Sweet & Maxwell.

de Baecque, Antoine & Toubiana, Serge, *François Truffaut* (1996). Paris: Gallimard.

de Beauvoir, Simone, *L'Amérique au jour le jour* (1948). Paris: Editions Paul Morithien.

de Tocqueville, Alexis, *Democracy in America* (1835) (trans. Henry Reeve, 2 vols. 1961). London: Saunders & Otley.

Dickinson, Margaert & Street, Sarah, *Cinema and State: The Film Industry and the British Government 1927-84* (1985). London: British Film Institute.

Dorfman, Ariel & Mattelart, Armand, *Para Leer el Pato Donald* (1973), Chile: Ediciones Universtarias de Valparaiso, translated as *How to read Donald Duck: Imperialist ideology in the Disney comic* (David Kunzle trans., 1975). New York, International General.

Duhamel, Georges, *Scènes de la vie future* (1930). Paris; Mercure de France.

Duigan, Peter & Gann, L.H., *An Ambivalent Heritage: Euro-American Relations* (1984). Stanford: Hoover Institution on War, Revolution and Peace, Stanford University Press.

Dyson, Kenneth & Humphreys, Peter, *Broadcasting and New Media Policies in Western Europe* (1988). London, Routledge.

Farran, Susan, *The French Legal System* (1993), London: Sweet & Maxwell.

Faÿ, Bernard, *La Civilization Américaine* (1939). Paris. Sagittaire.

Fiedler, Leslie A., *Love and Death in the American Novel* (rev. ed. 1966; reissued 1992). Harmondsworth: Penguin.

Fitzgerald, F. Scott, *The Letters of F. Scott Fitzgerald* (Andrew Turnbull ed., 1963).

Fitz-Simon, Christopher, *The Boys* (1994). London, Nick Hern Books.

Flanner, Janet, *Paris Was Yesterday 1925-1939* (1972). New York: Viking Press.

Forbes, Jill and Kelly, Michael (eds.), *French Cultural Studies: An Introduction* (1995). Oxford: Clarendon Press.

Foreign Relations of the United States (1969). Washington: US Government Printing Office.

Foucault, Michel, *Language, Counter-Memory, Practice* (Donald H. Bouchard ed. & Trans., Sherry Simon trans., 1977). Oxford, Blackwell.

Françon, André, *Cours de propriété littéraire, artistique et industrielle* (1994). Paris: Les Cours de Droit.

Frankel, Joseph, *British Foreign Policy 1945-1973* (1975). London: Oxford University Press, for the Royal Institute of International Affairs.

Fugate, Wilbur L. & Simowitz, Lee H., *Foreign Commerce & the Antitrust Laws* (4th ed. 1991). New York, Aspen Law and Business.

Furet, François, *Interpreting the French Revolution* (1981). Cambridge: Cambridge University Press.

Gabler, Neal, *An Empire Of Their Own: How The Jews Invented Hollywood* (1988). London; W.H. Allen.

Garçon, François, *De Blum à Pétain: cinéma et société française (1936-1944)* (1984). Paris: Cerf.

Gautier, Pierre-Yves, *Propriété littéraire et artistique* (1991). Paris, PUF.

Goldstein, Paul, *Copyright's Highway:* From Gutenberg to the Celestial Jukebox (1994) New York: Hill and Wang.

Gramsci, Antonio, *Selections from the Prison Notebooks* (Quentin Hoare & Geoffrey Nowell-Smith, eds. & trans. 1971). London; Lawrence & Wishart.

Guback, Thomas, *The International Film Industry* (1969). Bloomington: Indiana University Press.

Guide to GATT Law and Practice (6th ed. 1994). Lanham MD: World Trade Organisation Bernan Press.

Hale, John, *The Civilization of Europe in the Renaissance* (1994). London: Harper Collins.

Hamilton, Ian, *Writers in Hollywood* (1991). London: Minerva.

Harley, John Eugene, *World-Wide Influences of the Cinema* (1940). Los Angeles: University of Southern California Press.

Hayward, Susan, *French National Cinema* (1993). London: Routledge.

Hudec, Robert E., *The GATT Legal System and World Trade Diplomacy* (2nd ed. 1990). Salem. NH. Butterworth Legal Publishers.

Hutchinson, John & Smith, Anthony D. (eds.), *Nationalism* (1994). Oxford: Oxford University Press.

Huxley, Aldous, *Brave New World* (1932). London: Chatto and Windus.

Jacobs, Lewis, *The Rise of the American Film* (1939). New York: Harcourt Brace & Co.

Jardin, André, *Restoration and Reaction, 1815-1848* (1983). Cambridge: Cambridge University Press.

Jarvie, Ian C., *Hollywood's Overseas Campaign* (1992). Cambridge, New York: Cambridge University Press.

Jones, Howard Mumford, *America and French Culture 1750-1848* (1927; reissued ed. 1973). Westport, Conn.: Greenwood Press.

– *O Strange New World: American Culture: The Formative Years* (1964). New York: Viking Press.

Jones, Maldwyn A., *The Limits Of Liberty* (1983). Oxford: Oxford University Press.

Judt, Tony, *Past Imperfect: French Intellectuals 1944-1956* (1992). Berkeley, London: University of California Press.

Katz, Ephraim, *The Macmillan International Film Encyclopedia* (3rd ed. rev. Fred Klein & Donald Dean Nolen, 1998). London: Macmillan.

Keegan, John, *Six Armies in Normandy* (1982). Harmondsworth: Penguin.

Kieffer, Philippe & Chamard, Marie-Eve, *La Télé: Dix ans d'histoires secrètes* (1992). Paris: Flammarion.

Kracauer, Siegfried, *From Caligari to Hitler* (1947). London, New York: Dennis Dobson.

Kreimeier, Klaus, *Histoire du Cinéma Allemand: la UFA* (Olivier Mannoni, trans. 1994). Paris: Flammarion.

Kroes, R. *et al.* (eds.), *Receptions: American Mass Culture in Europe* (1993). Amsterdam, VU University Press.

Kuisel, Richard F., *Seducing the French: The Dilemma of Americanization* (1993). Berkerley, London: University of California Press.

Lacouture, Jean, *Léon Blum* (1977). Paris: Seuil.

Lang, Jack & Bredin, Jean-Denis, *Éclats* (1978). Paris: J.-C. Simoen.

Donald Lazere, ed., *Americn Media and Mass Cultures* (1987) Berkeley, London, University of California Press.

Larsen, Peter (ed.) *Import/Export: International Flow of Television Fiction* (1990). Paris: UNESCO.

Lealand, Geoffrey, *American Television Programmes on British Screens* (1994). London: British Film Institute Broadcasting Research Unit.

Leglise, Paul, *Histoire de la Politique du Cinéma Français* (1969). Paris: Film Editions.

Lucas, A. & H-J., *Traité de la propriété littéraire et artistique* (1994). Paris: Éditions Litec.

Maarek, Philippe J., *La Censure Cinématographique* (1982). Paris: Éditions Litec.

Mathy, Jean-Philippe, *Extrême-Orient: French Intellectuals and America* (1993).Chicago, London: University of Chicago Press.

Mayer, Pierre, *Droit international privé* (5th ed., 1994). Paris: Montchrestien.

Mayeur, Jean-Marie & Reberioux, Madeleine, *The Third Empire from its Origins to the Great War, 1871-1914* (1984). Cambridge: Cambridge University Press.

Moley, Raymond, *The Hays Office* (1945). Indianapolis, New York, Bobbs. Merrill Co.

Murray, Bruce, *Film and the German Left in the Weimar Republic* (1990). Austin, University of Texas Press.

North American Free Trade Agreement (1993) Ottawa: Canada Communication Group.

Pells, Richard, *Not Like Us: How Europeans Have Loved, Hated and Transformed American Culture Since World War II* (1997). New York, Basic Books.

Plessis, Alain, *The Rise and Fall of the Second Empire, 1852-1871* (1985). Cambridge, Cambridge University Press.

Pomaret, Charles, *L'Amérique à la conquête de l'Europe* (1931). Paris: Librarie Armand Colin.

Post Robert, ed., *Law and the order of Culture* (1991) Berkeley, Oxford: University of California Press.

Powdermaker, Hortense, *Hollywood: The Dream Factory* (1950). Boston, Little Brown & Co.

Pragnell, A., *Television in Europe: Quality and Value in a Time of Change* (1985). Manchester: European Institute for the Media.

Puttnam, David with Watson, Neil, *The Undeclared War: the struggle for control of the world's film industry* (1997). London, Harper Collins.

Recht, Pierre, *Le Droit d'Auteur, une nouvelle forme de propriété* (1969). Paris, Librarie Générale de Droit et de Jurisprudence, Gembloux, Editions J. Duculot.

Reisz, Karel & Millar, Gavin, *The Technique of Film Editing* (2nd ed. 1968). London and New York, Focal Press.

Revel, Jean-François, *Without Marx or Jesus* (J.F. Bernard, trans. 1971). London, McGibbon and Kee.

Rey-Debove & Gagnon, Gilberte, *Dictionnaire Des Anglicismes* (1988). Paris: Le Robert.

Rioux, Jean-Pierre, *The Fourth Republic, 1944-1958* (1987). Cambridge: Cambridge University Press.

Robert, Paul, *Le Petit Robert* (Rey, A & Rey-Debove, J., eds. 1985). Paris: Le Robert.

Robertson, David, *Sly and Able, A Political Biography of James F. Byrnes* (1994). New York, London: Norton.

Rocket, Kevin, *The Irish Filmography* (1996). Dublin: Red Mountain Media.

Roddick, Nick, *A New Deal in Entertainment: Warner Brothers in the 1930s* (1983). London: British Film Institute.

Rudden Bernard and Wyatt Derrick. *Basic Community Laws* (6th ed. 1996) Oxford: Oxford University Press.

Sadoul, Georges, *Le Cinéma français* (1962). Paris, Flammarion.

Sarris, Andrew, *The American Cinema* (1968). New York, Dutton.

Saunders, Thomas J., *Hollywood In Berlin: American Cinema and Weimar Germany* (1994). Berkeley: London, University of California Press.

Schiller, Herbert I., *Mass Communications and American Empire* (2nd ed., 1972).

Sepstrup, Preben, *Transnationalization of Television in Western Europe* (1990). London: John Libbey.

Servan-Schreiber, Jacques, *Le défi américain* (1967). Paris; Denöel.

Siclier, Jacques, *La France de Pétain et son cinéma* (1981).

Spurlin, Paul Merrill, *The Enlightenment in America* (1984). Athens, Ga.: University of Georgia.

Sturges, Preston, *Preston Sturges* (Sandy Sturges ed., 1990). New York, Simon and Schuster.

Swann, Paul, *The Hollywood Feature Film in Postwar Britain* (1987). London, Sydney: Croom Helm.

Taylor, John, *Storming The Magic Kingdom: Wall Street, The Raiders And The Battle For Disney* (1987). London, Viking.

Thibau, Jacques, *La France colonisée* (1980). Paris; Flammarion.

Thompson, Kristin, *Exporting Entertainment: America in the World film Market 1907-34* (1985). London: British Film Institute.

Truffaut, François, *Hitchcock* (rev. ed., 1988). London: Paladin.

Twain, Mark, *The Innocents Abroad* (1869) (Signet ed., with Afterword by Leslie A. Fiedler, 1980). New York: New American Library. London: New English Library.

Unkovic, Dennis *et al.*, *International Opportunities and the Export Trading Company Act of 1982* (1984).

Vogel, Harold, *Entertainment Industry Economics* (2nd ed., 1990; 3rd ed., 1994; 4th ed., 1998). Cambridge, New York: Cambridge University Press.

Year book of European Law, Oxford, Clarendon Press. Wells, Alan, *Picture Tube Imperialism?* (1972). Moryknoll, N.Y.: Orbis Books.

Wyatt, Derrick & Dashwood, Alan, *Wyatt & Dashwood's European Community Law* (5th. ed., 1994). London: Sweet & Maxwell.

Legal decisions

European Union

Case 22/70, [E.R.T.A.] 1971 E.C.R. 273, 1971 C.M.L.R. 335 (1971).

Case 155/73, Guiseppe Sacchi, 1974 E.C.R. 409, 2 C.M.L.R. 177 (1974).

Case 62/79, Coditel v. Cine Vog Films, 1980 E.C.R. 881, 2 C.M.L.R. 362 (1980).

Case 89/85, Re Wood Pulp Cartel, 1988 E.C.R. 5193, 4 C.M.L.R. 901 (1988).

Cases 241-242/91, Radio Téléfis Eireann and another v. European Commission (1995) ECR I-743

England

Donaldson v. Becket, 98 E.R. 257 (H.L. 1774).

France

Cass. civ. 1ère, 7 February, 1973, *Sté Les Productions Fox Europa v. Luntz*, Dalloz (1973) J. 363.

Cass. civ, 1ère, 8 January, 1980, *Dubuffet v. Régie Nationale de Usines Renault*, Revue Internationale du droit d'auteur (April 1994).

Cass. civ. 1ère, 28 May, 1991, *Consorts Huston v. Sté Turner Entertainment*, Revue internationale du droit d'auteur (July 1991) 197.

Paris, 4ème ch. B., 6 July 1989, *Soc. Turner Entertainment Co. v. Consorts Huston et autres*, Dalloz (1990) J. 152.

Paris, 1ère ch., 26 November 1990, *Carle v. TF1*, Images Juridiques, Jan. 15, 1991.

Trib. civ. Seine, 1ère ch., 6-7 April 1949, *Prévert et Carné v. Sté Pathé*, Gazette du Palais 1949, 249.

United States

Edison v. American Mutoscope Co., 114 F. 926 (2d Cir. 1902), cert. denied, 186 US 486 (1902)

Edison v. American Mutoscope & Biograph Co., 151 F. 767 (2d Cir. 1907)

Motion Picture Patents Co. v. Champion Film Co., 183 F. 986 (C.C.S.D.N.Y. 1910)

Motion Picture Patents Co. v. Indep. Moving Pictures Co. of Am., 200 F. 411 (2d Cir. 1912)

Motion Picture Patents Co. v. Calehuff Supply Co. Inc., 251 F. 598 (3d. Cir. 1918)

Motion Picture Patent Co. v. Laemmle, 178 F. 104 (C.C.S.D.N.Y. 1910)

United States v. Motion Picture Patents Co., 225 F. 800 (E.D. Pa. 1915), appeal dismissed per stipulation, 247 US 524 (1918)

Sony Corp. of America v. Universal City Studios, 464 US 417 (1984).

Wheaton v. Peters, 33 US (8 Pet) 591 (1834).

Treaties, Statutes and Decrees

Treaties and international agreements

Canada-United States Free Trade Agreement, *International Law Materials* 27 (1988) 281.

Joint Declaration of the Government of the United States of America and the Government of the French Republic on Motion Pictures, *Treaties and Other International Acts Series*. no. 1841.

North American Free Trade Agreement (1993).

Understanding between the Government of the United States of America and the Provisional Government of the French Republic With Respect to the Exhibition of American Motion Pictures in France, *Department of State Bulletin* (June 9, 1946) 999.

France

Code Civil (Dalloz 1998)

Code de la propriété intellectuelle, loi no. 92-587 du 1er juillet 1992.

Decret No. 87-36 du 26 janvier 1987, *J.O.* Jan 27, 1986, 946.

Decret No. 90-66 du 17 janvier 1990, *J.O.* Jan 18, 1990, *G.P.* Jan. 31-Feb 1, 1990, 321.

Loi no. 57-298 du 11 mars 1957 sur la propriété littéraire et artistique

Loi No. 86-1067 du 30 septembre 1986 relative à la liberté de communication, *J.O.* Oct 1. 1986, *G.P.* Oct. 8-9 1986 504.

Loi No. 92-61 du 18 janvier 1992, Modifiant les articles 27, 28, 31 et 70 de la loi no. 86-1067 du 30 septembre 1986 relative à la liberté de communication, *J.O.* Jan. 21, 1992.

Rome

Justinian, *Institutes.*

United States

Berne Convention Implementation Act of 1988, Pub. L. No. 100-568, 102 Stat. 285.

Copyright Act, 17 U.S.C. §§ 101 *et seq.*

Visual Artists Rights Act of 1990, Pub. L. 101-650. Title VI, 104 Stat. 5128.

Webb-Pomerene Act of 1919, 15 U.S.C. §§ 61-65.

Motion Pictures

A Clockwork Orange (Polaris, 1971).
A Hard Day's Night (Proscenium, 1964).
Arrivé d'un train à La Ciotat (Lumière, 1895).
Barry Lyndon (Hawk/Peregrine, 1975).
Dangerous Liaisons (Warner/Lorimar/NFH, 1988).
Das Cabinet des Dr. Caligari (Decla-Bioscop, 1919).
Du Rififi chez des hommes [Rififi] (Indus/Pathé/Prima, 1955).
Escamotage d'une dame chez Robert Houdin (Meliès, 1896).
Gone with The Wind (MGM/Selznick International, 1939).
I Married a Witch (United Artists/Cinema Guild, 1942).
It Happened One Night (Columbia Pictures, 1934).
Jean de Florette (Renn Productions/Films A2/Rai2/DD Productions, 1986).
Jurassic Park (Universal/Amblin, 1993).
King and Country (BHE, 1964).
La battaglia di Algeri (Casbah/Igor, 1965).

La grande illusion (Réalisations d'Art Cinématographique, 1937).

La nuit fantastique (U.T.C., 1942).

La sortie des usines Lumière (Lumière 1895).

L'affaire Dreyfus (Meliès 1899).

Les anges du peché [Angels of the Street] (Synops-Roland Tual, 1943).

Les dames du Bois de Boulogne [Ladies of the Park] (Consortium du Film, 1946).

Les enfants du paradis [Children of Paradise] (Pathé, 1945).

Les visiteurs du soir [The Devil's Envoys] (André Paulvé, 1942).

L'eternel retour [Love Eternal] (André Paulvé, 1943).

Manon des sources, (Renn Productions/Films A2/Rai2/DD Productions, 1986).

Metropolis (UFA, 1926).

Missing (Universal/Polygram, 1982).

Monsieur Klein (Lira/Adel/Nova/Mondial Te-Fi, 1976).

My Beautiful Laundrette (Working Title/SAF/Channel 4, 1985).

Napoléon (WESTI/Société Générale de Films, 1927).

New York in a Blizzard (Edison, 1901).

Night and the City (TCF, 1950).

Passion [Madame Dubarry] (Union-UFA, 1919).

Pépé le Moko (Paris Film, 1936).

Pote tin Kyriaki [Never on Sunday] (Lopert/Melinafilm, 1959).

Pretty Baby (Paramount, 1978).

Return to Glennascaul (Dublin Gate, 1951).

Sous les toits de Paris (Tobis, 1930).

Sullivan's Travels (Paramount Pictures, 1941).

Sunset Boulevard (Paramount Pictures, 1950).

Tearing Down the Spanish Flag (Vitagraph, 1898).

The Age of Innocence (Columbia, 1993).

The Go-Between (World Film Services, 1970).

The Great Bull Fight (Edison, 1901).

The Knack (Woodfall, 1965).

The Lady From Shanghai (Columbia Pictures, 1948).

The Servant (Springbok, 1963).

2001: A Space Odyssey (Stanley Kubrick, 1968).

Un carnet de bal [Life Dances On] (Lévy/Strauss/Sigma, 1937).

Voyage à la lune (Meliès 1902).

Z (Reggane/ONCIC, 1968).

Zazie dans le Métro (Nouvelles Editions, 1960).